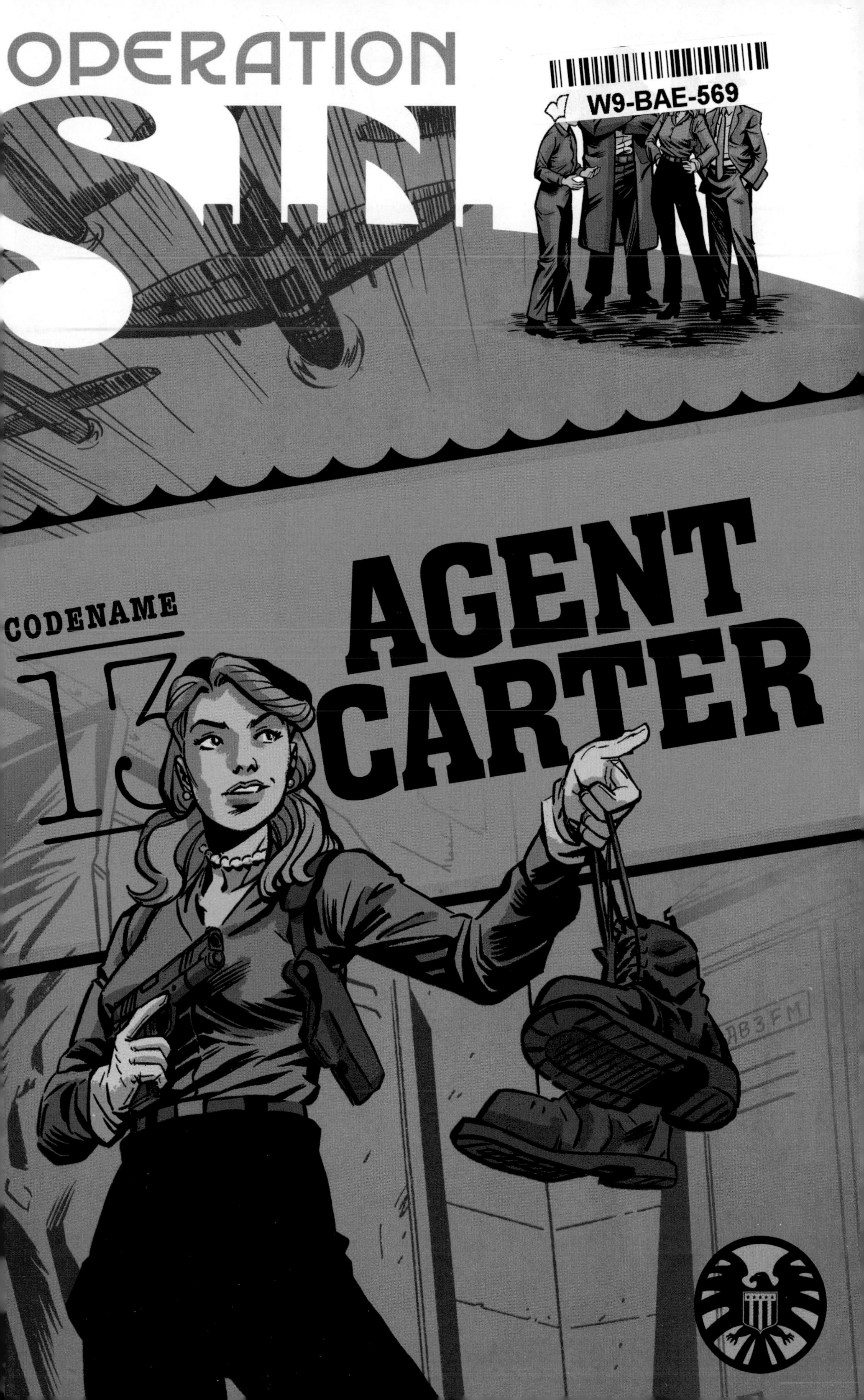
OPERATION
S.I.N.
CODENAME
13
AGENT
CARTER

OPERATION S.I.N.

OPERATION: S.I.N. — AGENT CARTER. Contains material originally published in magazine form as OPERATION: S.I.N. #1-5 and CAPTAIN AMERICA AND THE FIRST THIRTEEN #1. First printing 2015. ISBN# 978-0-7851-9713-3. Published by MARVEL WORLDWIDE, INC., a subsidiary of MARVEL ENTERTAINMENT, LLC. OFFICE OF PUBLICATION: 135 West 50th Street, New York, NY 10020. Copyright © 2015 MARVEL No similarity between any of the names, characters, persons, and/or institutions in this magazine with those of any living or dead person or institution is intended, and any such similarity which may exist is purely coincidental. **Printed in the U.S.A.** ALAN FINE, President, Marvel Entertainment; DAN BUCKLEY, President, TV, Publishing and Brand Management; JOE QUESADA, Chief Creative Officer; TOM BREVOORT, SVP of Publishing; DAVID BOGART, SVP of Operations & Procurement, Publishing; C.B. CEBULSKI, VP of International Development & Brand Management; DAVID GABRIEL, SVP Print, Sales & Marketing; JIM O'KEEFE, VP of Operations & Logistics; DAN CARR, Executive Director of Publishing Technology; SUSAN CRESPI, Editorial Operations Manager; ALEX MORALES, Publishing Operations Manager; STAN LEE, Chairman Emeritus. For information regarding advertising in Marvel Comics or on Marvel.com, please contact Jonathan Rheingold, VP of Custom Solutions & Ad Sales, at jrheingold@marvel.com. For Marvel subscription inquiries, please call 800-217-9158. **Manufactured between 6/24/2015 and 7/27/2015 by R.R. DONNELLEY, INC., SALEM, VA, USA.**

10 9 8 7 6 5 4 3 2 1

AGENT CARTER

Writer: **Kathryn Immonen**
Artist: **Rich Ellis**
Colorist: **Jordan Boyd**
Letterer: **VC's Joe Sabino**
Cover Artist: **Michael Komarck**
Editor: **Jon Moisan**

CAPTAIN AMERICA AND THE FIRST THIRTEEN

Writer: **Kathryn Immonen**
Artist: **Ramón Pérez**
Colorist: **John Rauch**

Letterer: **Jared K. Fletcher**
Cover Art: **Greg Tocchini**
Editor: **Rachel Pinnelas**

Supervising Editor: **Tom Brevoort**

PEGGY CARTER CREATED BY STAN LEE & JACK KIRBY

Collection Editor: **Jennifer Grünwald**
Assistant Editor: **Sarah Brunstad**
Associate Managing Editor: **Alex Starbuck**
Editor, Special Projects: **Mark D. Beazley**
Senior Editor, Special Projects: **Jeff Youngquist**
SVP Print, Sales & Marketing: **David Gabriel**
Book Designer: **Jay Bowen**

Editor in Chief: **Axel Alonso**
Chief Creative Officer: **Joe Quesada**
Publisher: **Dan Buckley**
Executive Producer: **Alan Fine**

1

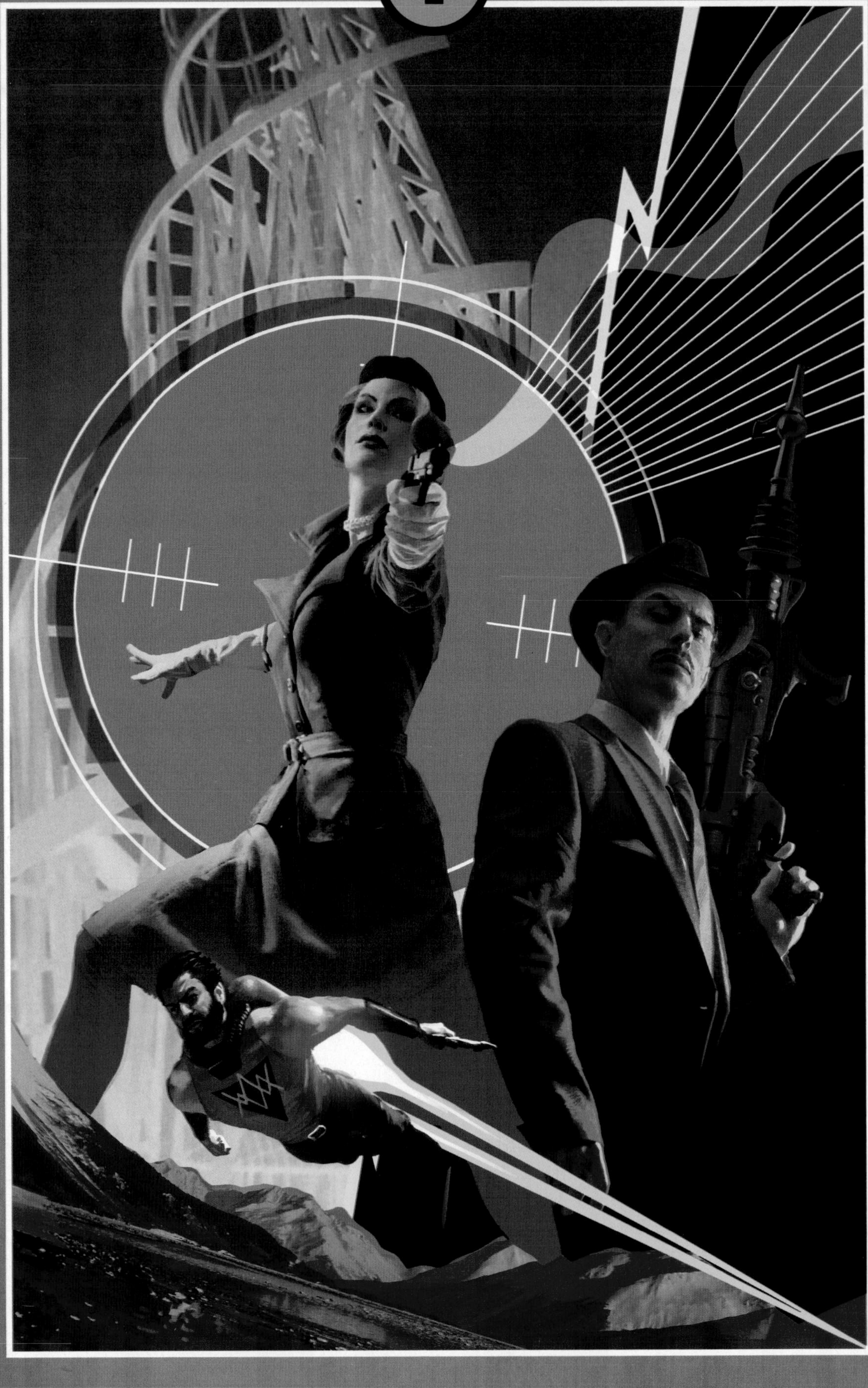

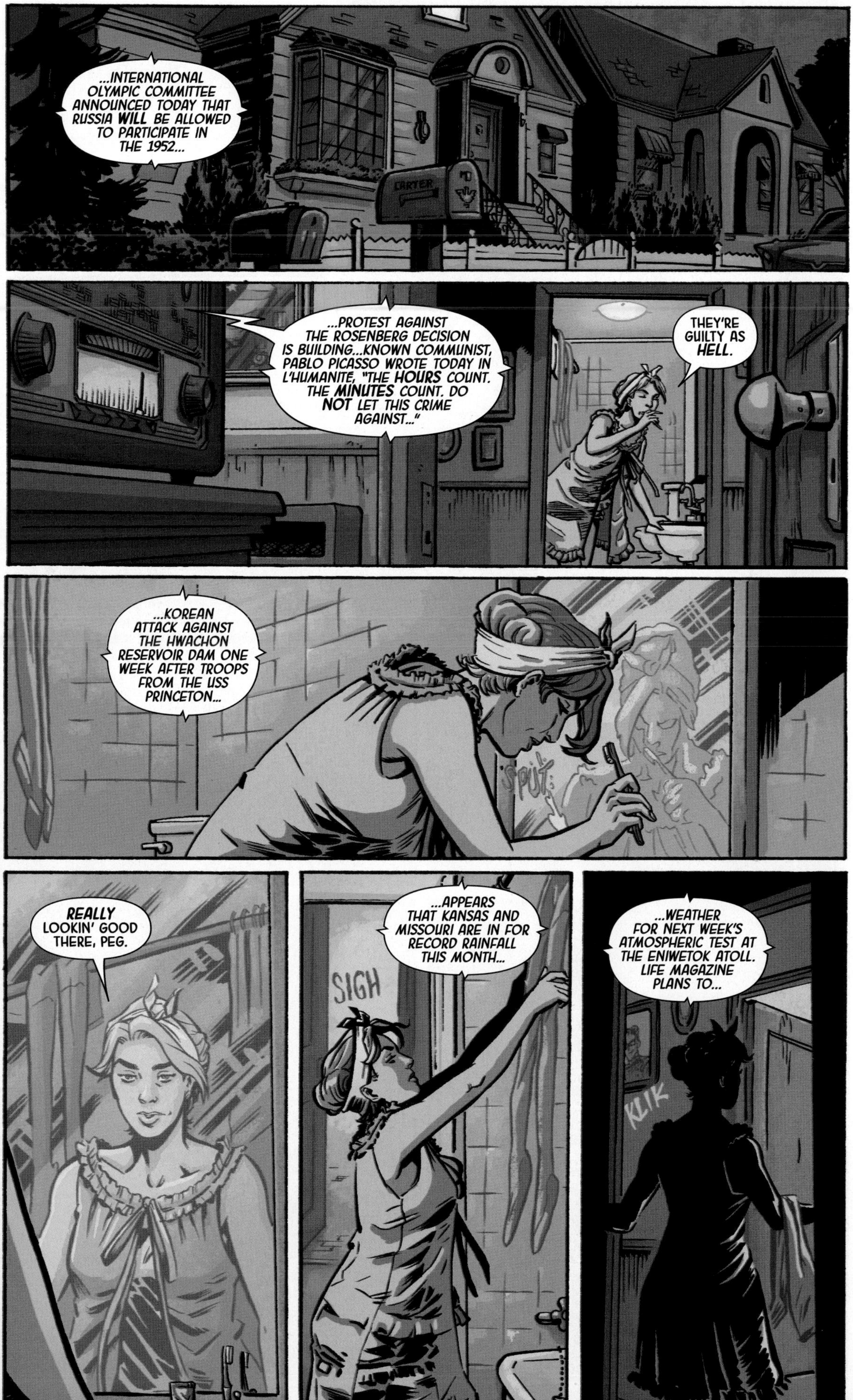
...INTERNATIONAL OLYMPIC COMMITTEE ANNOUNCED TODAY THAT RUSSIA WILL BE ALLOWED TO PARTICIPATE IN THE 1952...
CARTER
...PROTEST AGAINST THE ROSENBERG DECISION IS BUILDING...KNOWN COMMUNIST, PABLO PICASSO WROTE TODAY IN L'HUMANITÉ, "THE HOURS COUNT. THE MINUTES COUNT. DO NOT LET THIS CRIME AGAINST..."
THEY'RE GUILTY AS HELL.
...KOREAN ATTACK AGAINST THE HWACHON RESERVOIR DAM ONE WEEK AFTER TROOPS FROM THE USS PRINCETON...
SPUT
REALLY LOOKIN' GOOD THERE, PEG.
...APPEARS THAT KANSAS AND MISSOURI ARE IN FOR RECORD RAINFALL THIS MONTH...
SIGH
...WEATHER FOR NEXT WEEK'S ATMOSPHERIC TEST AT THE ENIWETOK ATOLL. LIFE MAGAZINE PLANS TO...
KLIK

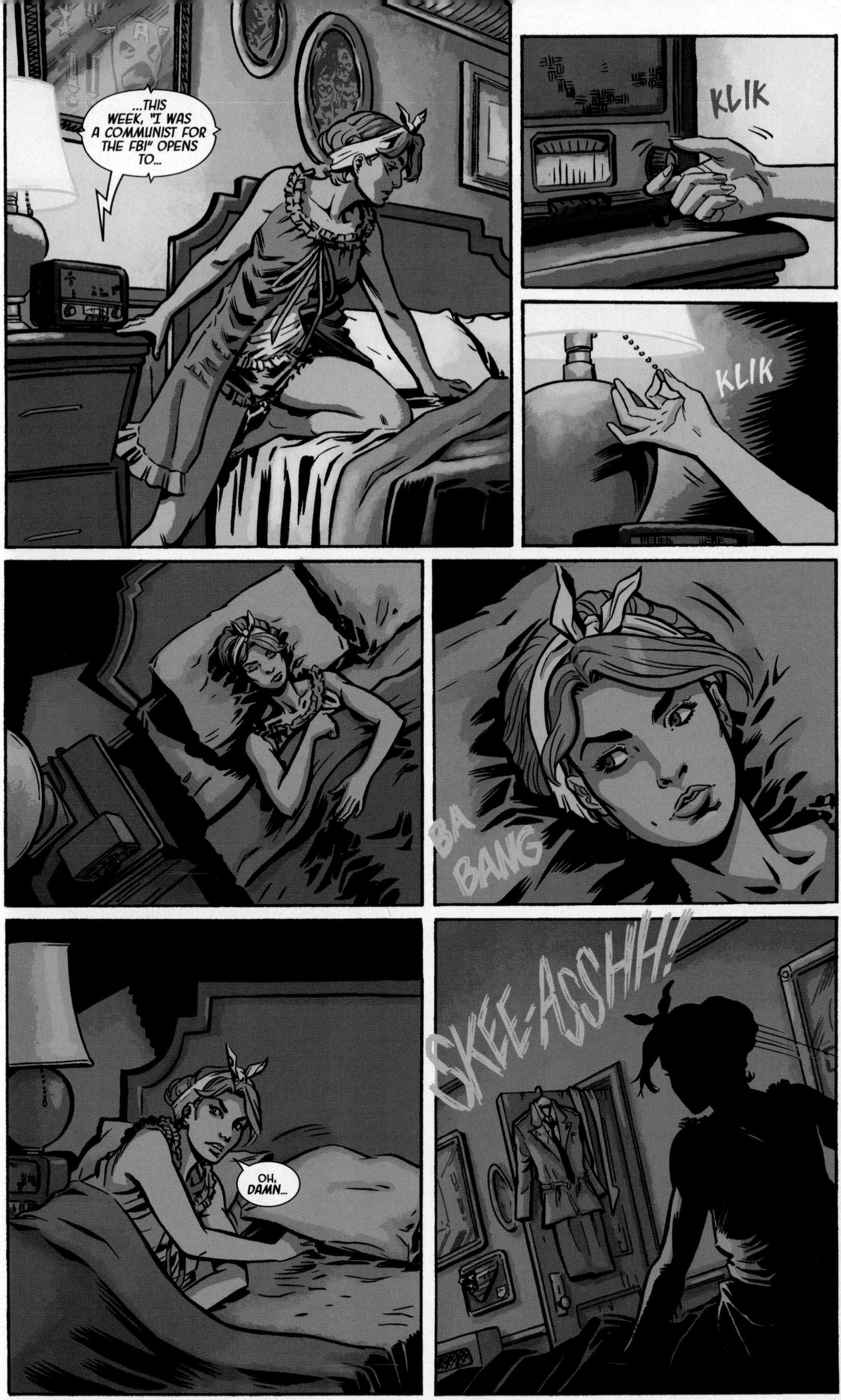
...THIS WEEK, "I WAS A COMMUNIST FOR THE FBI" OPENS TO...
KLIK
KLIK
BA BANG
OH, DAMN...
SKEE-ASSHH!

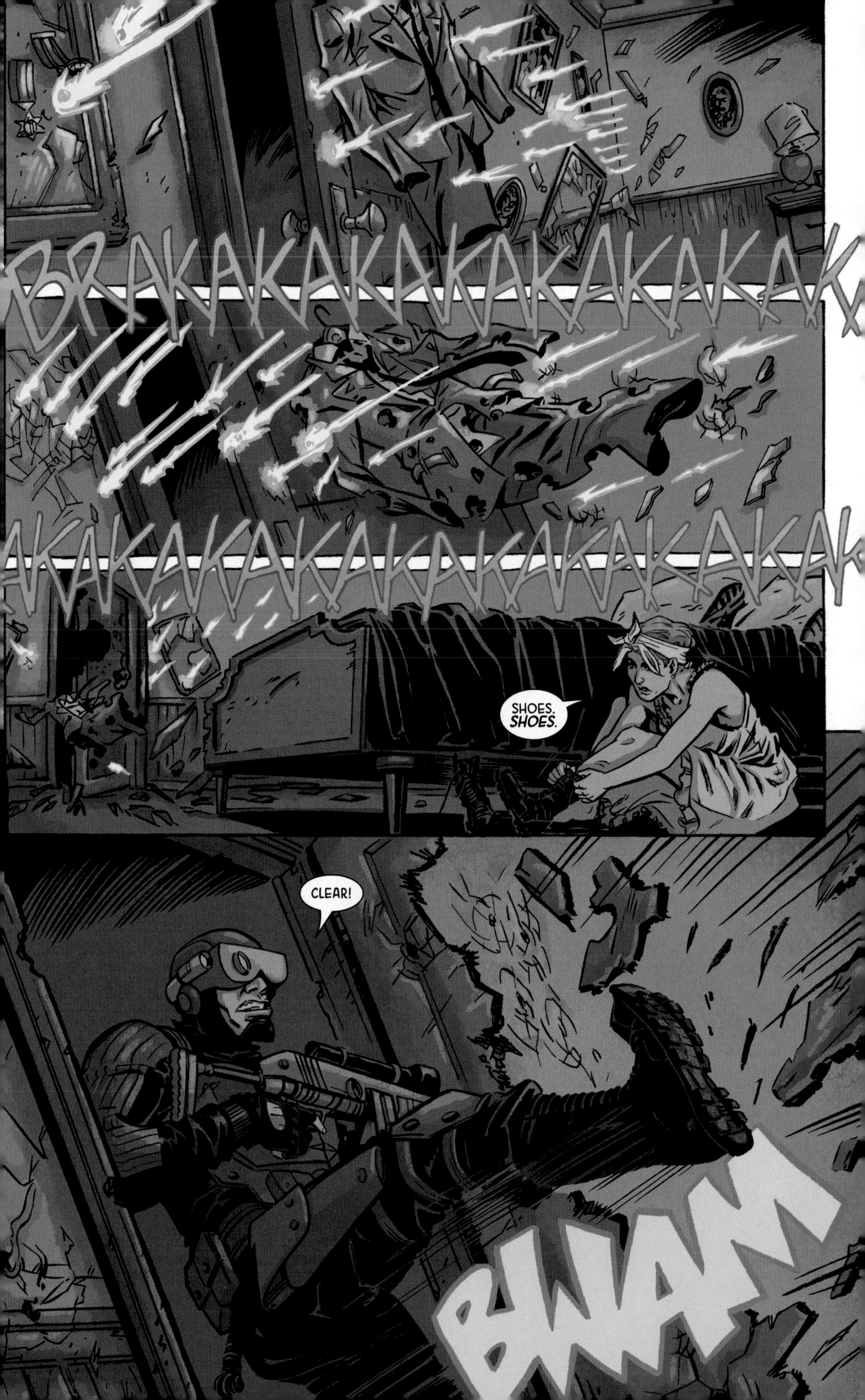
BRAKAKAKAKAKAKAKAKAKAK
AKAKAKAKAKAKAKAKAKAKAK
SHOES. SHOES.
CLEAR!
BWAM

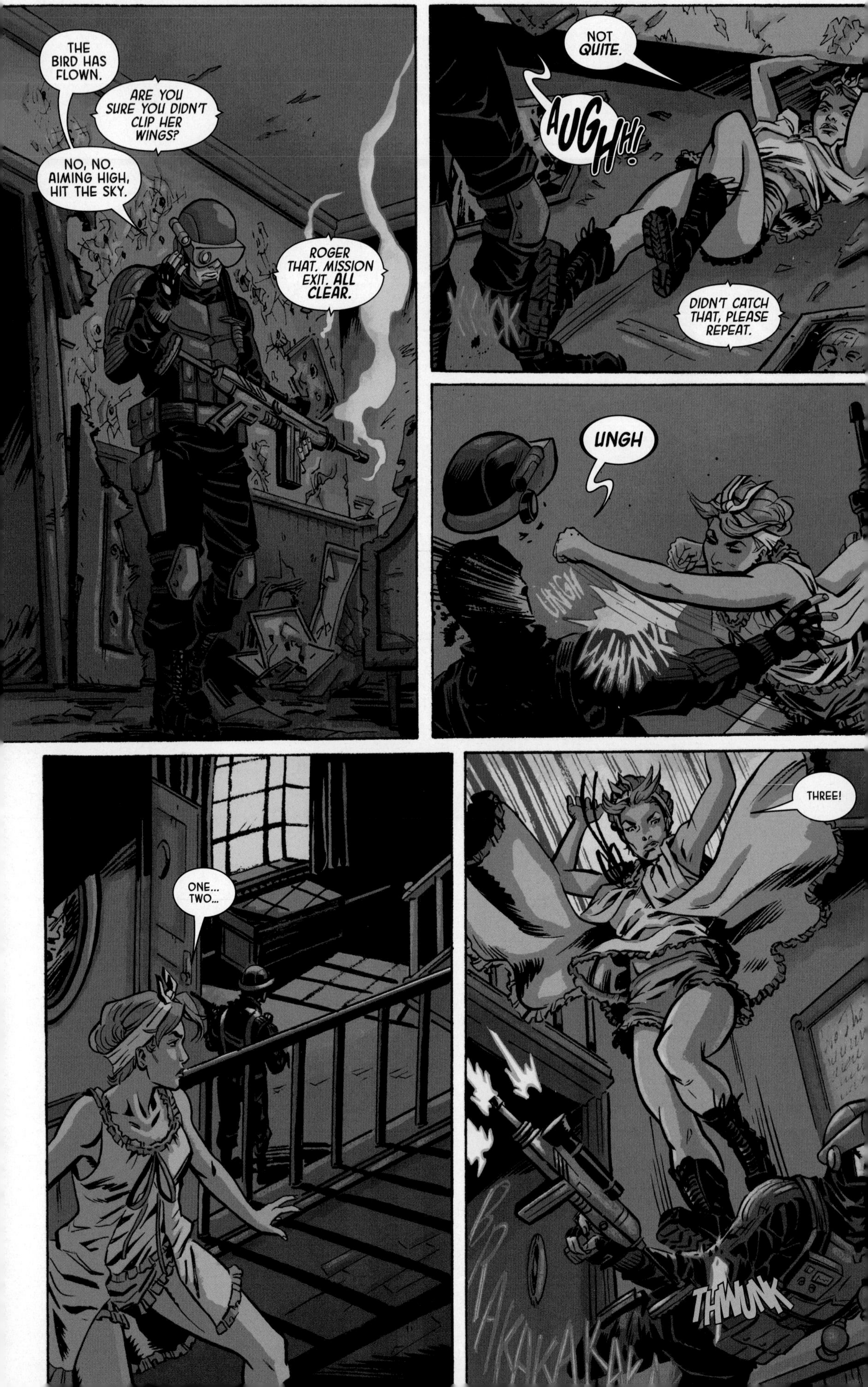
THE BIRD HAS FLOWN.
ARE YOU SURE YOU DIDN'T CLIP HER WINGS?
NO, NO. AIMING HIGH, HIT THE SKY.
ROGER THAT. MISSION EXIT. ALL CLEAR.
NOT QUITE.
AUGHH!
DIDN'T CATCH THAT, PLEASE REPEAT.
UNGH
ONE... TWO...
THREE!
THWUNK

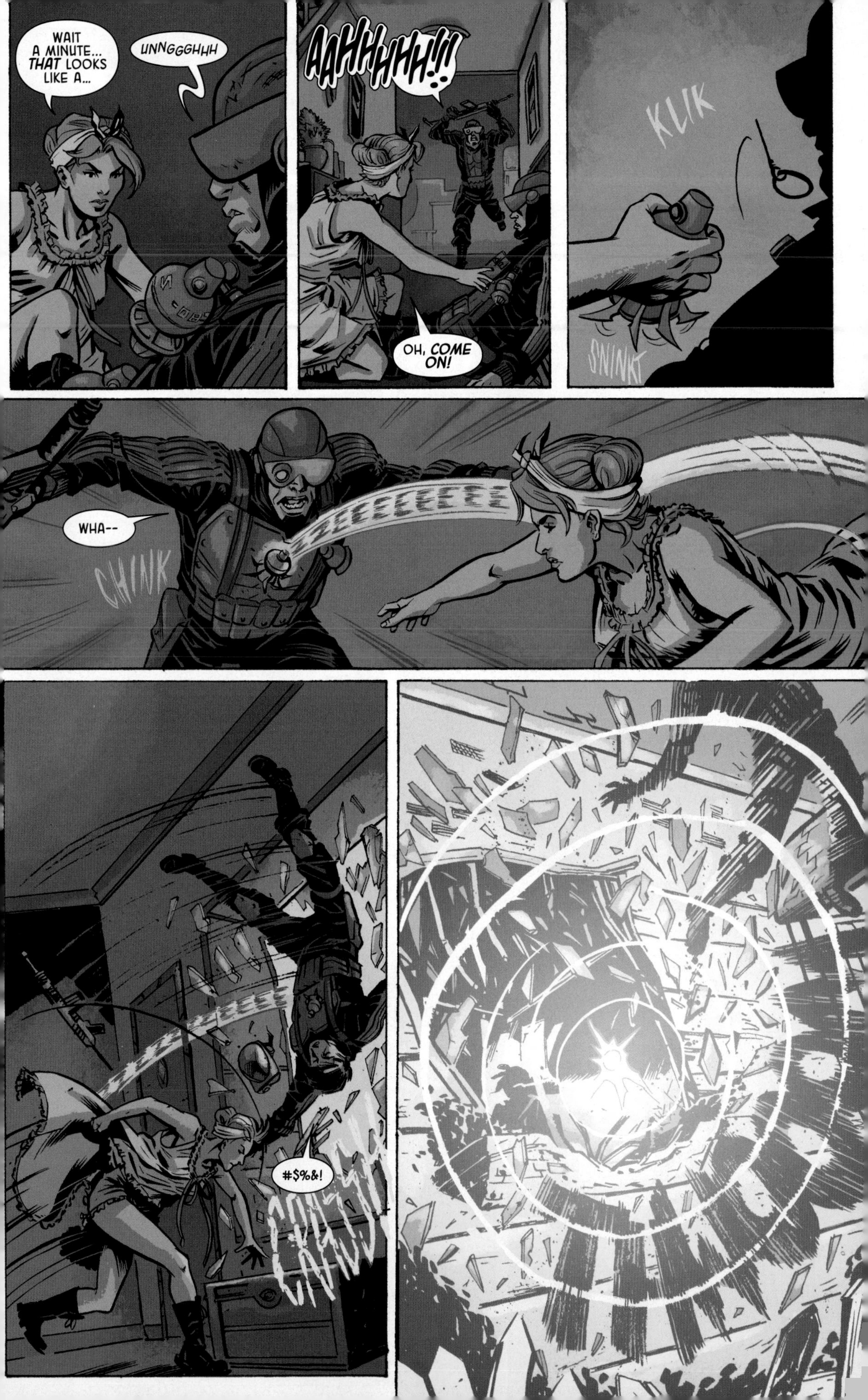
WAIT A MINUTE... THAT LOOKS LIKE A...
UNNGGGHHH
AAHHHHHH!!!
OH, COME ON!
KLIK
SNIKT
WHA--
CHINK
#$%&!

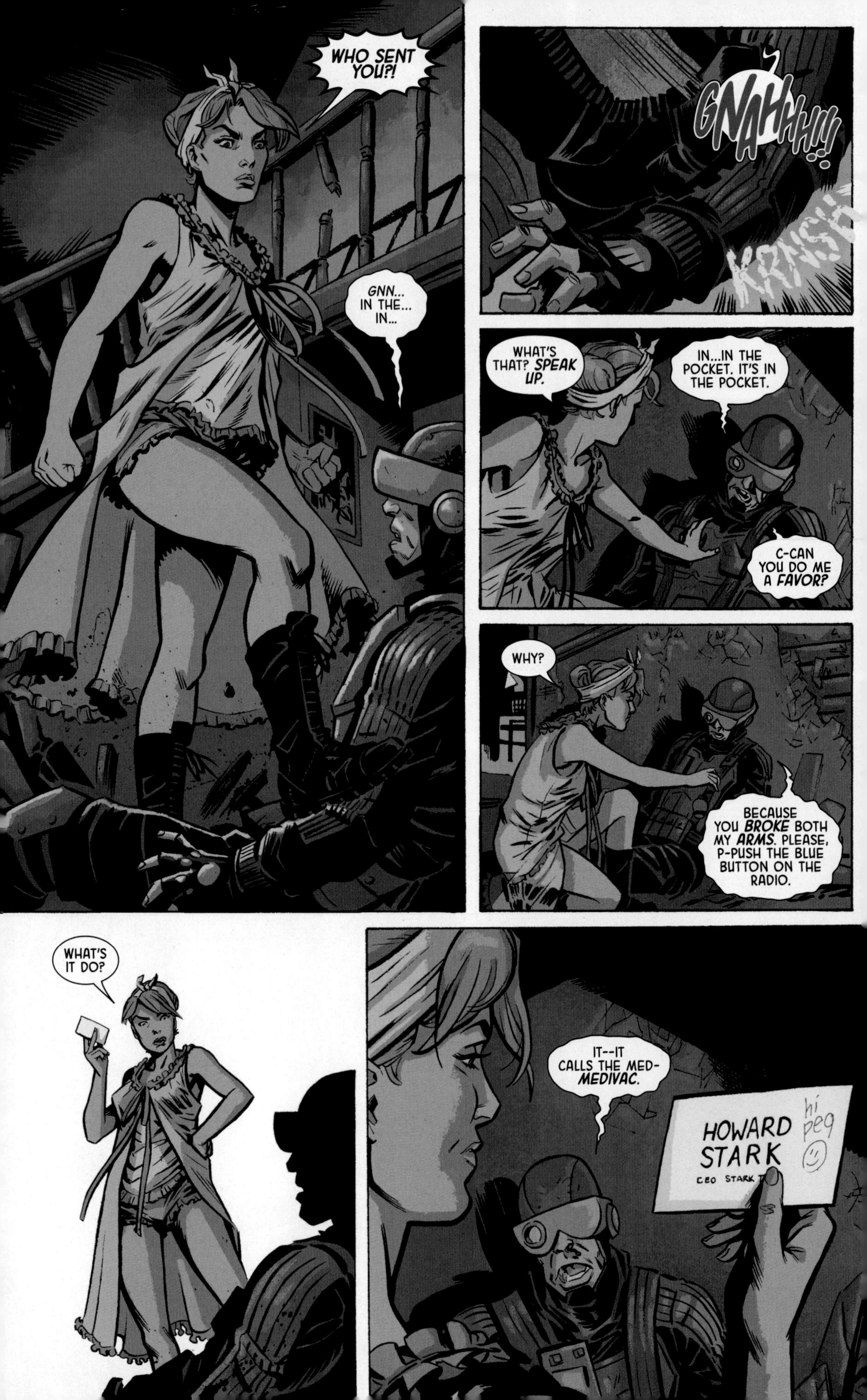
WHO SENT YOU?!
GNN... IN THE... IN...
GNAHHHH!!!
KRASH
WHAT'S THAT? SPEAK UP.
IN...IN THE POCKET. IT'S IN THE POCKET.
C-CAN YOU DO ME A FAVOR?
WHY?
BECAUSE YOU BROKE BOTH MY ARMS. PLEASE, P-PUSH THE BLUE BUTTON ON THE RADIO.
WHAT'S IT DO?
IT--IT CALLS THE MED-MEDIVAC.
HOWARD STARK
CEO STARK
hi peg

Subject:
Peggy Carter

Codename(s):
Agent 13, Mademoiselle

Findings:
A former **WWII resistance fighter** in Nazi-occupied Europe, Ms. Carter has been known to have romantic affiliations with the super hero known as **Captain America**, though the relationship ended when he was killed in action. Peggy has had an additional known affiliation with **S.H.I.E.L.D.** engineer and inventor **Howard Stark**, read: **non-romantic**. Ms. Carter has not been an active agent for many years.

Recorder's Notes:
Keep a careful eye on Agent Carter.

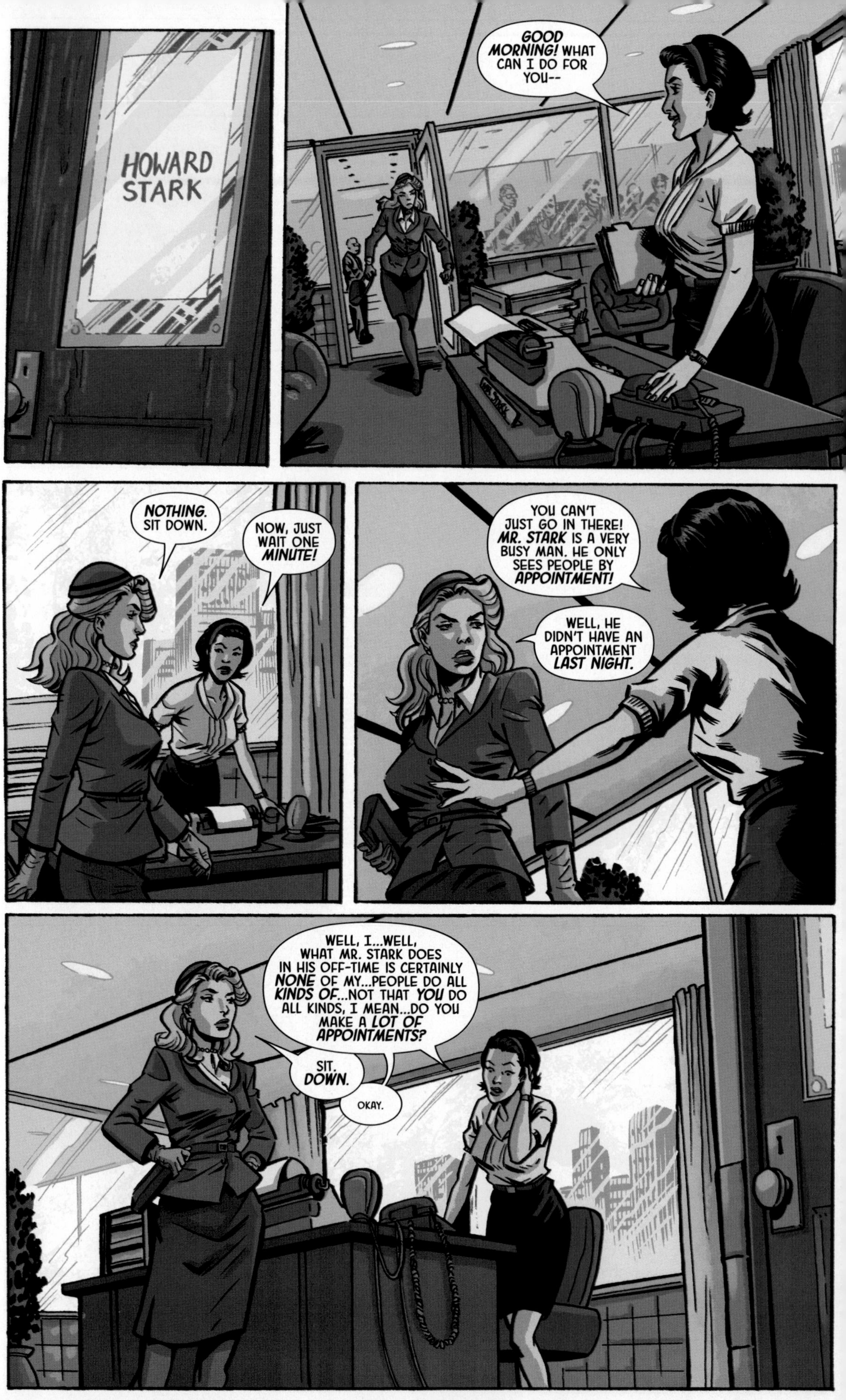
HOWARD STARK
GOOD MORNING! WHAT CAN I DO FOR YOU--
NOTHING. SIT DOWN.
NOW, JUST WAIT ONE MINUTE!
YOU CAN'T JUST GO IN THERE! MR. STARK IS A VERY BUSY MAN. HE ONLY SEES PEOPLE BY APPOINTMENT!
WELL, HE DIDN'T HAVE AN APPOINTMENT LAST NIGHT.
WELL, I...WELL, WHAT MR. STARK DOES IN HIS OFF-TIME IS CERTAINLY NONE OF MY...PEOPLE DO ALL KINDS OF...NOT THAT YOU DO ALL KINDS, I MEAN...DO YOU MAKE A LOT OF APPOINTMENTS?
SIT. DOWN.
OKAY.

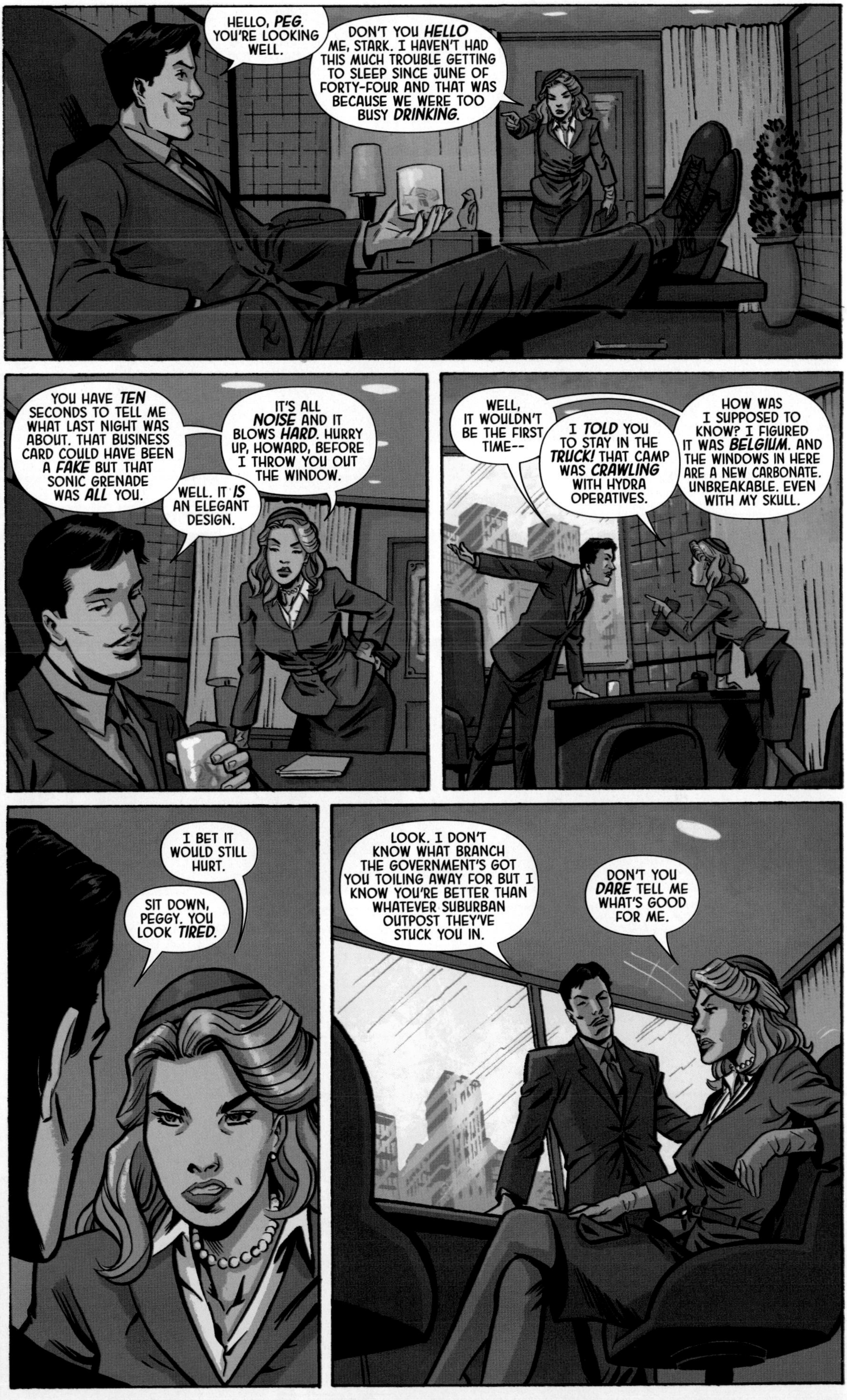
HELLO, PEG. YOU'RE LOOKING WELL.
DON'T YOU HELLO ME, STARK. I HAVEN'T HAD THIS MUCH TROUBLE GETTING TO SLEEP SINCE JUNE OF FORTY-FOUR AND THAT WAS BECAUSE WE WERE TOO BUSY DRINKING.
YOU HAVE TEN SECONDS TO TELL ME WHAT LAST NIGHT WAS ABOUT. THAT BUSINESS CARD COULD HAVE BEEN A FAKE BUT THAT SONIC GRENADE WAS ALL YOU.
WELL. IT IS AN ELEGANT DESIGN.
IT'S ALL NOISE AND IT BLOWS HARD. HURRY UP, HOWARD, BEFORE I THROW YOU OUT THE WINDOW.
WELL, IT WOULDN'T BE THE FIRST TIME--
I TOLD YOU TO STAY IN THE TRUCK! THAT CAMP WAS CRAWLING WITH HYDRA OPERATIVES.
HOW WAS I SUPPOSED TO KNOW? I FIGURED IT WAS BELGIUM. AND THE WINDOWS IN HERE ARE A NEW CARBONATE. UNBREAKABLE. EVEN WITH MY SKULL.
I BET IT WOULD STILL HURT.
SIT DOWN, PEGGY. YOU LOOK TIRED.
LOOK. I DON'T KNOW WHAT BRANCH THE GOVERNMENT'S GOT YOU TOILING AWAY FOR BUT I KNOW YOU'RE BETTER THAN WHATEVER SUBURBAN OUTPOST THEY'VE STUCK YOU IN.
DON'T YOU DARE TELL ME WHAT'S GOOD FOR ME.

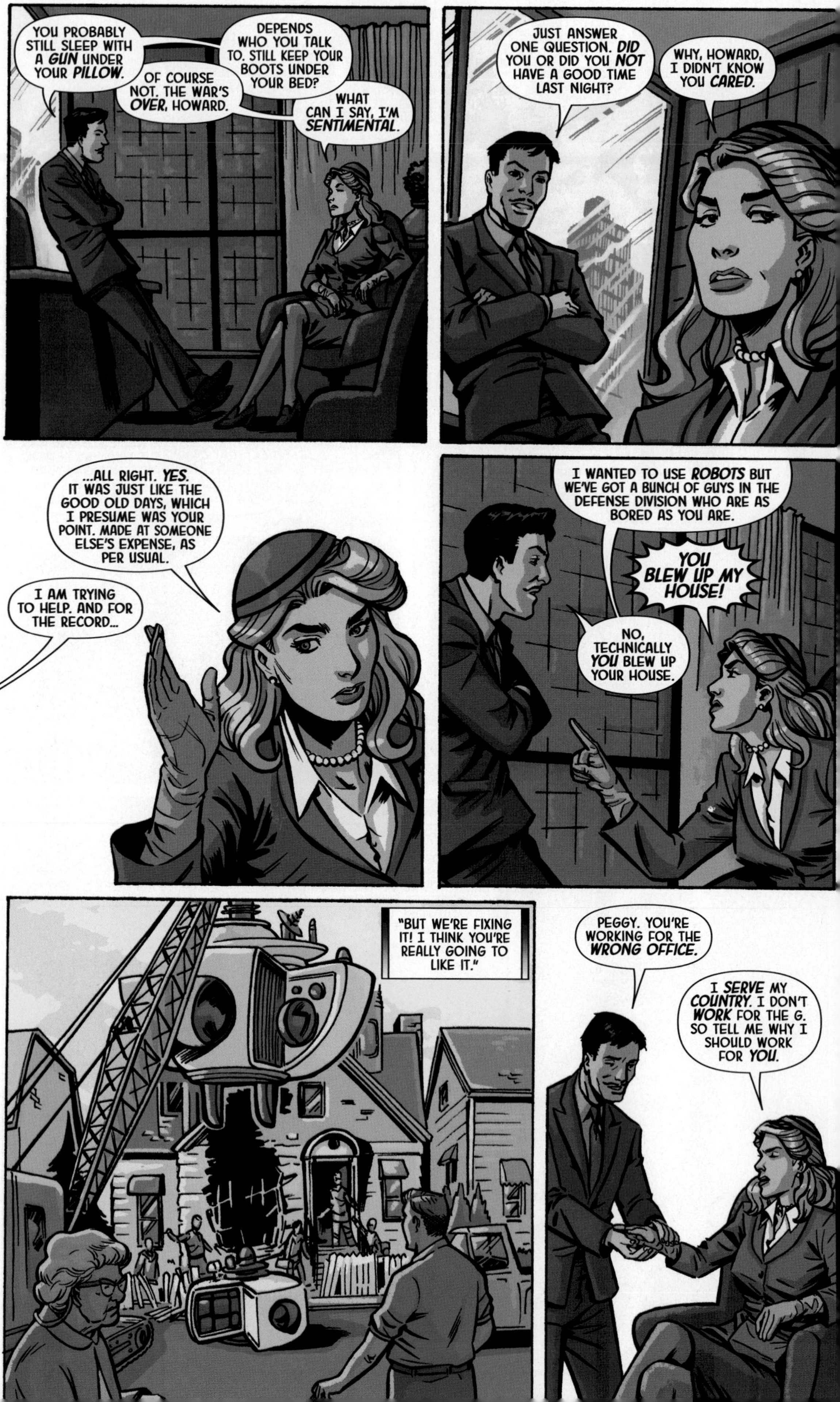
YOU PROBABLY STILL SLEEP WITH A GUN UNDER YOUR PILLOW.
DEPENDS WHO YOU TALK TO. STILL KEEP YOUR BOOTS UNDER YOUR BED?
OF COURSE NOT. THE WAR'S OVER, HOWARD.
WHAT CAN I SAY, I'M SENTIMENTAL.
JUST ANSWER ONE QUESTION. DID YOU OR DID YOU NOT HAVE A GOOD TIME LAST NIGHT?
WHY, HOWARD, I DIDN'T KNOW YOU CARED.
...ALL RIGHT. YES. IT WAS JUST LIKE THE GOOD OLD DAYS, WHICH I PRESUME WAS YOUR POINT. MADE AT SOMEONE ELSE'S EXPENSE, AS PER USUAL.
I AM TRYING TO HELP. AND FOR THE RECORD...
I WANTED TO USE ROBOTS BUT WE'VE GOT A BUNCH OF GUYS IN THE DEFENSE DIVISION WHO ARE AS BORED AS YOU ARE.
YOU BLEW UP MY HOUSE!
NO, TECHNICALLY YOU BLEW UP YOUR HOUSE.
"BUT WE'RE FIXING IT! I THINK YOU'RE REALLY GOING TO LIKE IT."
PEGGY. YOU'RE WORKING FOR THE WRONG OFFICE.
I SERVE MY COUNTRY. I DON'T WORK FOR THE G. SO TELL ME WHY I SHOULD WORK FOR YOU.

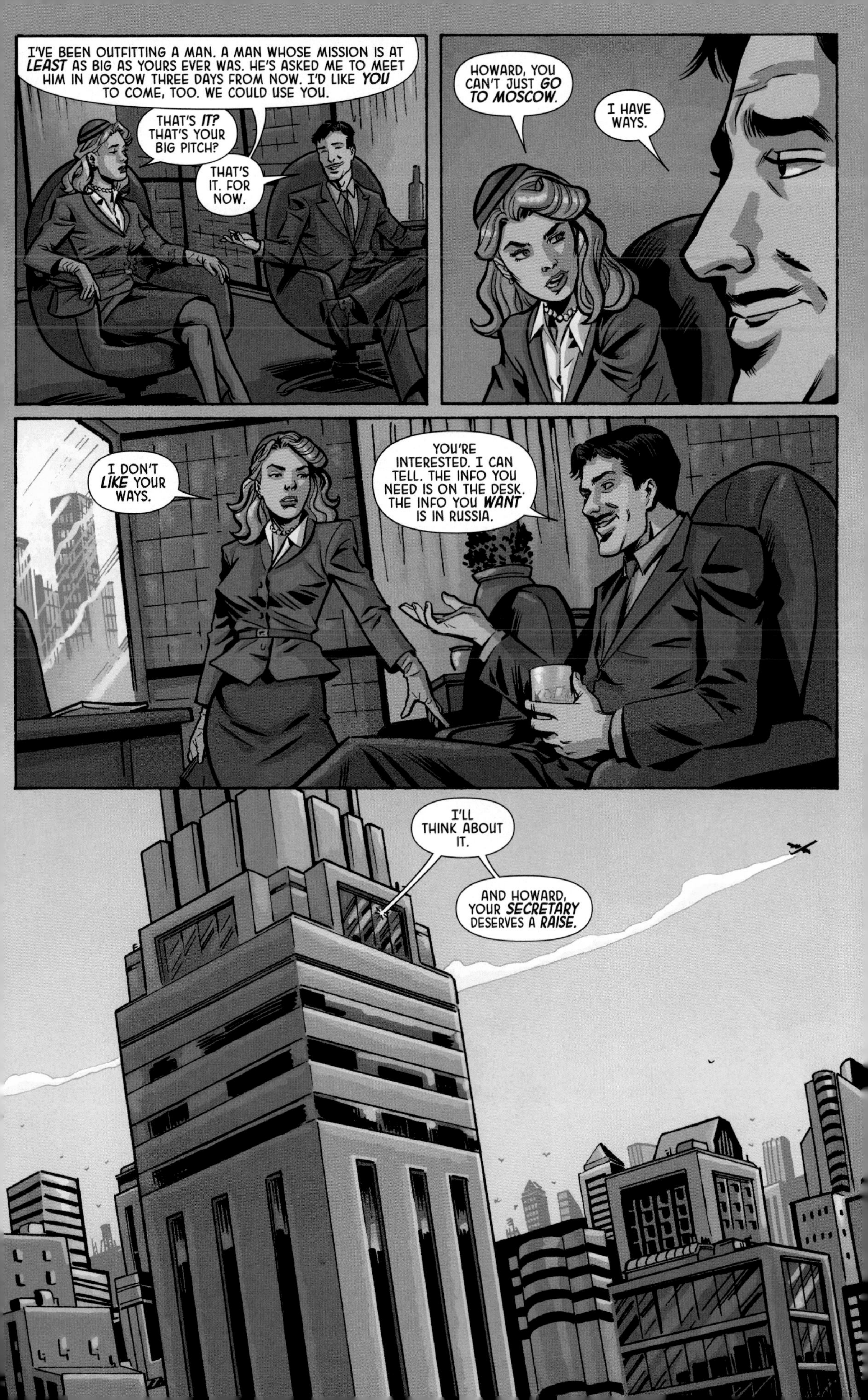
I'VE BEEN OUTFITTING A MAN. A MAN WHOSE MISSION IS AT LEAST AS BIG AS YOURS EVER WAS. HE'S ASKED ME TO MEET HIM IN MOSCOW THREE DAYS FROM NOW. I'D LIKE YOU TO COME, TOO. WE COULD USE YOU.
THAT'S IT? THAT'S YOUR BIG PITCH?
THAT'S IT. FOR NOW.
HOWARD, YOU CAN'T JUST GO TO MOSCOW.
I HAVE WAYS.
I DON'T LIKE YOUR WAYS.
YOU'RE INTERESTED. I CAN TELL. THE INFO YOU NEED IS ON THE DESK. THE INFO YOU WANT IS IN RUSSIA.
I'LL THINK ABOUT IT.
AND HOWARD, YOUR SECRETARY DESERVES A RAISE.

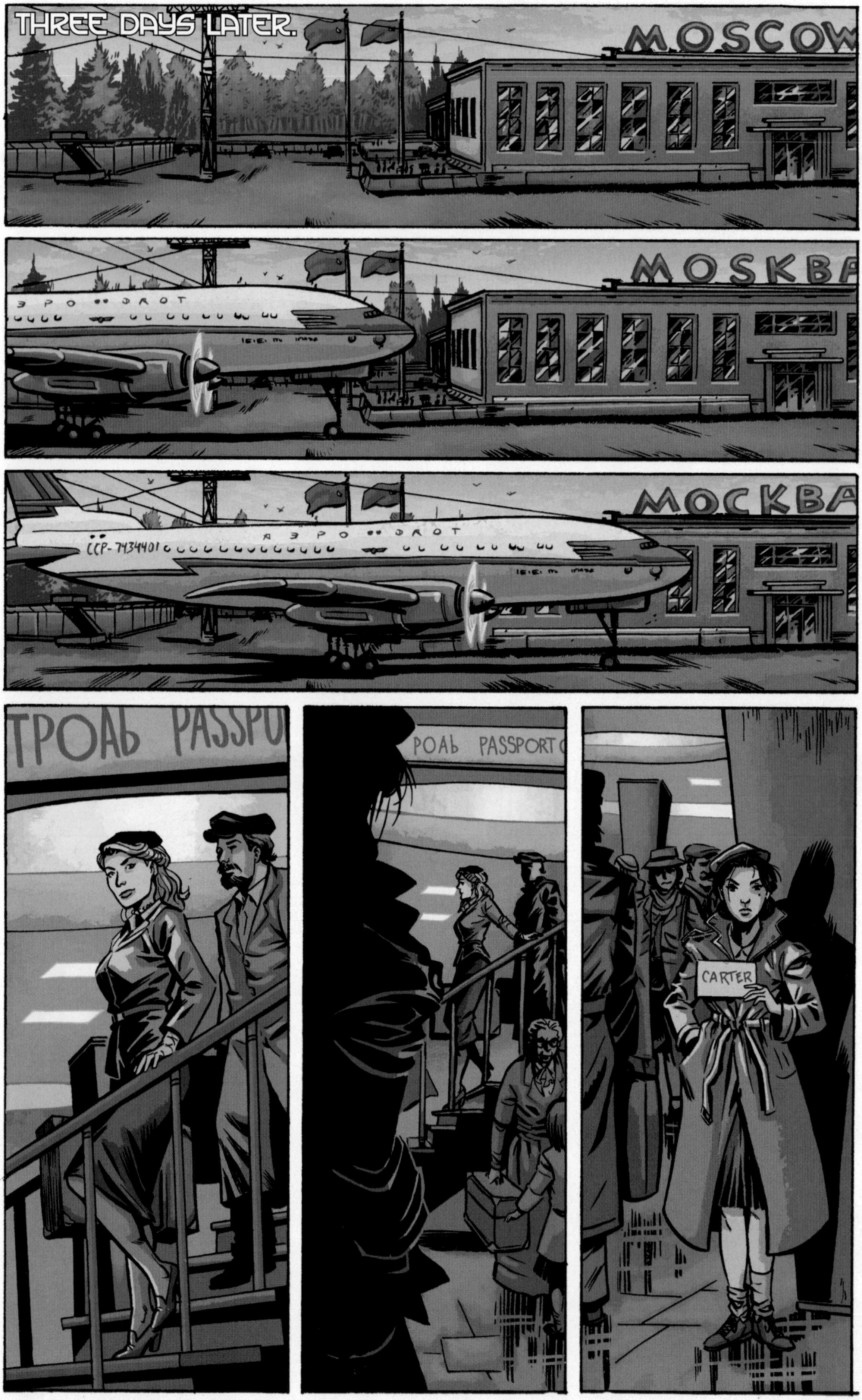
THREE DAYS LATER.
MOSCOW
MOSKBA
CCP-7434401
MOCKBA
TPOAb PASSPO
POAb PASSPORT
CARTER

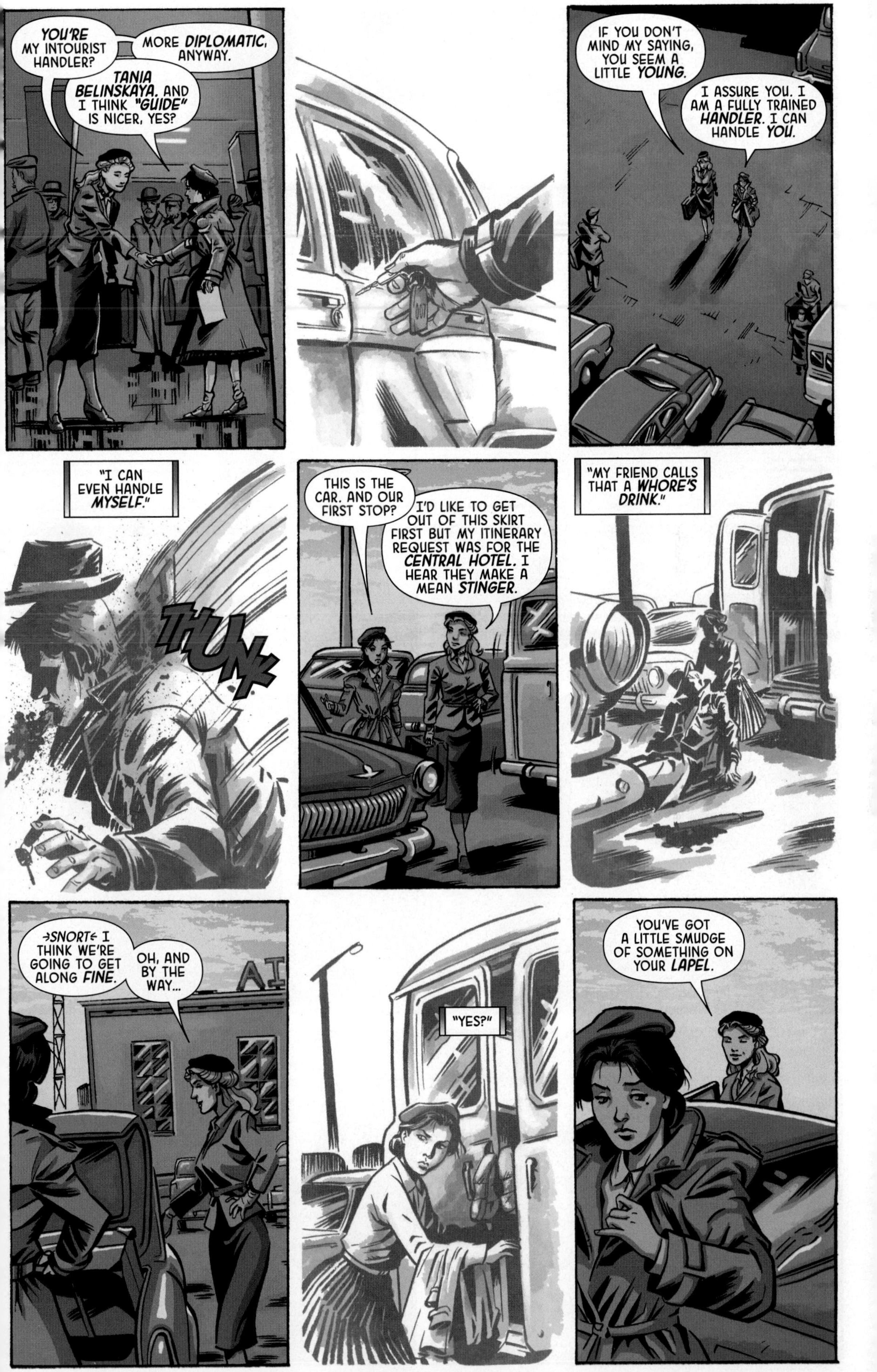
YOU'RE MY INTOURIST HANDLER?
MORE DIPLOMATIC, ANYWAY.
TANIA BELINSKAYA. AND I THINK "GUIDE" IS NICER, YES?
IF YOU DON'T MIND MY SAYING, YOU SEEM A LITTLE YOUNG.
I ASSURE YOU. I AM A FULLY TRAINED HANDLER. I CAN HANDLE YOU.
"I CAN EVEN HANDLE MYSELF."
THUNK
THIS IS THE CAR. AND OUR FIRST STOP?
I'D LIKE TO GET OUT OF THIS SKIRT FIRST BUT MY ITINERARY REQUEST WAS FOR THE CENTRAL HOTEL. I HEAR THEY MAKE A MEAN STINGER.
"MY FRIEND CALLS THAT A WHORE'S DRINK."
→SNORT← I THINK WE'RE GOING TO GET ALONG FINE.
OH, AND BY THE WAY...
"YES?"
YOU'VE GOT A LITTLE SMUDGE OF SOMETHING ON YOUR LAPEL.

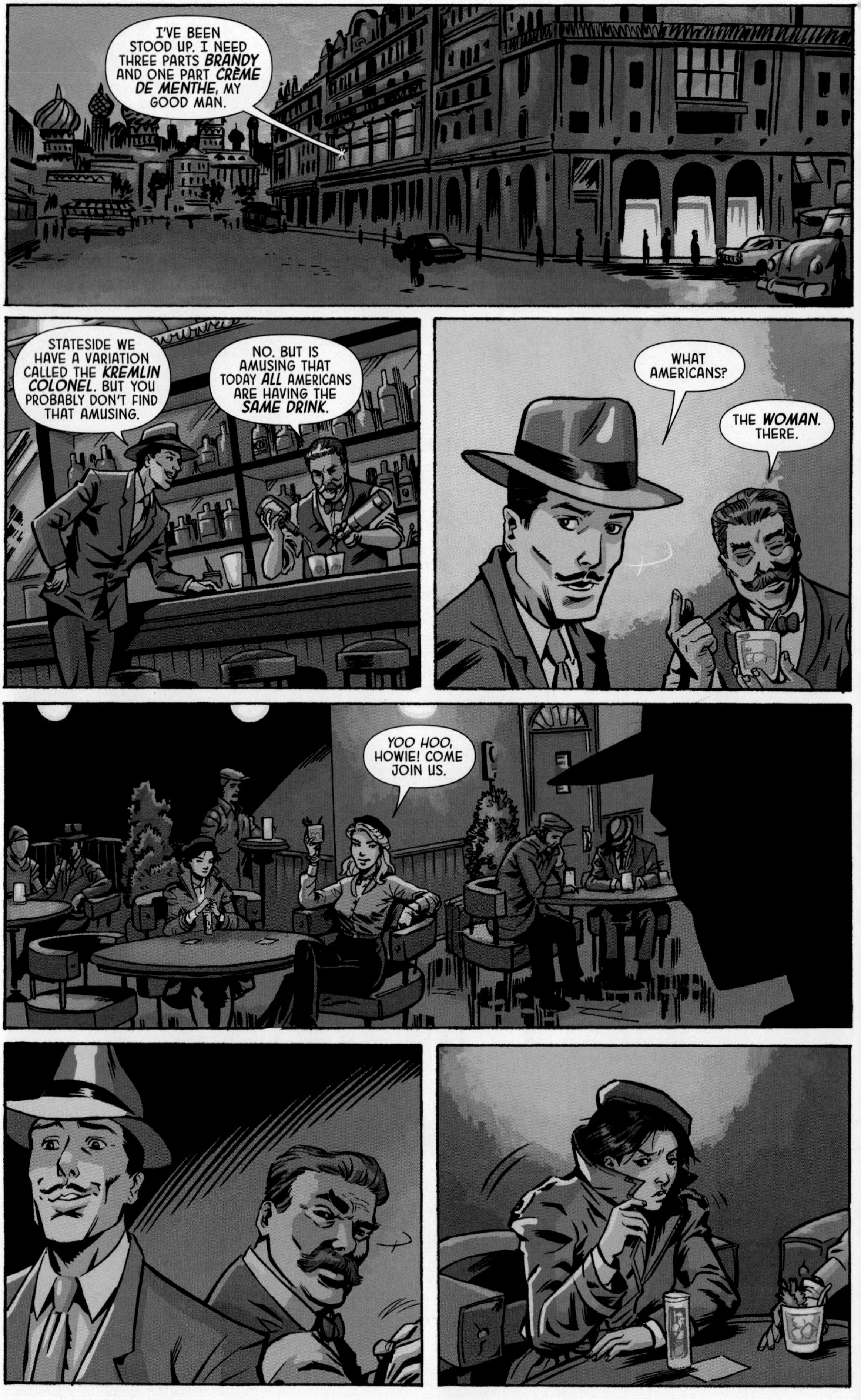
I'VE BEEN STOOD UP. I NEED THREE PARTS BRANDY AND ONE PART CRÈME DE MENTHE, MY GOOD MAN.
STATESIDE WE HAVE A VARIATION CALLED THE KREMLIN COLONEL. BUT YOU PROBABLY DON'T FIND THAT AMUSING.
NO. BUT IS AMUSING THAT TODAY ALL AMERICANS ARE HAVING THE SAME DRINK.
WHAT AMERICANS?
THE WOMAN. THERE.
YOO HOO, HOWIE! COME JOIN US.

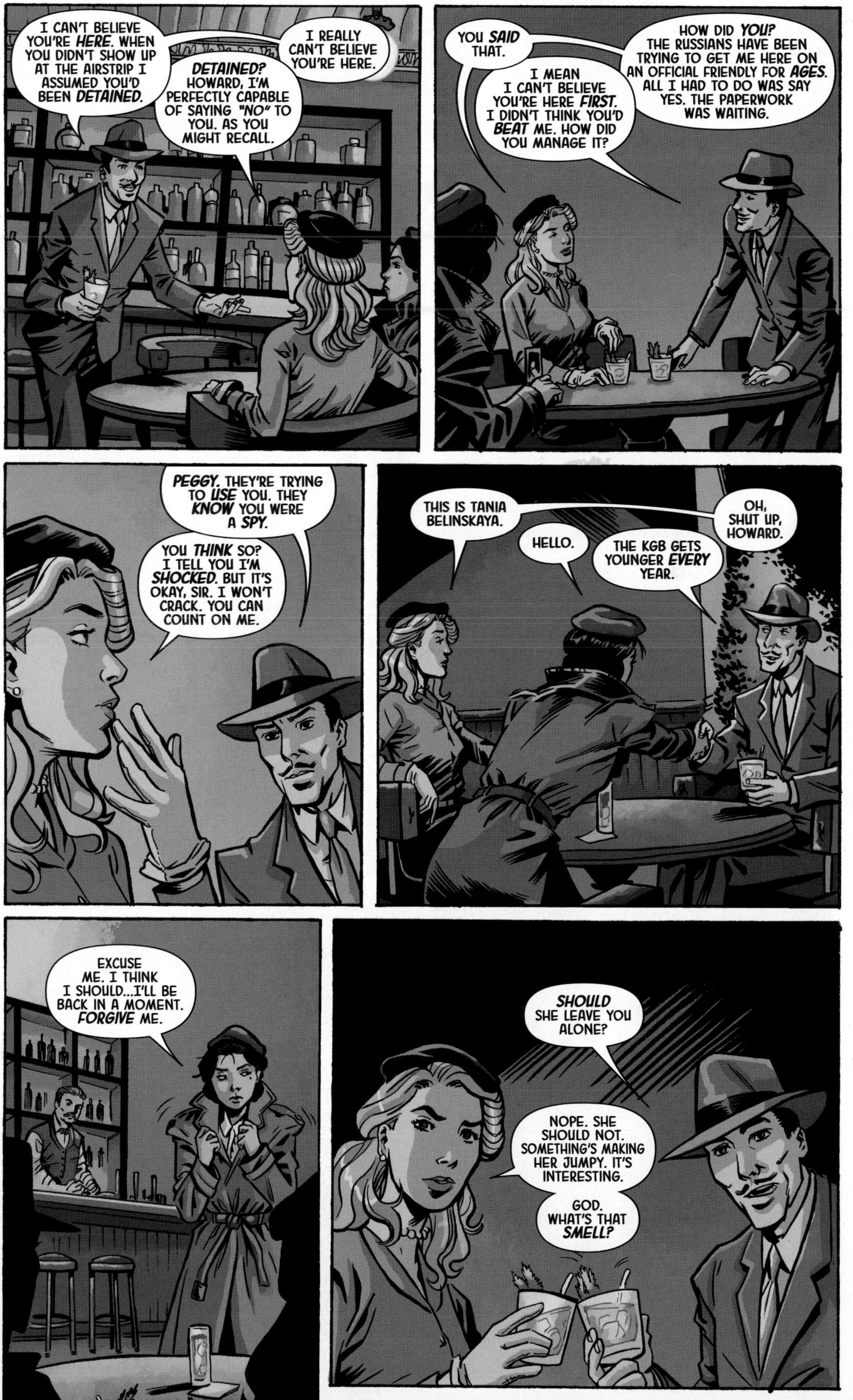
I CAN'T BELIEVE YOU'RE HERE. WHEN YOU DIDN'T SHOW UP AT THE AIRSTRIP I ASSUMED YOU'D BEEN DETAINED.
I REALLY CAN'T BELIEVE YOU'RE HERE.
DETAINED? HOWARD, I'M PERFECTLY CAPABLE OF SAYING "NO" TO YOU. AS YOU MIGHT RECALL.
YOU SAID THAT.
I MEAN I CAN'T BELIEVE YOU'RE HERE FIRST. I DIDN'T THINK YOU'D BEAT ME. HOW DID YOU MANAGE IT?
HOW DID YOU? THE RUSSIANS HAVE BEEN TRYING TO GET ME HERE ON AN OFFICIAL FRIENDLY FOR AGES. ALL I HAD TO DO WAS SAY YES. THE PAPERWORK WAS WAITING.
PEGGY. THEY'RE TRYING TO USE YOU. THEY KNOW YOU WERE A SPY.
YOU THINK SO? I TELL YOU I'M SHOCKED. BUT IT'S OKAY, SIR. I WON'T CRACK. YOU CAN COUNT ON ME.
THIS IS TANIA BELINSKAYA.
HELLO.
THE KGB GETS YOUNGER EVERY YEAR.
OH, SHUT UP, HOWARD.
EXCUSE ME. I THINK I SHOULD...I'LL BE BACK IN A MOMENT. FORGIVE ME.
SHOULD SHE LEAVE YOU ALONE?
NOPE. SHE SHOULD NOT. SOMETHING'S MAKING HER JUMPY. IT'S INTERESTING.
GOD. WHAT'S THAT SMELL?

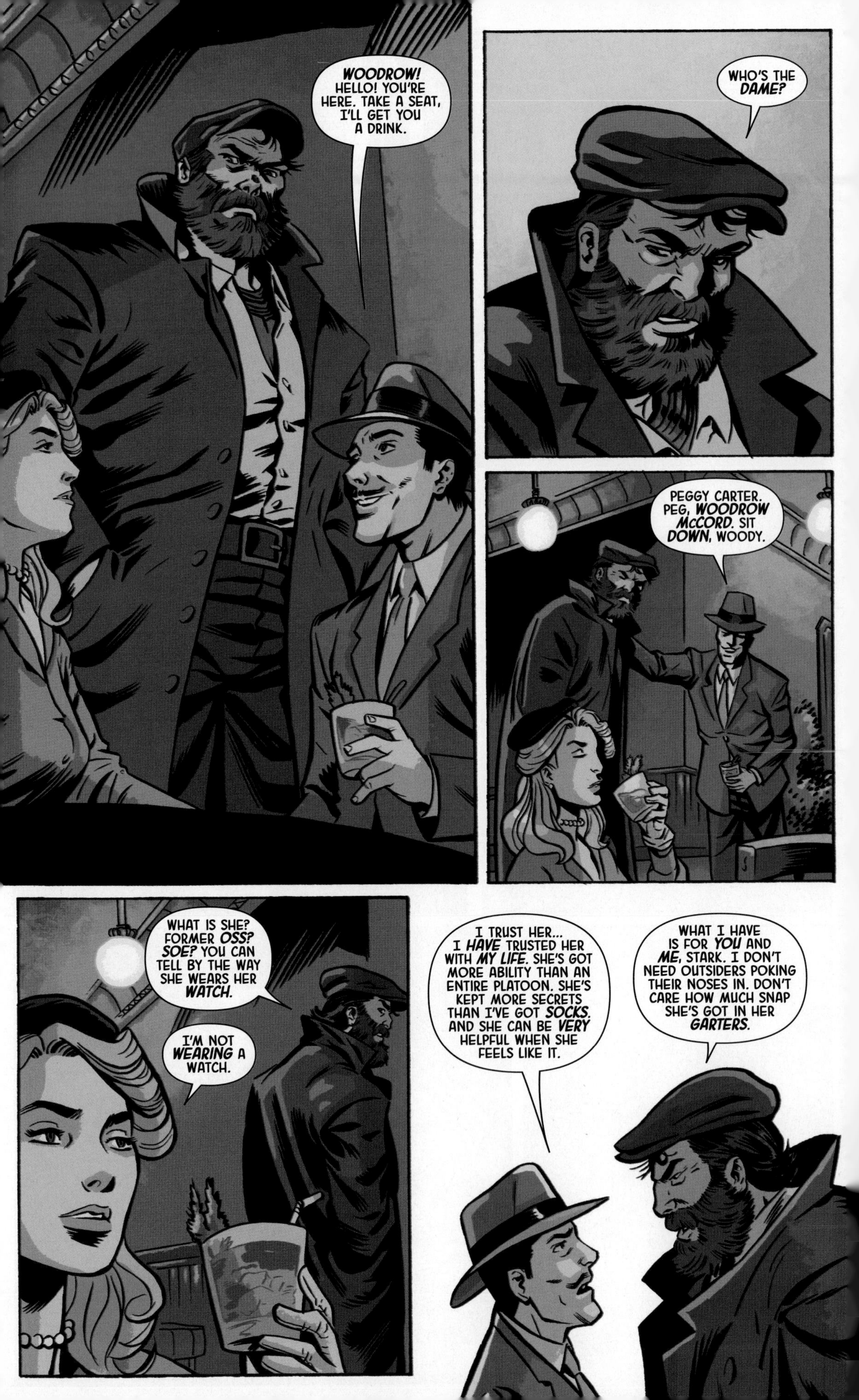
WOODROW! HELLO! YOU'RE HERE. TAKE A SEAT, I'LL GET YOU A DRINK.
WHO'S THE DAME?
PEGGY CARTER. PEG, WOODROW McCORD. SIT DOWN, WOODY.
WHAT IS SHE? FORMER OSS? SOE? YOU CAN TELL BY THE WAY SHE WEARS HER WATCH.
I'M NOT WEARING A WATCH.
I TRUST HER... I HAVE TRUSTED HER WITH MY LIFE. SHE'S GOT MORE ABILITY THAN AN ENTIRE PLATOON. SHE'S KEPT MORE SECRETS THAN I'VE GOT SOCKS. AND SHE CAN BE VERY HELPFUL WHEN SHE FEELS LIKE IT.
WHAT I HAVE IS FOR YOU AND ME, STARK. I DON'T NEED OUTSIDERS POKING THEIR NOSES IN. DON'T CARE HOW MUCH SNAP SHE'S GOT IN HER GARTERS.

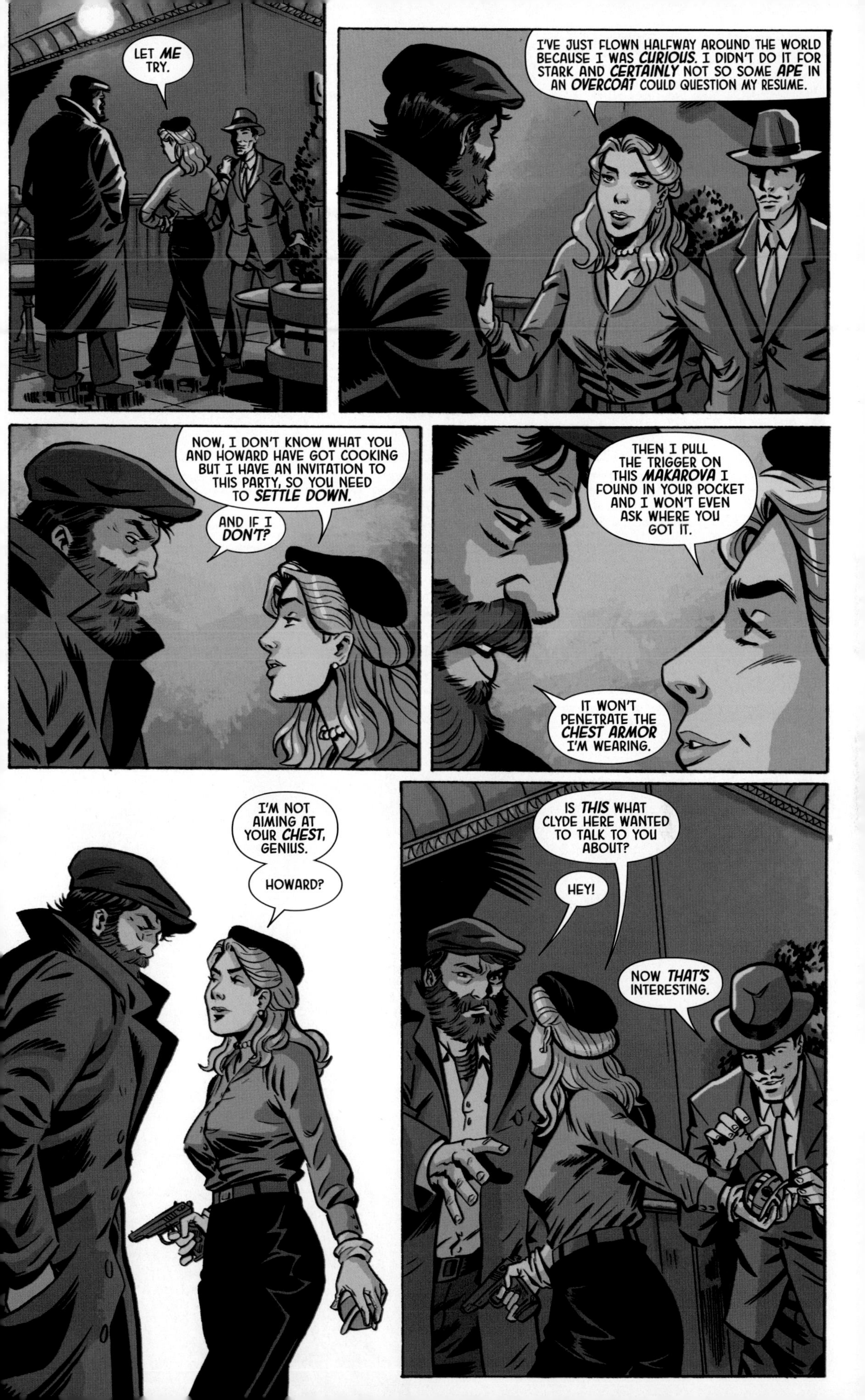
LET ME TRY.
I'VE JUST FLOWN HALFWAY AROUND THE WORLD BECAUSE I WAS CURIOUS. I DIDN'T DO IT FOR STARK AND CERTAINLY NOT SO SOME APE IN AN OVERCOAT COULD QUESTION MY RESUME.
NOW, I DON'T KNOW WHAT YOU AND HOWARD HAVE GOT COOKING BUT I HAVE AN INVITATION TO THIS PARTY, SO YOU NEED TO SETTLE DOWN.
AND IF I DON'T?
THEN I PULL THE TRIGGER ON THIS MAKAROVA I FOUND IN YOUR POCKET AND I WON'T EVEN ASK WHERE YOU GOT IT.
IT WON'T PENETRATE THE CHEST ARMOR I'M WEARING.
I'M NOT AIMING AT YOUR CHEST, GENIUS.
HOWARD?
IS THIS WHAT CLYDE HERE WANTED TO TALK TO YOU ABOUT?
HEY!
NOW THAT'S INTERESTING.

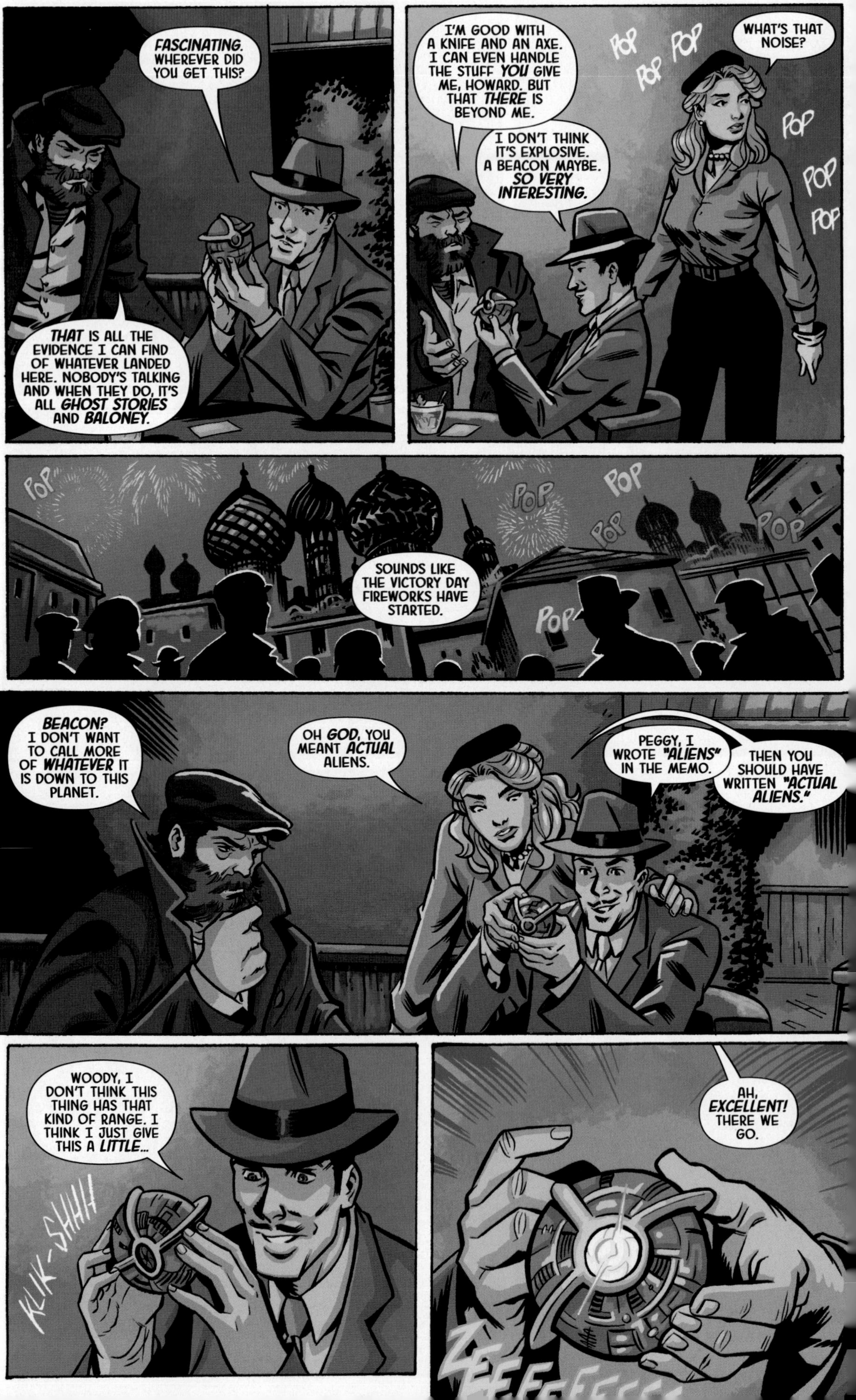
FASCINATING. WHEREVER DID YOU GET THIS?
THAT IS ALL THE EVIDENCE I CAN FIND OF WHATEVER LANDED HERE. NOBODY'S TALKING AND WHEN THEY DO, IT'S ALL GHOST STORIES AND BALONEY.
I'M GOOD WITH A KNIFE AND AN AXE. I CAN EVEN HANDLE THE STUFF YOU GIVE ME, HOWARD. BUT THAT THERE IS BEYOND ME.
I DON'T THINK IT'S EXPLOSIVE. A BEACON MAYBE. SO VERY INTERESTING.
POP POP POP
WHAT'S THAT NOISE?
POP POP POP
POP
POP POP
POP POP
SOUNDS LIKE THE VICTORY DAY FIREWORKS HAVE STARTED.
POP
BEACON? I DON'T WANT TO CALL MORE OF WHATEVER IT IS DOWN TO THIS PLANET.
OH GOD, YOU MEANT ACTUAL ALIENS.
PEGGY, I WROTE "ALIENS" IN THE MEMO.
THEN YOU SHOULD HAVE WRITTEN "ACTUAL ALIENS."
WOODY, I DON'T THINK THIS THING HAS THAT KIND OF RANGE. I THINK I JUST GIVE THIS A LITTLE...
KLIK-SHHH
AH, EXCELLENT! THERE WE GO.

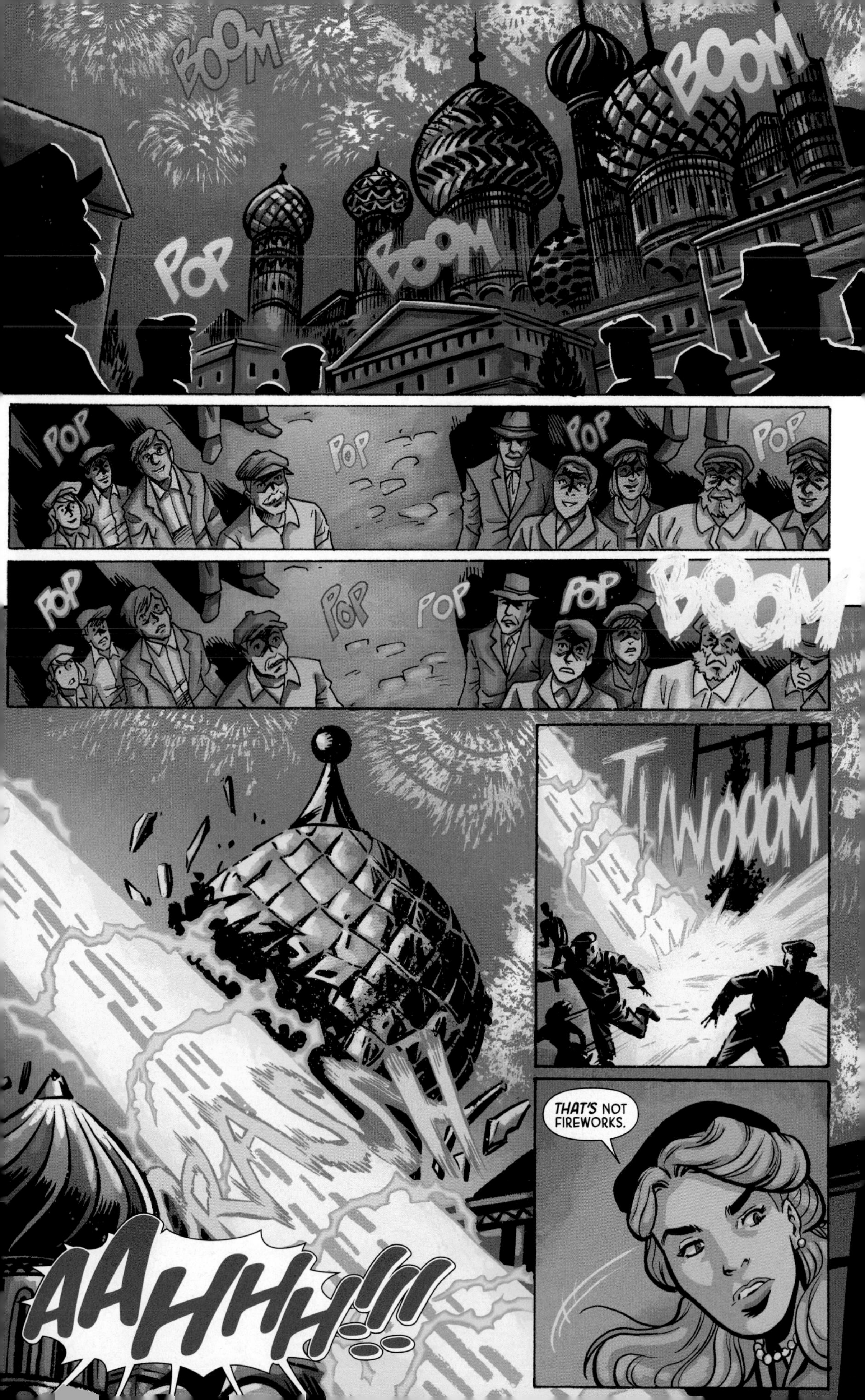
BOOM
BOOM
POP
BOOM
POP
POP
POP
POP
POP
POP
POP
POP
POP
BOOM
TWOOOM
CRASH
AAHHH!!!
THAT'S NOT FIREWORKS.

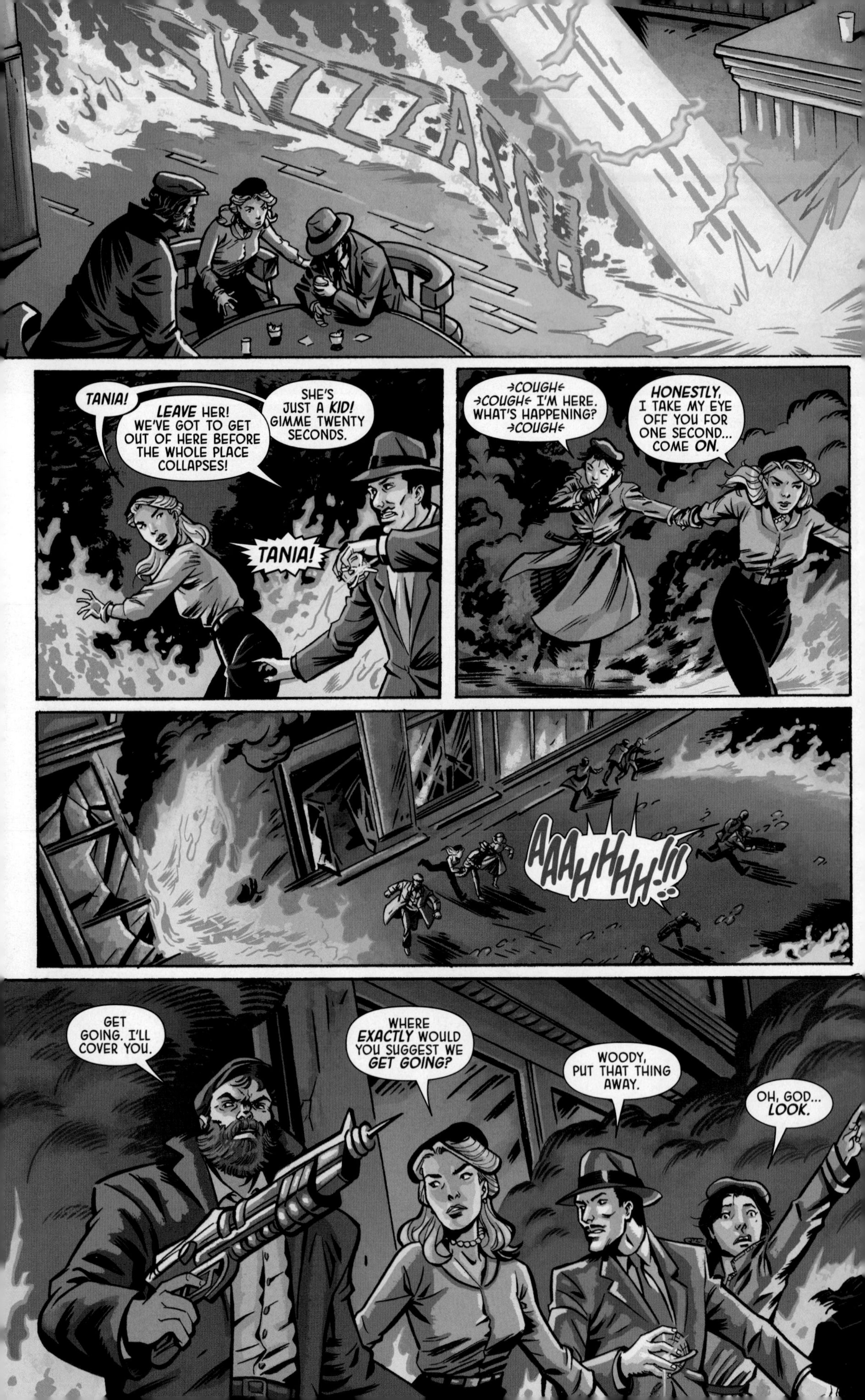
SKZZASCH
TANIA!
LEAVE HER! WE'VE GOT TO GET OUT OF HERE BEFORE THE WHOLE PLACE COLLAPSES!
SHE'S JUST A KID! GIMME TWENTY SECONDS.
TANIA!
>COUGH< >COUGH< I'M HERE. WHAT'S HAPPENING? >COUGH<
HONESTLY, I TAKE MY EYE OFF YOU FOR ONE SECOND... COME ON.
AAAHHHH!!!
GET GOING. I'LL COVER YOU.
WHERE EXACTLY WOULD YOU SUGGEST WE GET GOING?
WOODY, PUT THAT THING AWAY.
OH, GOD... LOOK.

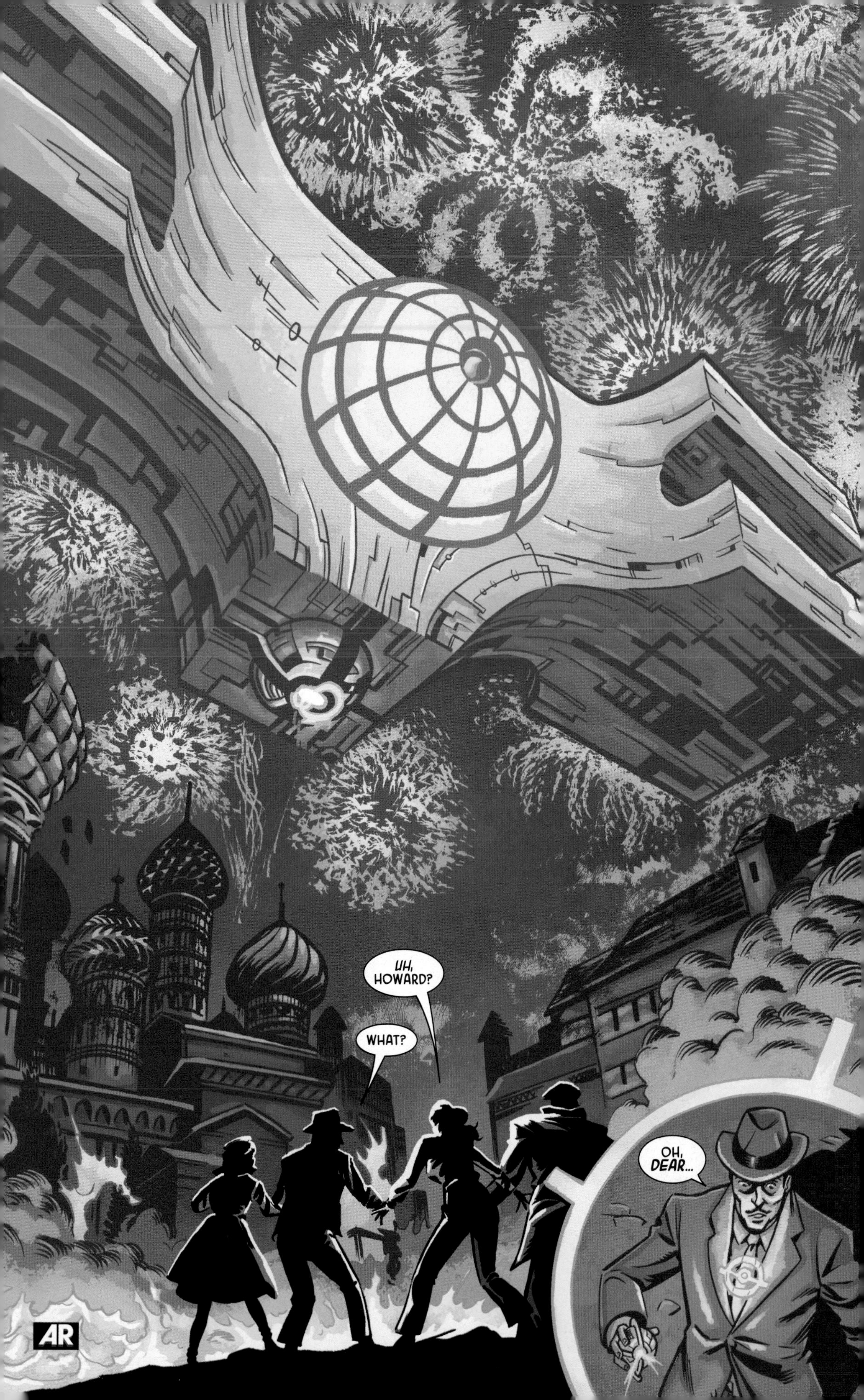
UH, HOWARD?
WHAT?
OH, DEAR...

2

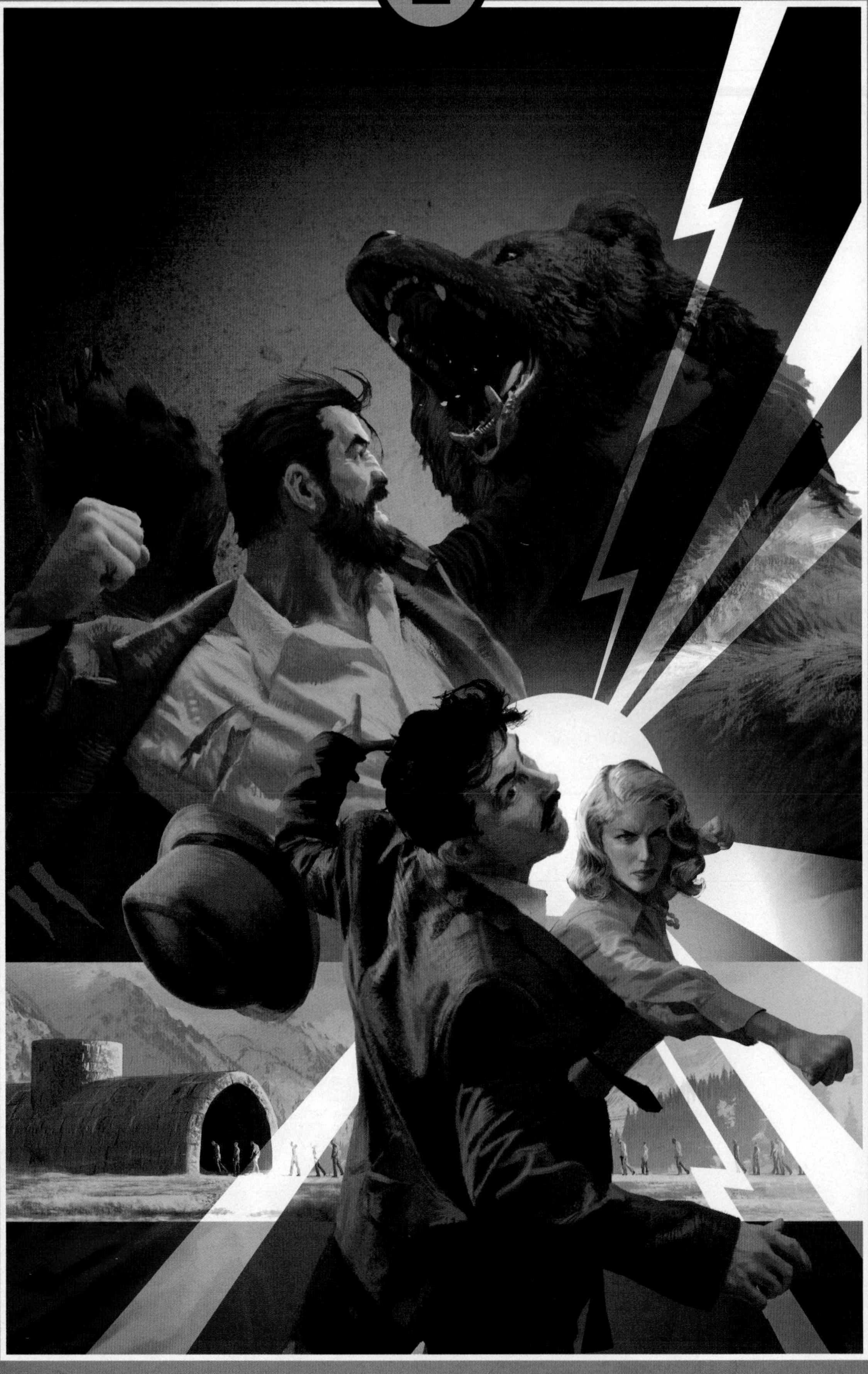

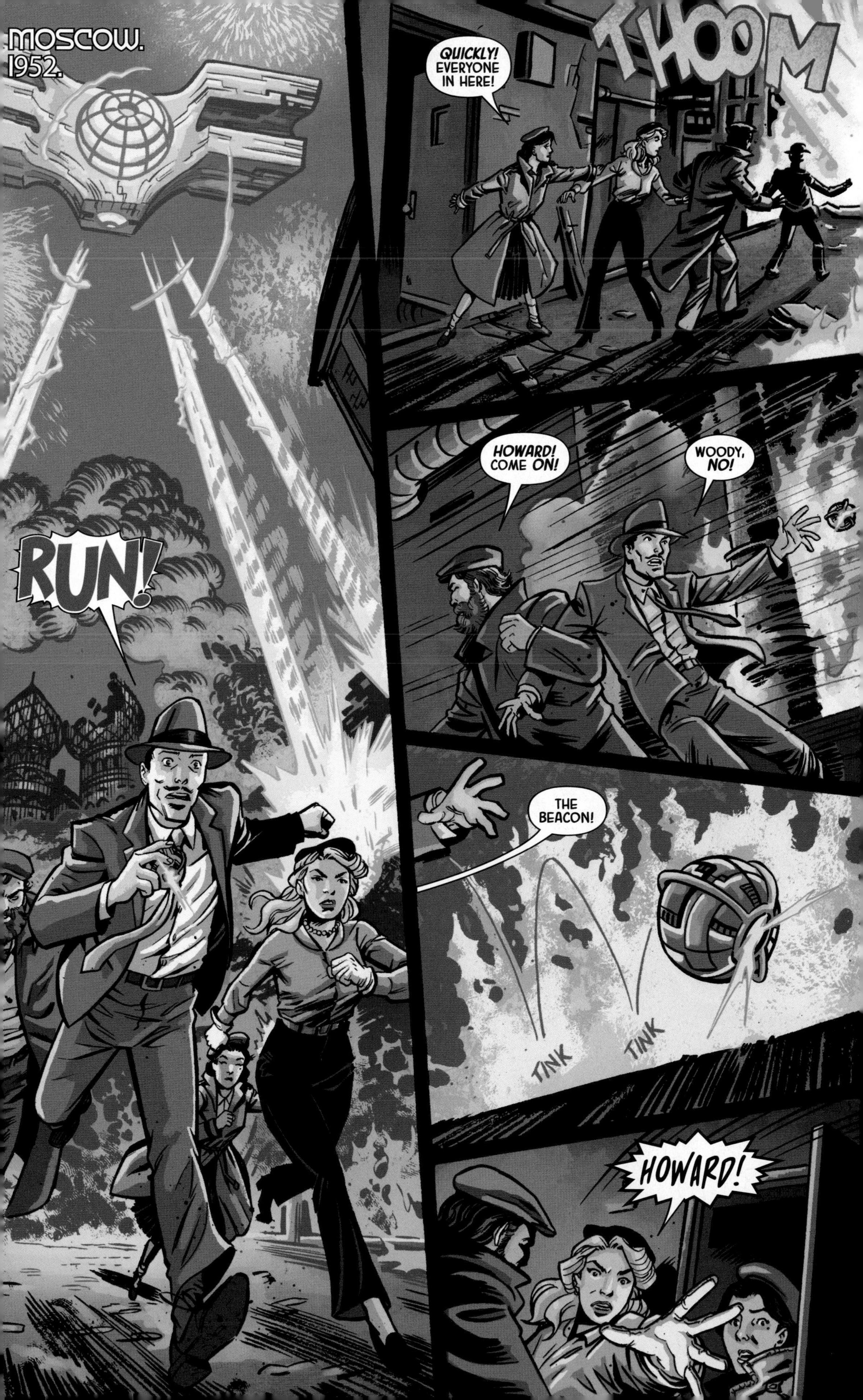
MOSCOW.
1952.
RUN!
QUICKLY! EVERYONE IN HERE!
THOOM
HOWARD! COME ON!
WOODY, NO!
THE BEACON!
TINK
TINK
HOWARD!

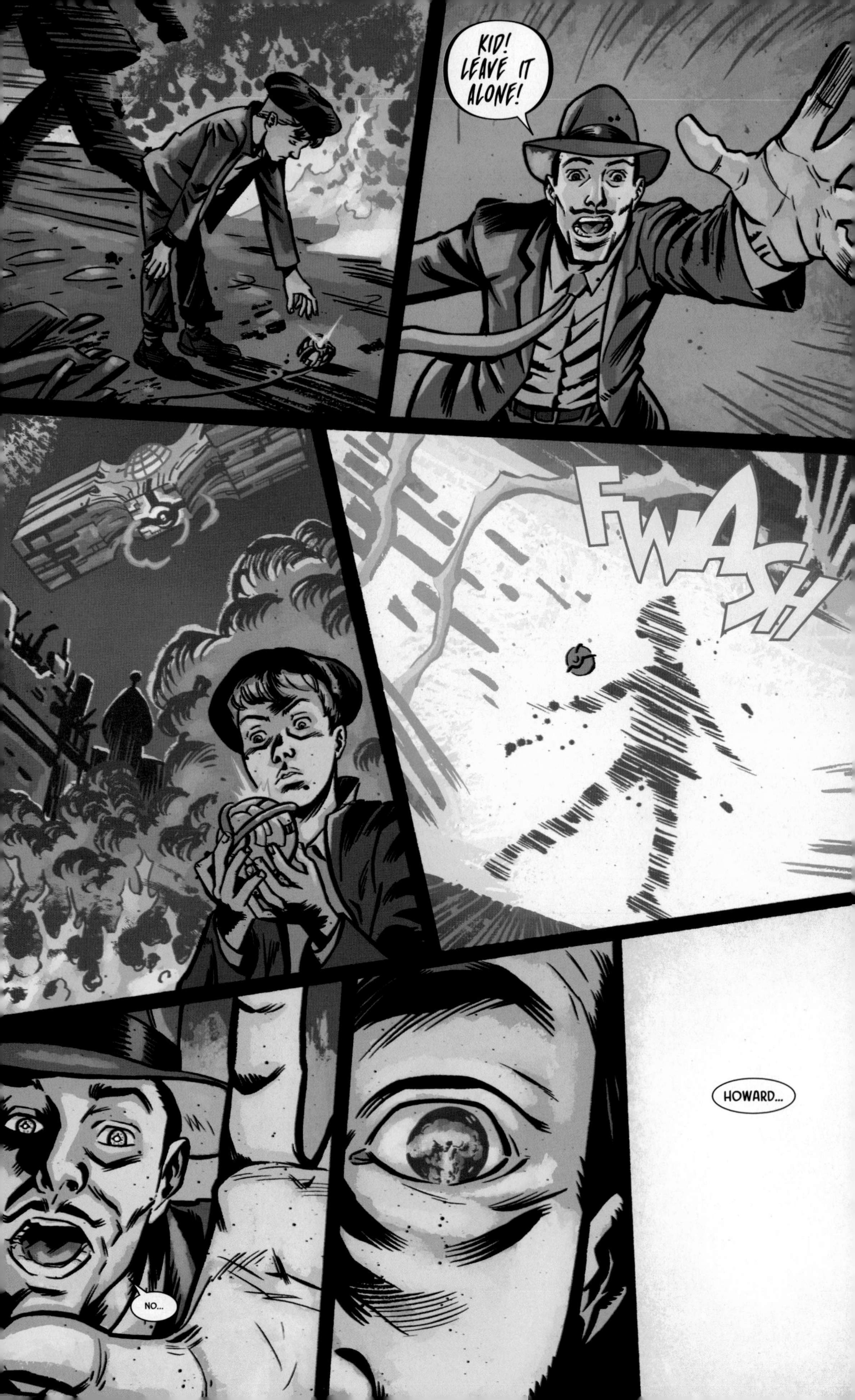
KID! LEAVE IT ALONE!
FWASH
HOWARD...
NO...

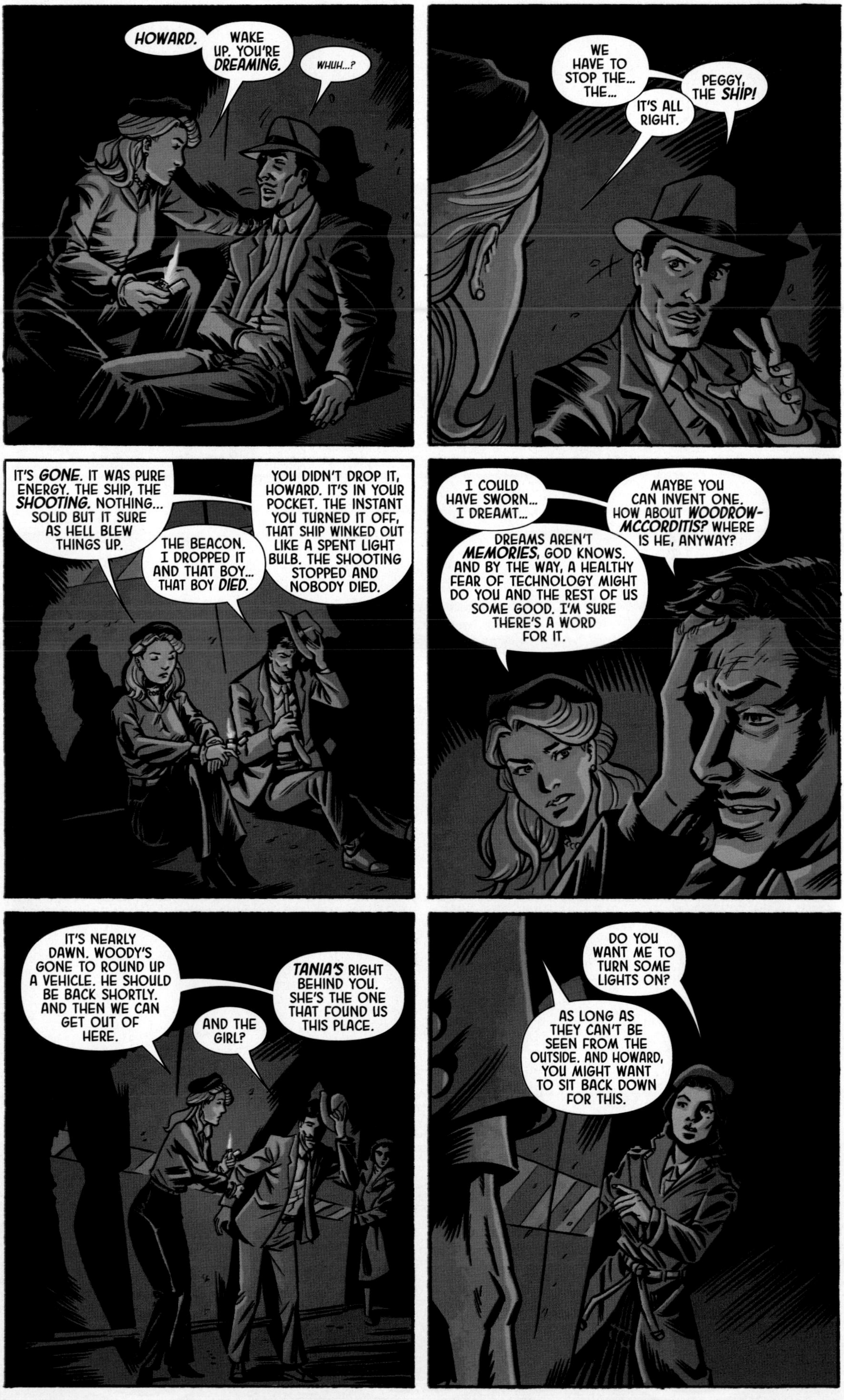
HOWARD.
WAKE UP. YOU'RE DREAMING.
WHUH...?
WE HAVE TO STOP THE... THE...
PEGGY, THE SHIP!
IT'S ALL RIGHT.
IT'S GONE. IT WAS PURE ENERGY. THE SHIP, THE SHOOTING. NOTHING... SOLID BUT IT SURE AS HELL BLEW THINGS UP.
THE BEACON. I DROPPED IT AND THAT BOY... THAT BOY DIED.
YOU DIDN'T DROP IT, HOWARD. IT'S IN YOUR POCKET. THE INSTANT YOU TURNED IT OFF, THAT SHIP WINKED OUT LIKE A SPENT LIGHT BULB. THE SHOOTING STOPPED AND NOBODY DIED.
I COULD HAVE SWORN... I DREAMT...
DREAMS AREN'T MEMORIES, GOD KNOWS. AND BY THE WAY, A HEALTHY FEAR OF TECHNOLOGY MIGHT DO YOU AND THE REST OF US SOME GOOD. I'M SURE THERE'S A WORD FOR IT.
MAYBE YOU CAN INVENT ONE. HOW ABOUT WOODROW-MCCORDITIS? WHERE IS HE, ANYWAY?
IT'S NEARLY DAWN. WOODY'S GONE TO ROUND UP A VEHICLE. HE SHOULD BE BACK SHORTLY. AND THEN WE CAN GET OUT OF HERE.
AND THE GIRL?
TANIA'S RIGHT BEHIND YOU. SHE'S THE ONE THAT FOUND US THIS PLACE.
DO YOU WANT ME TO TURN SOME LIGHTS ON?
AS LONG AS THEY CAN'T BE SEEN FROM THE OUTSIDE. AND HOWARD, YOU MIGHT WANT TO SIT BACK DOWN FOR THIS.

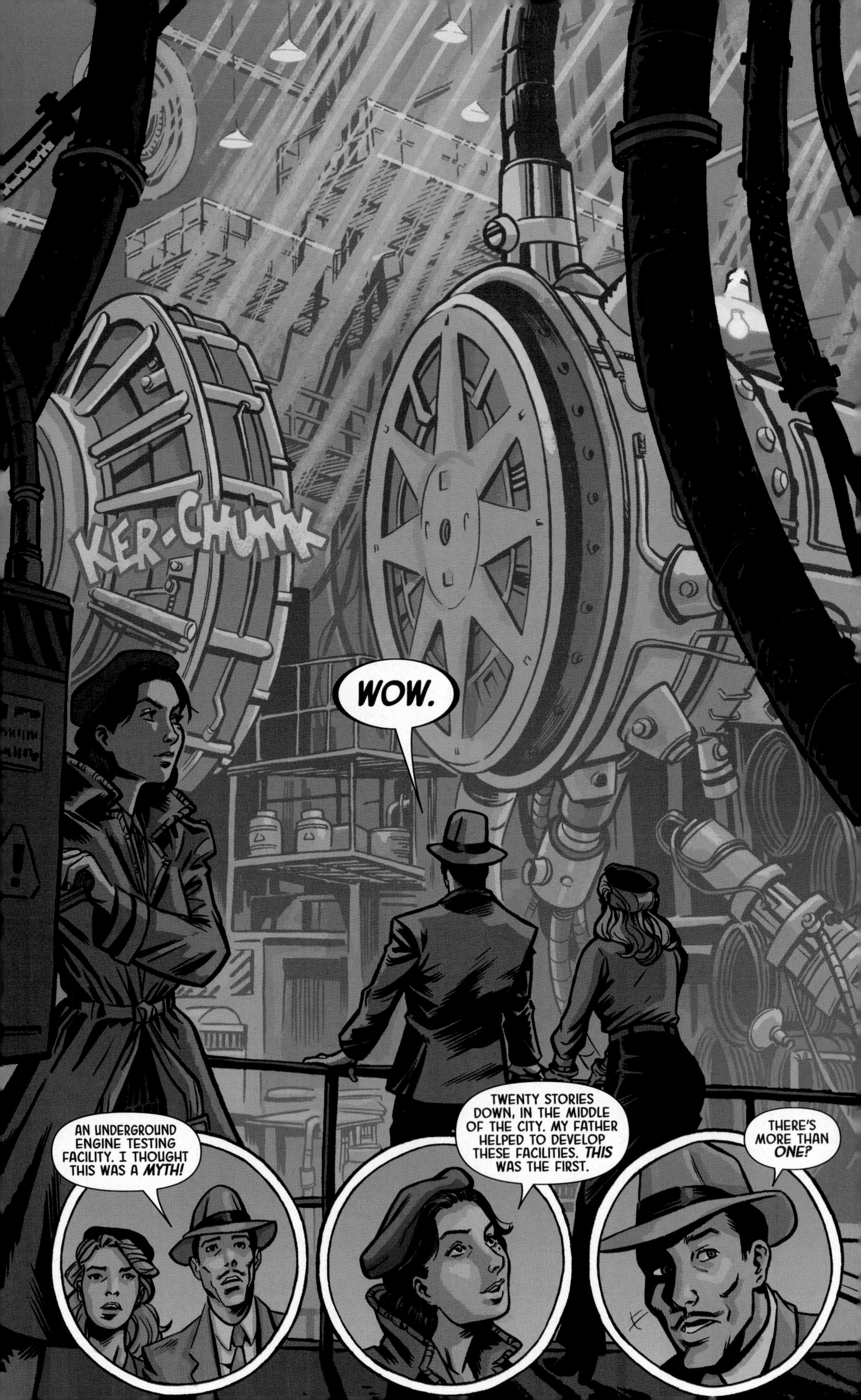
KER-CHUNK
WOW.
AN UNDERGROUND ENGINE TESTING FACILITY. I THOUGHT THIS WAS A *MYTH!*
TWENTY STORIES DOWN, IN THE MIDDLE OF THE CITY. MY FATHER HELPED TO DEVELOP THESE FACILITIES. *THIS* WAS THE FIRST.
THERE'S MORE THAN *ONE?*

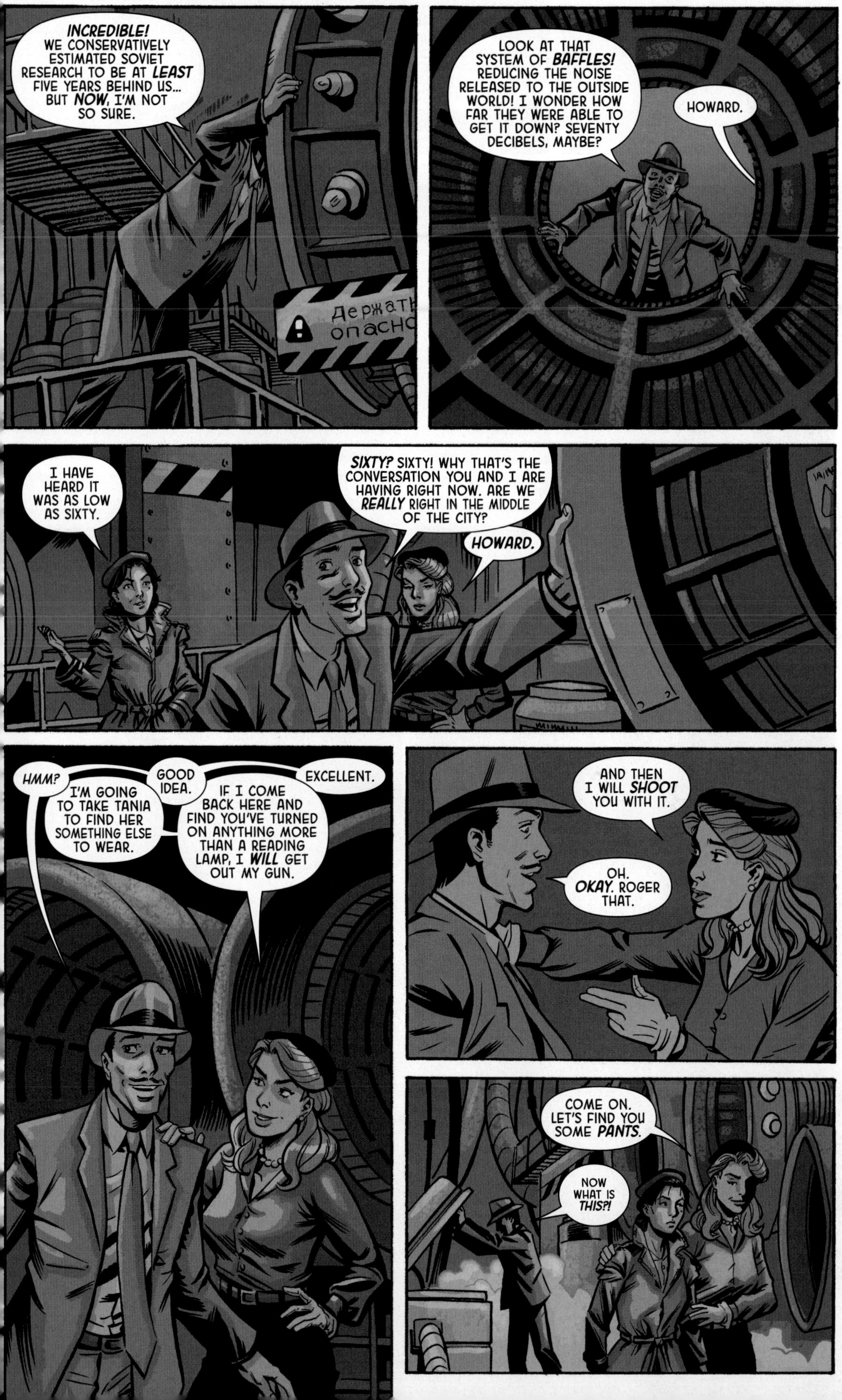
INCREDIBLE! WE CONSERVATIVELY ESTIMATED SOVIET RESEARCH TO BE AT LEAST FIVE YEARS BEHIND US... BUT NOW, I'M NOT SO SURE.
Держат
опасн
LOOK AT THAT SYSTEM OF BAFFLES! REDUCING THE NOISE RELEASED TO THE OUTSIDE WORLD! I WONDER HOW FAR THEY WERE ABLE TO GET IT DOWN? SEVENTY DECIBELS, MAYBE?
HOWARD.
I HAVE HEARD IT WAS AS LOW AS SIXTY.
SIXTY? SIXTY! WHY THAT'S THE CONVERSATION YOU AND I ARE HAVING RIGHT NOW. ARE WE REALLY RIGHT IN THE MIDDLE OF THE CITY?
HOWARD.
HMM?
I'M GOING TO TAKE TANIA TO FIND HER SOMETHING ELSE TO WEAR.
GOOD IDEA.
IF I COME BACK HERE AND FIND YOU'VE TURNED ON ANYTHING MORE THAN A READING LAMP, I WILL GET OUT MY GUN.
EXCELLENT.
AND THEN I WILL SHOOT YOU WITH IT.
OH. OKAY. ROGER THAT.
COME ON. LET'S FIND YOU SOME PANTS.
NOW WHAT IS THIS?!

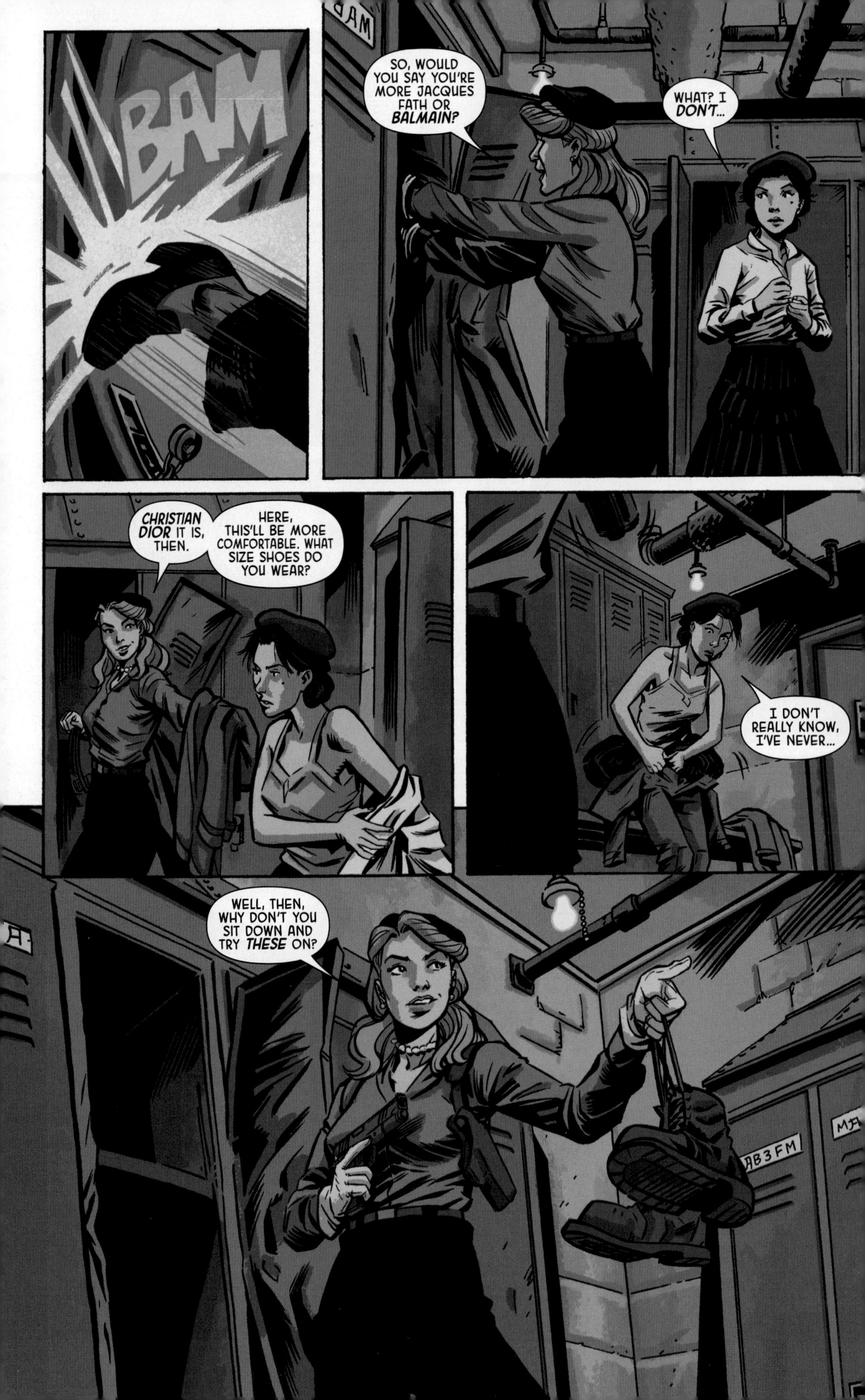
BAM
SO, WOULD YOU SAY YOU'RE MORE JACQUES FATH OR BALMAIN?
WHAT? I DON'T...
CHRISTIAN DIOR IT IS, THEN.
HERE, THIS'LL BE MORE COMFORTABLE. WHAT SIZE SHOES DO YOU WEAR?
I DON'T REALLY KNOW, I'VE NEVER...
WELL, THEN, WHY DON'T YOU SIT DOWN AND TRY THESE ON?

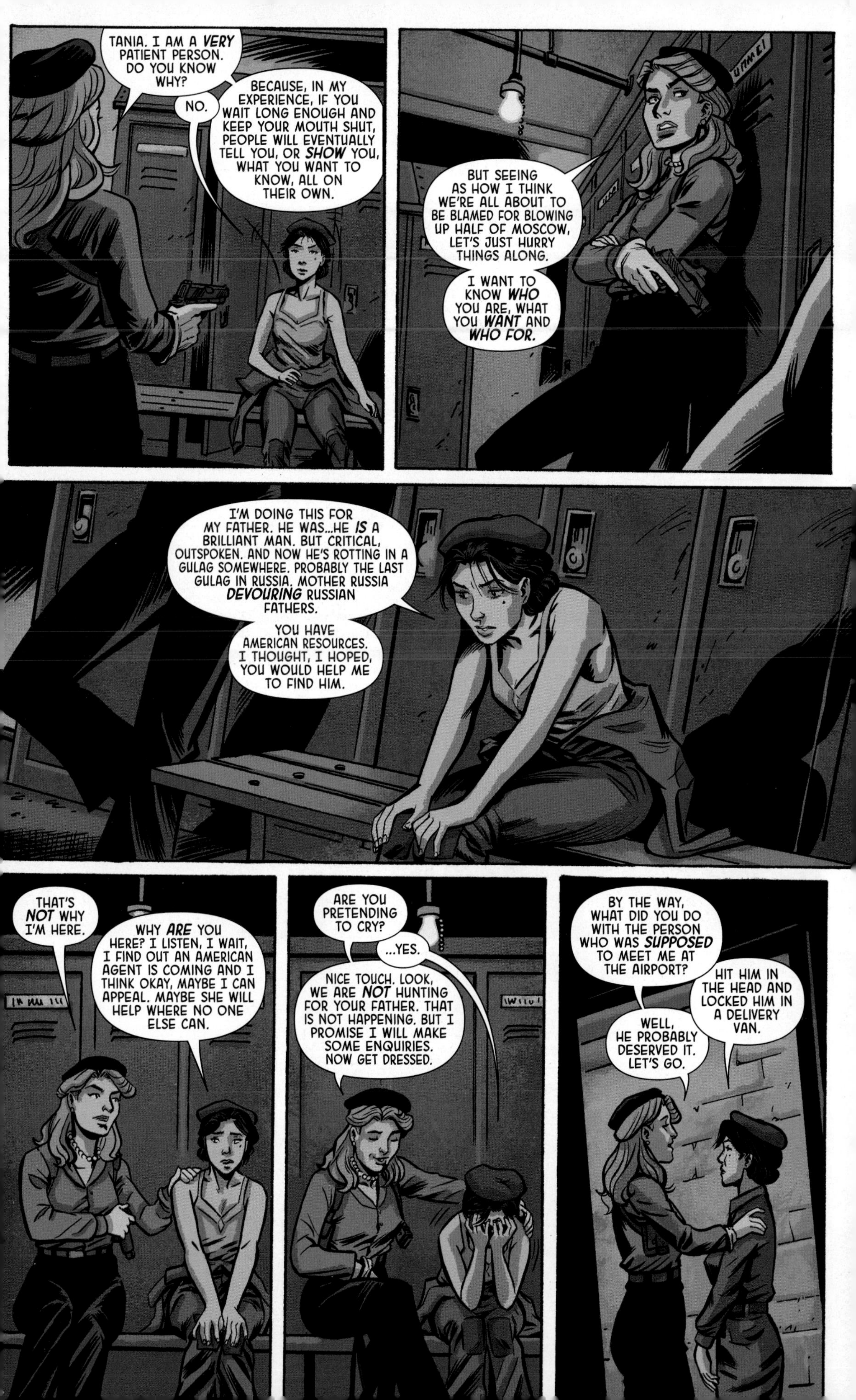
TANIA. I AM A VERY PATIENT PERSON. DO YOU KNOW WHY?
NO.
BECAUSE, IN MY EXPERIENCE, IF YOU WAIT LONG ENOUGH AND KEEP YOUR MOUTH SHUT, PEOPLE WILL EVENTUALLY TELL YOU, OR SHOW YOU, WHAT YOU WANT TO KNOW, ALL ON THEIR OWN.
BUT SEEING AS HOW I THINK WE'RE ALL ABOUT TO BE BLAMED FOR BLOWING UP HALF OF MOSCOW, LET'S JUST HURRY THINGS ALONG.
I WANT TO KNOW WHO YOU ARE, WHAT YOU WANT AND WHO FOR.
I'M DOING THIS FOR MY FATHER. HE WAS...HE IS A BRILLIANT MAN. BUT CRITICAL, OUTSPOKEN. AND NOW HE'S ROTTING IN A GULAG SOMEWHERE. PROBABLY THE LAST GULAG IN RUSSIA. MOTHER RUSSIA DEVOURING RUSSIAN FATHERS.
YOU HAVE AMERICAN RESOURCES. I THOUGHT, I HOPED, YOU WOULD HELP ME TO FIND HIM.
THAT'S NOT WHY I'M HERE.
WHY ARE YOU HERE? I LISTEN, I WAIT, I FIND OUT AN AMERICAN AGENT IS COMING AND I THINK OKAY, MAYBE I CAN APPEAL. MAYBE SHE WILL HELP WHERE NO ONE ELSE CAN.
ARE YOU PRETENDING TO CRY?
...YES.
NICE TOUCH. LOOK, WE ARE NOT HUNTING FOR YOUR FATHER. THAT IS NOT HAPPENING. BUT I PROMISE I WILL MAKE SOME ENQUIRIES. NOW GET DRESSED.
BY THE WAY, WHAT DID YOU DO WITH THE PERSON WHO WAS SUPPOSED TO MEET ME AT THE AIRPORT?
HIT HIM IN THE HEAD AND LOCKED HIM IN A DELIVERY VAN.
WELL, HE PROBABLY DESERVED IT. LET'S GO.

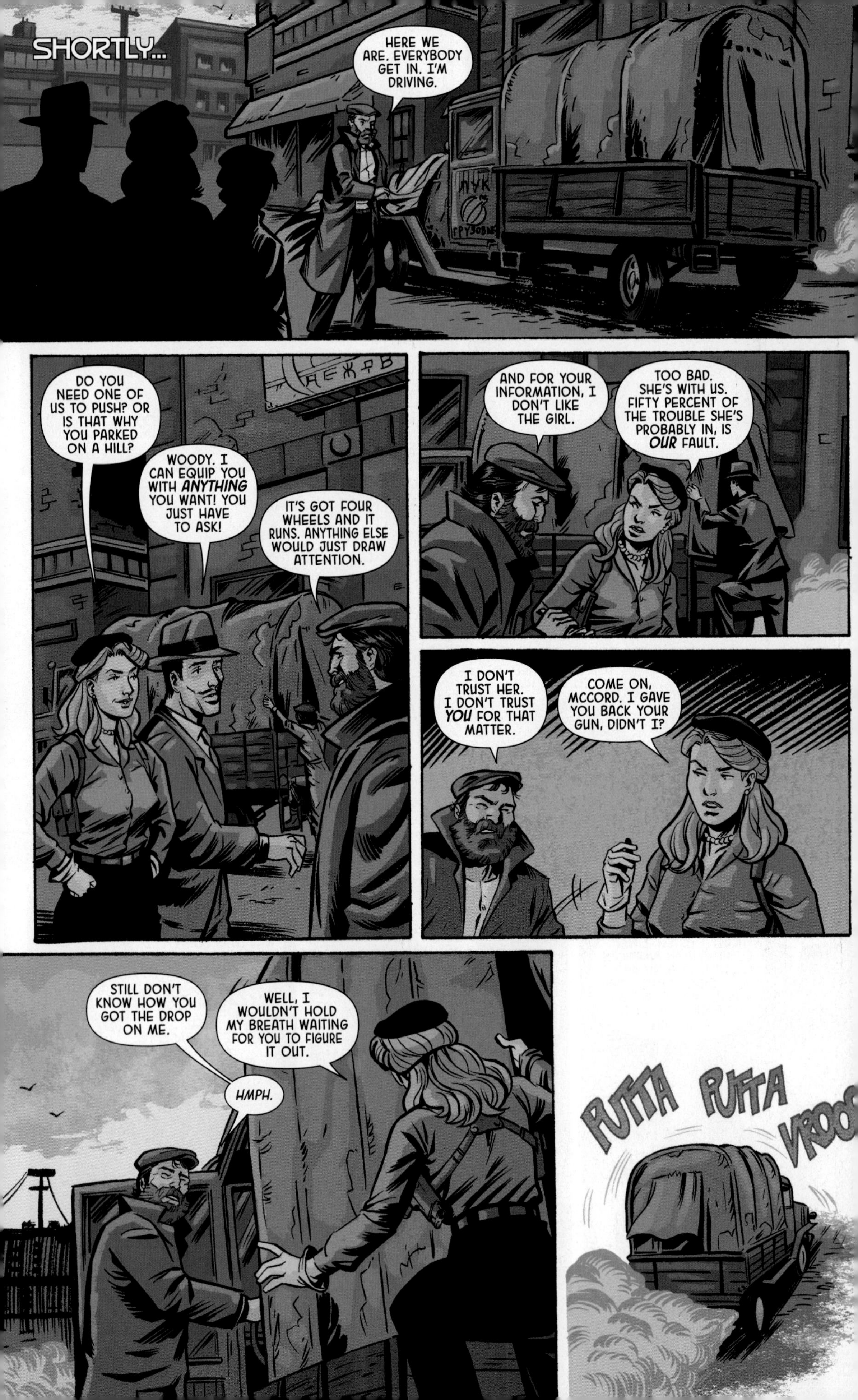
SHORTLY...
HERE WE ARE. EVERYBODY GET IN. I'M DRIVING.
DO YOU NEED ONE OF US TO PUSH? OR IS THAT WHY YOU PARKED ON A HILL?
WOODY. I CAN EQUIP YOU WITH ANYTHING YOU WANT! YOU JUST HAVE TO ASK!
IT'S GOT FOUR WHEELS AND IT RUNS. ANYTHING ELSE WOULD JUST DRAW ATTENTION.
AND FOR YOUR INFORMATION, I DON'T LIKE THE GIRL.
TOO BAD. SHE'S WITH US. FIFTY PERCENT OF THE TROUBLE SHE'S PROBABLY IN, IS OUR FAULT.
I DON'T TRUST HER. I DON'T TRUST YOU FOR THAT MATTER.
COME ON, MCCORD. I GAVE YOU BACK YOUR GUN, DIDN'T I?
STILL DON'T KNOW HOW YOU GOT THE DROP ON ME.
WELL, I WOULDN'T HOLD MY BREATH WAITING FOR YOU TO FIGURE IT OUT.
HMPH.
PUTTA PUTTA
VROO

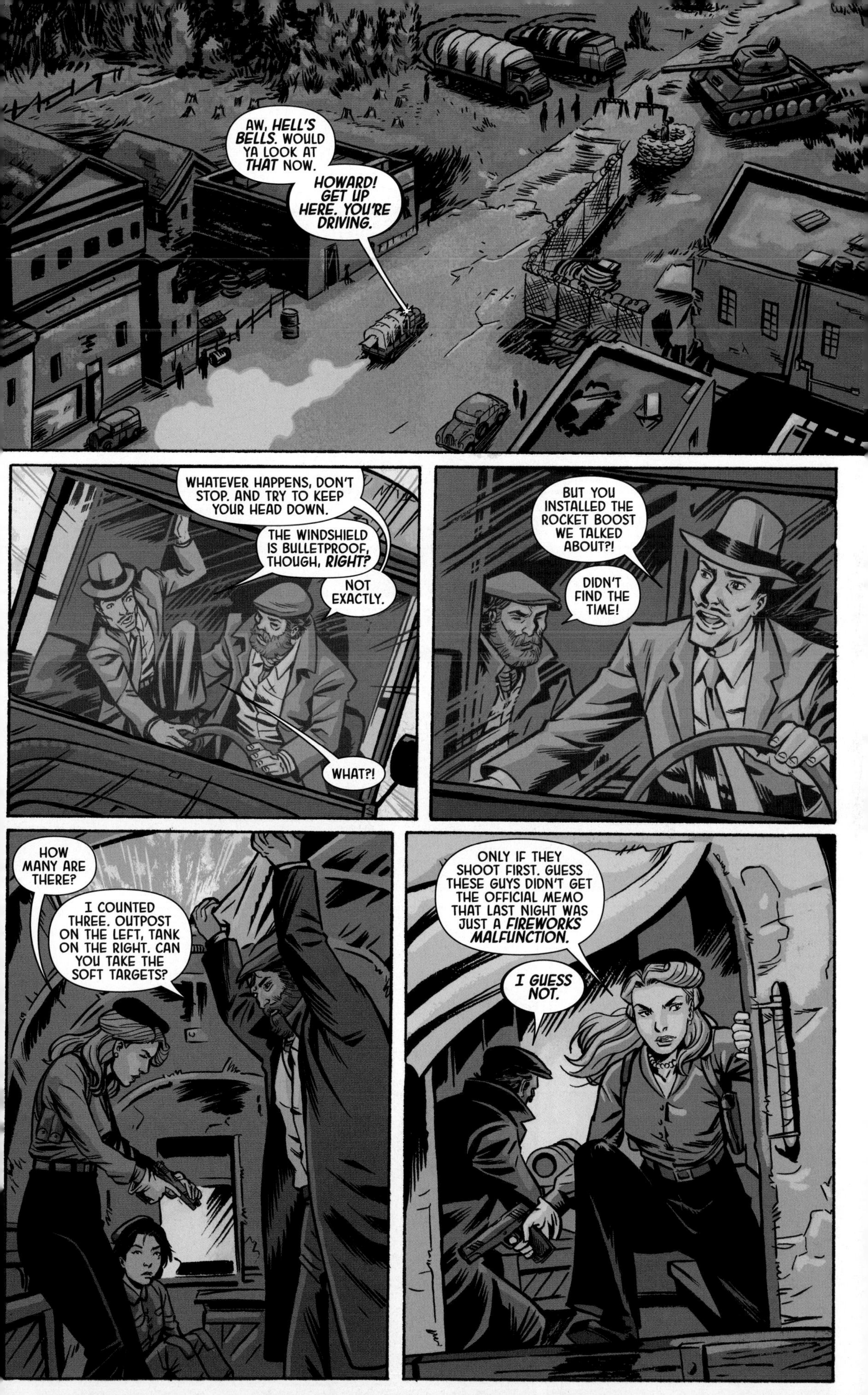
AW, HELL'S BELLS. WOULD YA LOOK AT THAT NOW.
HOWARD! GET UP HERE. YOU'RE DRIVING.
WHATEVER HAPPENS, DON'T STOP. AND TRY TO KEEP YOUR HEAD DOWN.
THE WINDSHIELD IS BULLETPROOF, THOUGH, RIGHT?
NOT EXACTLY.
WHAT?!
BUT YOU INSTALLED THE ROCKET BOOST WE TALKED ABOUT?!
DIDN'T FIND THE TIME!
HOW MANY ARE THERE?
I COUNTED THREE. OUTPOST ON THE LEFT, TANK ON THE RIGHT. CAN YOU TAKE THE SOFT TARGETS?
ONLY IF THEY SHOOT FIRST. GUESS THESE GUYS DIDN'T GET THE OFFICIAL MEMO THAT LAST NIGHT WAS JUST A FIREWORKS MALFUNCTION.
I GUESS NOT.

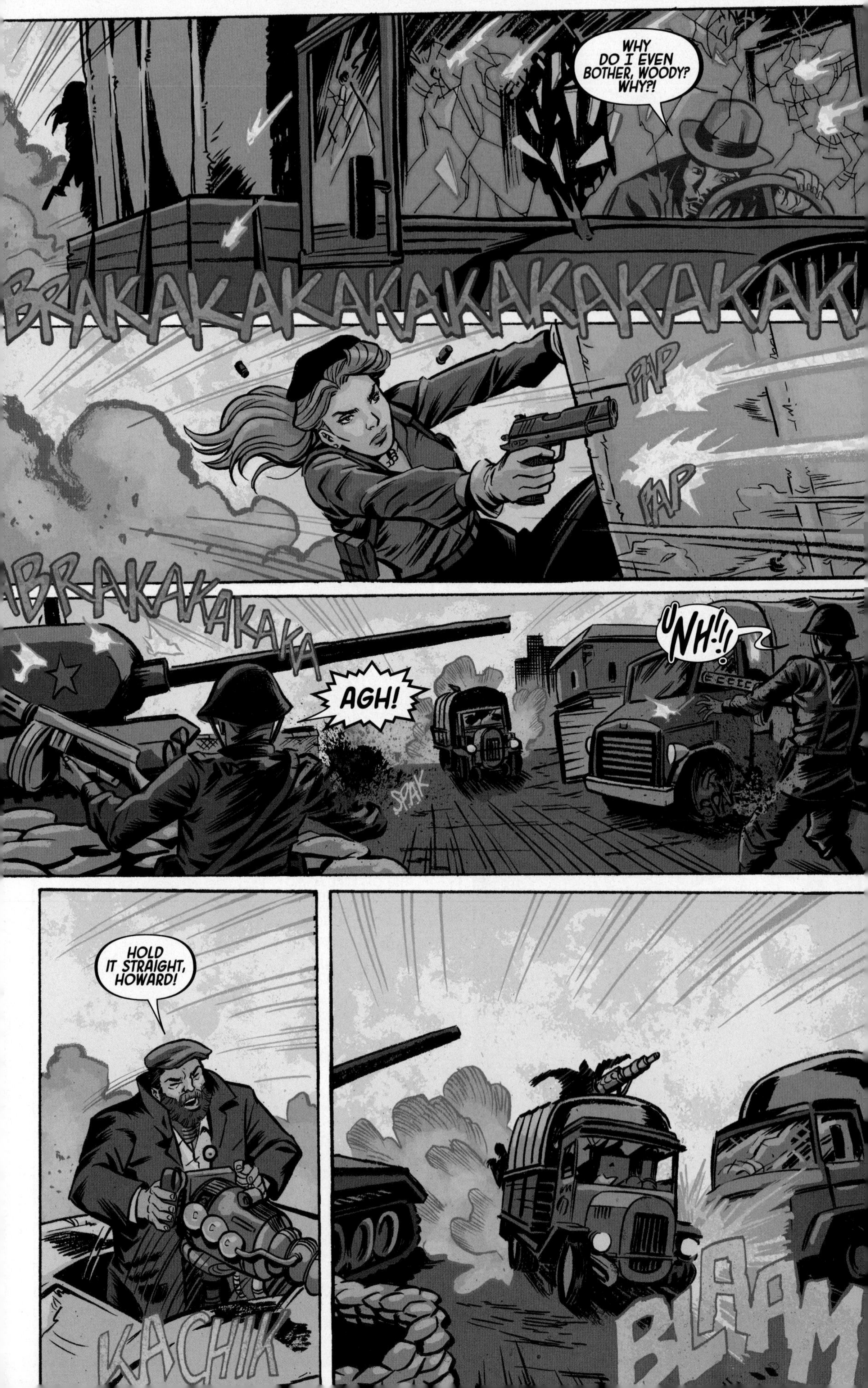
WHY DO I EVEN BOTHER, WOODY? WHY?!
BRAKAKAKAKAKAKAKAKAK
PAP
PAP
BRAKAKAKAKAKA
AGH!
UNH!!!
SPAK
SPAK
HOLD IT STRAIGHT, HOWARD!
KACHIK
BLAM

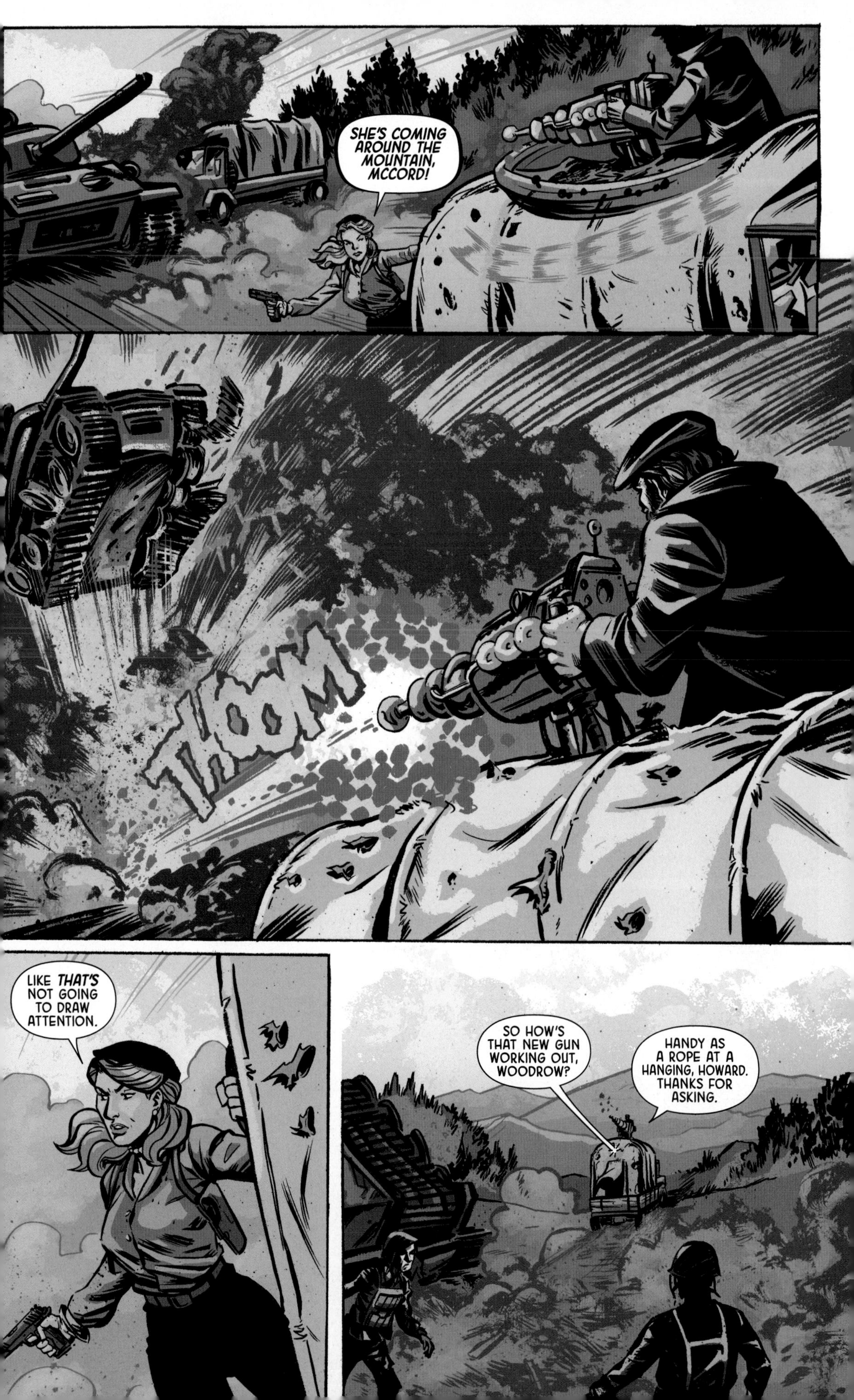
SHE'S COMING AROUND THE MOUNTAIN, MCCORD!
ZEEEEEEE
THOOM
LIKE THAT'S NOT GOING TO DRAW ATTENTION.
SO HOW'S THAT NEW GUN WORKING OUT, WOODROW?
HANDY AS A ROPE AT A HANGING, HOWARD. THANKS FOR ASKING.

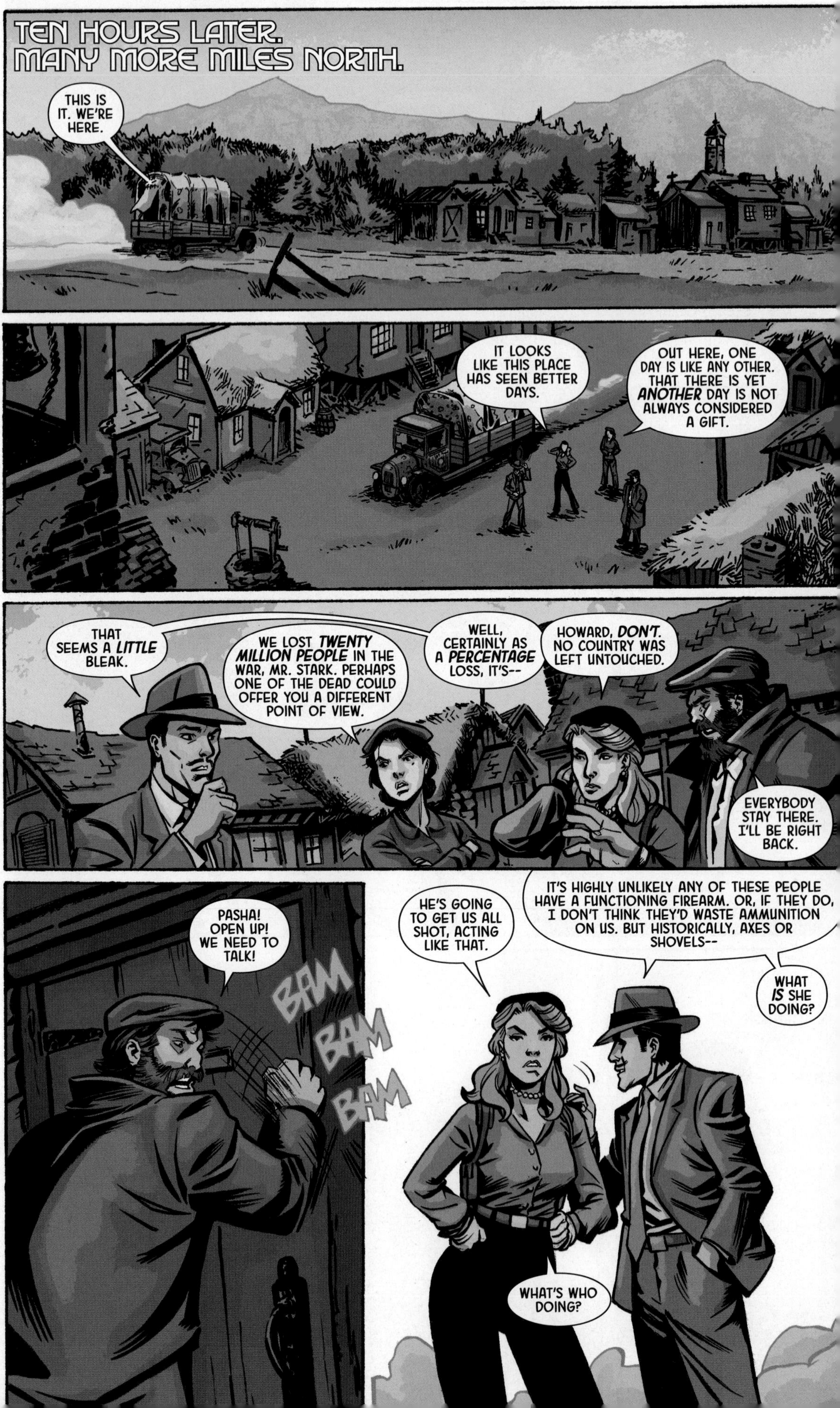
TEN HOURS LATER.
MANY MORE MILES NORTH.
THIS IS IT. WE'RE HERE.
IT LOOKS LIKE THIS PLACE HAS SEEN BETTER DAYS.
OUT HERE, ONE DAY IS LIKE ANY OTHER. THAT THERE IS YET *ANOTHER* DAY IS NOT ALWAYS CONSIDERED A GIFT.
THAT SEEMS A *LITTLE* BLEAK.
WE LOST *TWENTY MILLION PEOPLE* IN THE WAR, MR. STARK. PERHAPS ONE OF THE DEAD COULD OFFER YOU A DIFFERENT POINT OF VIEW.
WELL, CERTAINLY AS A *PERCENTAGE* LOSS, IT'S--
HOWARD, *DON'T*. NO COUNTRY WAS LEFT UNTOUCHED.
EVERYBODY STAY THERE. I'LL BE RIGHT BACK.
PASHA! OPEN UP! WE NEED TO TALK!
BAM
BAM
BAM
HE'S GOING TO GET US ALL SHOT, ACTING LIKE THAT.
IT'S HIGHLY UNLIKELY ANY OF THESE PEOPLE HAVE A FUNCTIONING FIREARM. OR, IF THEY DO, I DON'T THINK THEY'D WASTE AMMUNITION ON US. BUT HISTORICALLY, AXES OR SHOVELS--
WHAT *IS* SHE DOING?
WHAT'S WHO DOING?

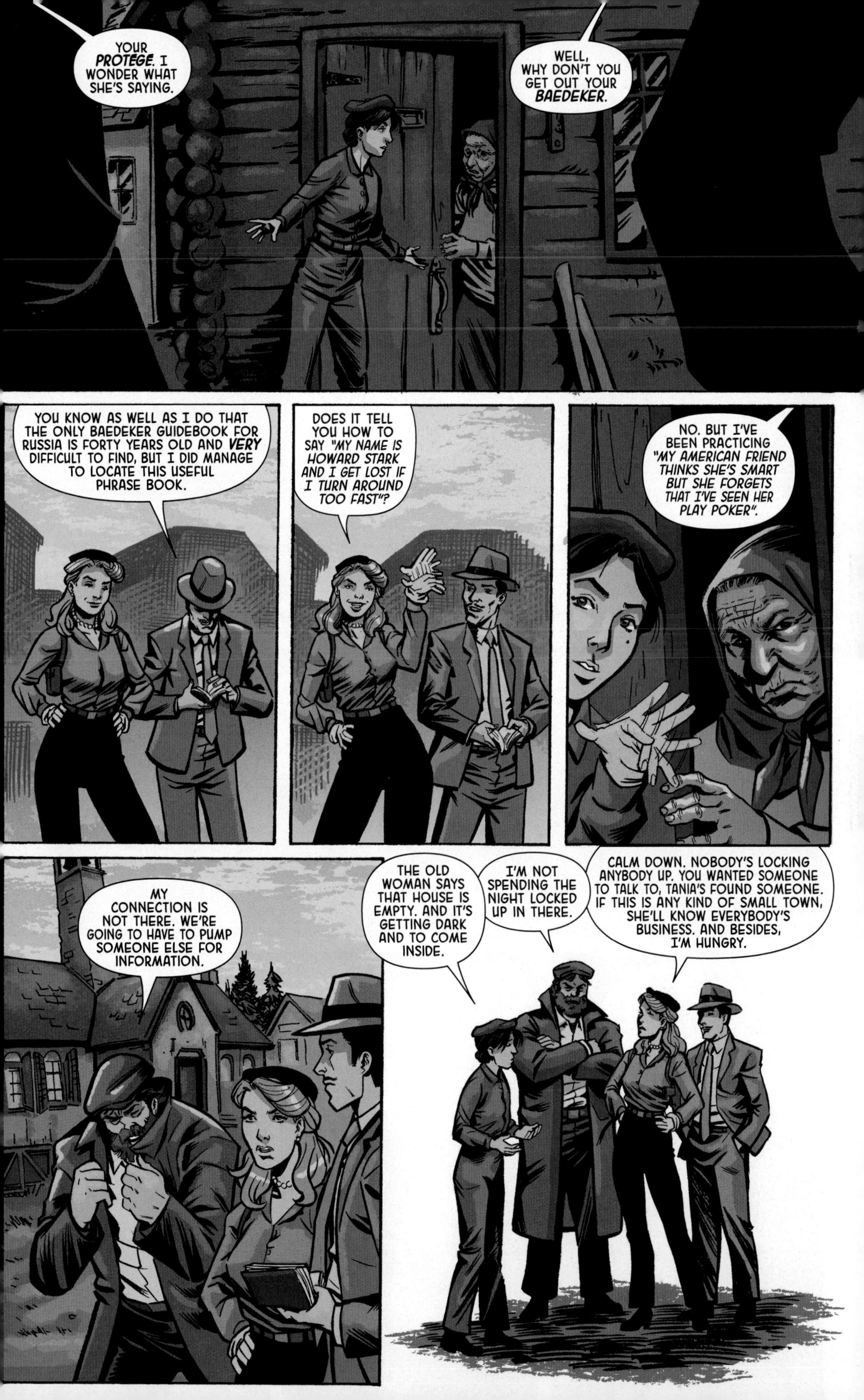
YOUR *PROTEGE*. I WONDER WHAT SHE'S SAYING.
WELL, WHY DON'T YOU GET OUT YOUR *BAEDEKER*.
YOU KNOW AS WELL AS I DO THAT THE ONLY BAEDEKER GUIDEBOOK FOR RUSSIA IS FORTY YEARS OLD AND *VERY* DIFFICULT TO FIND, BUT I DID MANAGE TO LOCATE THIS USEFUL PHRASE BOOK.
DOES IT TELL YOU HOW TO SAY *"MY NAME IS HOWARD STARK AND I GET LOST IF I TURN AROUND TOO FAST"*?
NO. BUT I'VE BEEN PRACTICING *"MY AMERICAN FRIEND THINKS SHE'S SMART BUT SHE FORGETS THAT I'VE SEEN HER PLAY POKER"*.
MY CONNECTION IS NOT THERE. WE'RE GOING TO HAVE TO PUMP SOMEONE ELSE FOR INFORMATION.
THE OLD WOMAN SAYS THAT HOUSE IS EMPTY. AND IT'S GETTING DARK AND TO COME INSIDE.
I'M NOT SPENDING THE NIGHT LOCKED UP IN THERE.
CALM DOWN. NOBODY'S LOCKING ANYBODY UP. YOU WANTED SOMEONE TO TALK TO, TANIA'S FOUND SOMEONE. IF THIS IS ANY KIND OF SMALL TOWN, SHE'LL KNOW EVERYBODY'S BUSINESS. AND BESIDES, I'M HUNGRY.

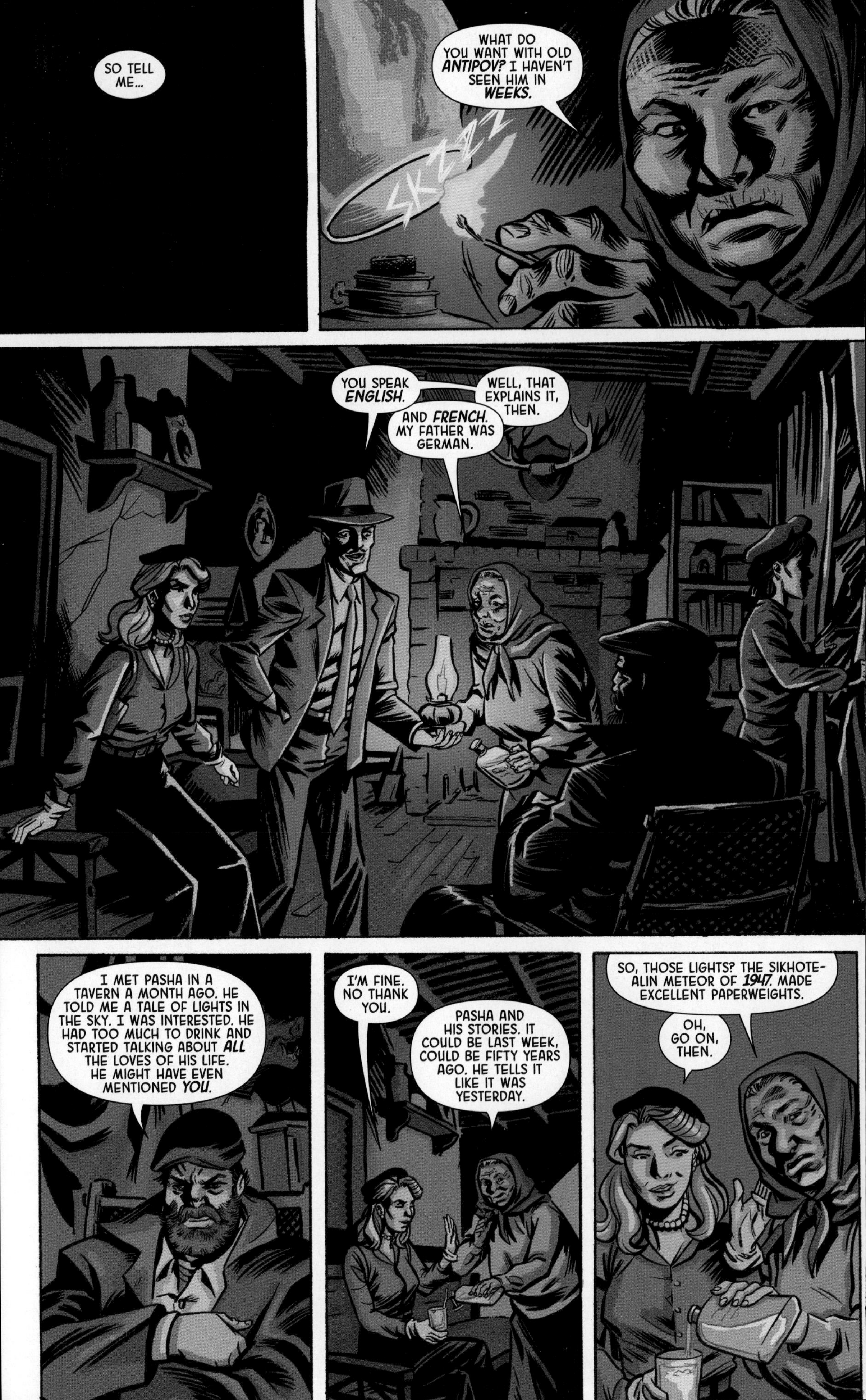
SO TELL ME...
WHAT DO YOU WANT WITH OLD ANTIPOV? I HAVEN'T SEEN HIM IN WEEKS.
SKZZZ
YOU SPEAK ENGLISH.
WELL, THAT EXPLAINS IT, THEN.
AND FRENCH. MY FATHER WAS GERMAN.
I MET PASHA IN A TAVERN A MONTH AGO. HE TOLD ME A TALE OF LIGHTS IN THE SKY. I WAS INTERESTED. HE HAD TOO MUCH TO DRINK AND STARTED TALKING ABOUT ALL THE LOVES OF HIS LIFE. HE MIGHT HAVE EVEN MENTIONED YOU.
I'M FINE. NO THANK YOU.
PASHA AND HIS STORIES. IT COULD BE LAST WEEK, COULD BE FIFTY YEARS AGO. HE TELLS IT LIKE IT WAS YESTERDAY.
SO, THOSE LIGHTS? THE SIKHOTE-ALIN METEOR OF 1947. MADE EXCELLENT PAPERWEIGHTS.
OH, GO ON, THEN.

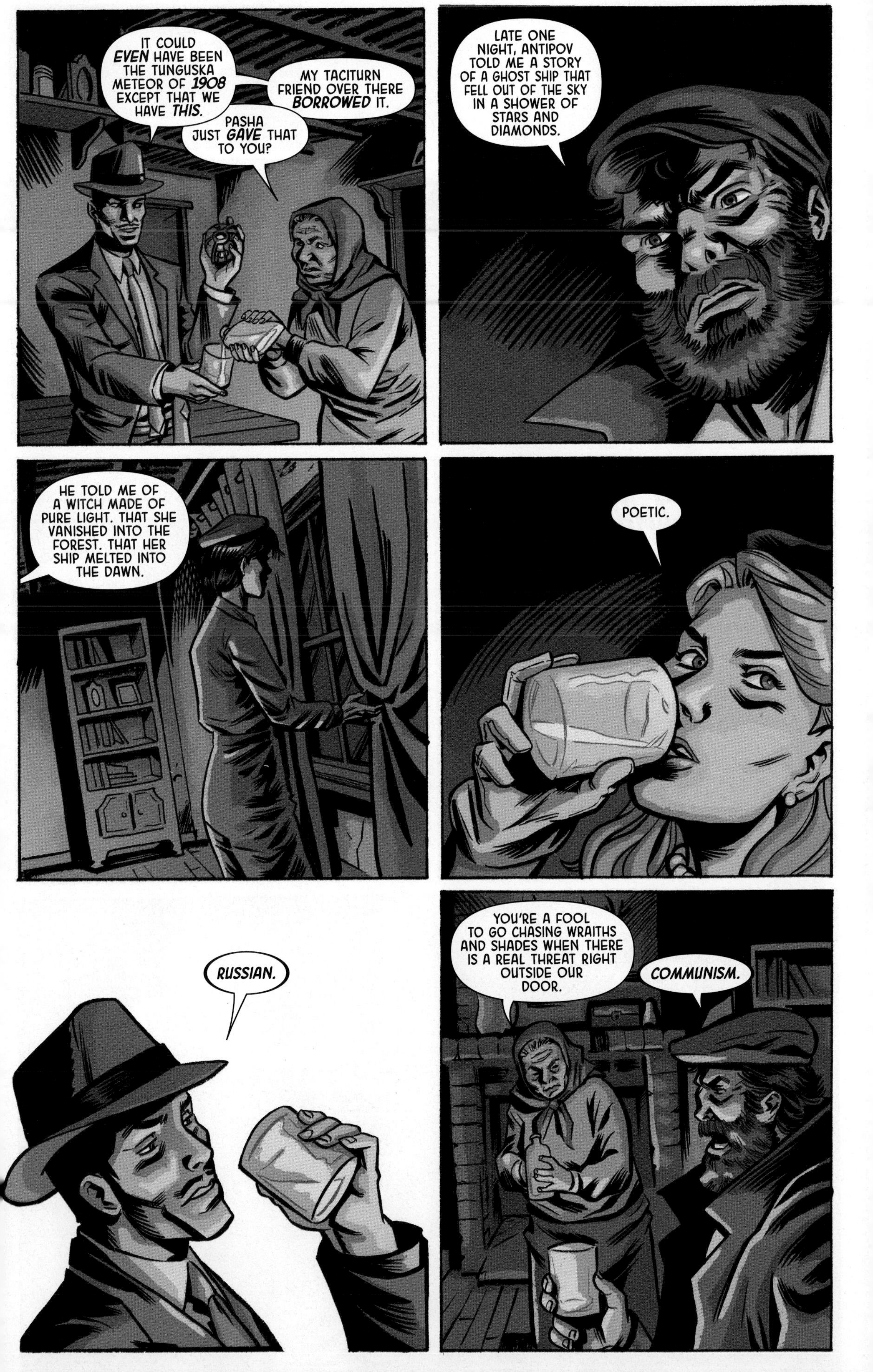
IT COULD EVEN HAVE BEEN THE TUNGUSKA METEOR OF 1908 EXCEPT THAT WE HAVE THIS.
MY TACITURN FRIEND OVER THERE BORROWED IT.
PASHA JUST GAVE THAT TO YOU?
LATE ONE NIGHT, ANTIPOV TOLD ME A STORY OF A GHOST SHIP THAT FELL OUT OF THE SKY IN A SHOWER OF STARS AND DIAMONDS.
HE TOLD ME OF A WITCH MADE OF PURE LIGHT. THAT SHE VANISHED INTO THE FOREST. THAT HER SHIP MELTED INTO THE DAWN.
POETIC.
RUSSIAN.
YOU'RE A FOOL TO GO CHASING WRAITHS AND SHADES WHEN THERE IS A REAL THREAT RIGHT OUTSIDE OUR DOOR.
COMMUNISM.

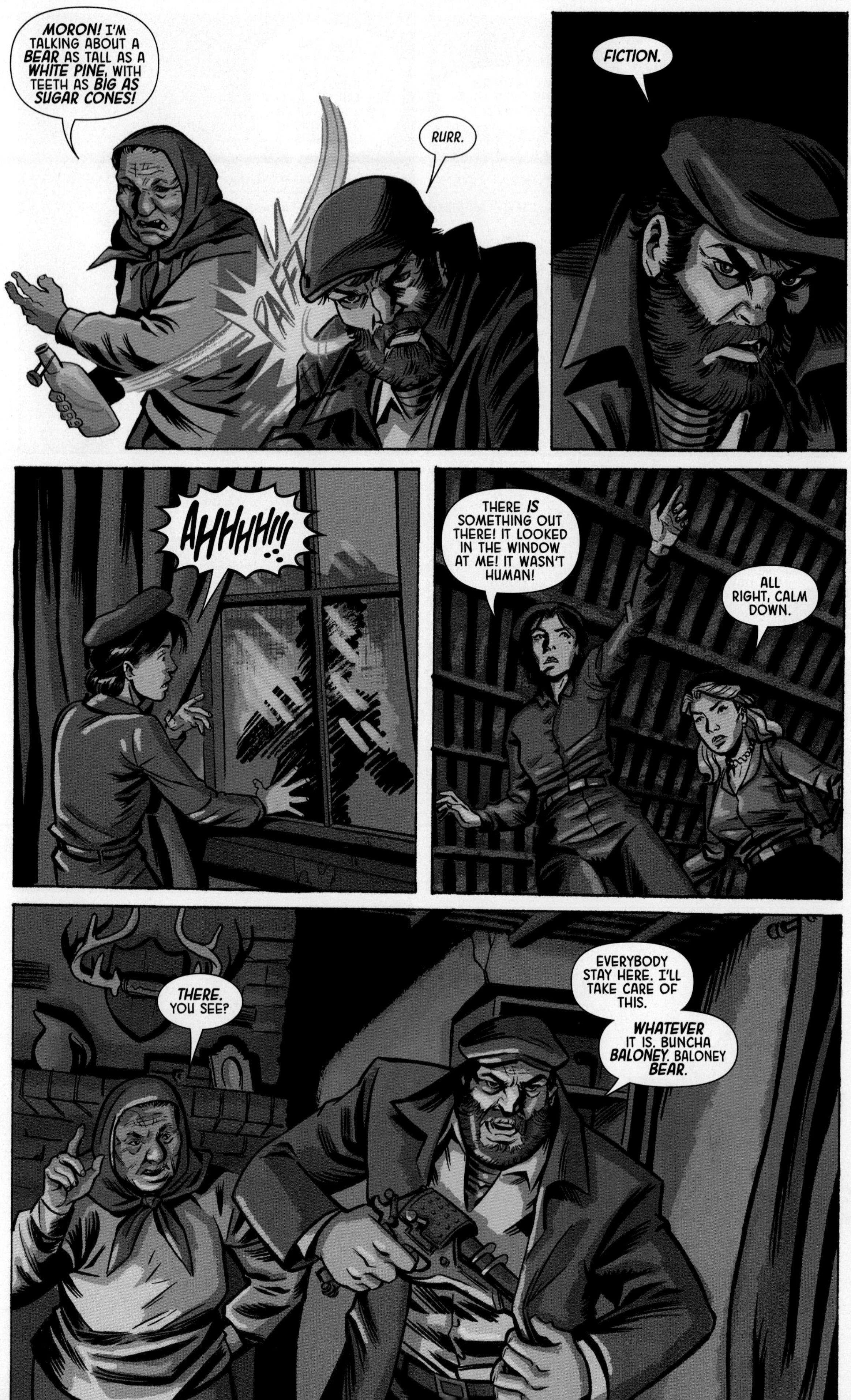

MORON! I'M TALKING ABOUT A BEAR AS TALL AS A WHITE PINE, WITH TEETH AS BIG AS SUGAR CONES!
PAFF!
RURR.
FICTION.
AHHHH!!!
THERE IS SOMETHING OUT THERE! IT LOOKED IN THE WINDOW AT ME! IT WASN'T HUMAN!
ALL RIGHT, CALM DOWN.
THERE. YOU SEE?
EVERYBODY STAY HERE. I'LL TAKE CARE OF THIS.
WHATEVER IT IS. BUNCHA BALONEY. BALONEY BEAR.

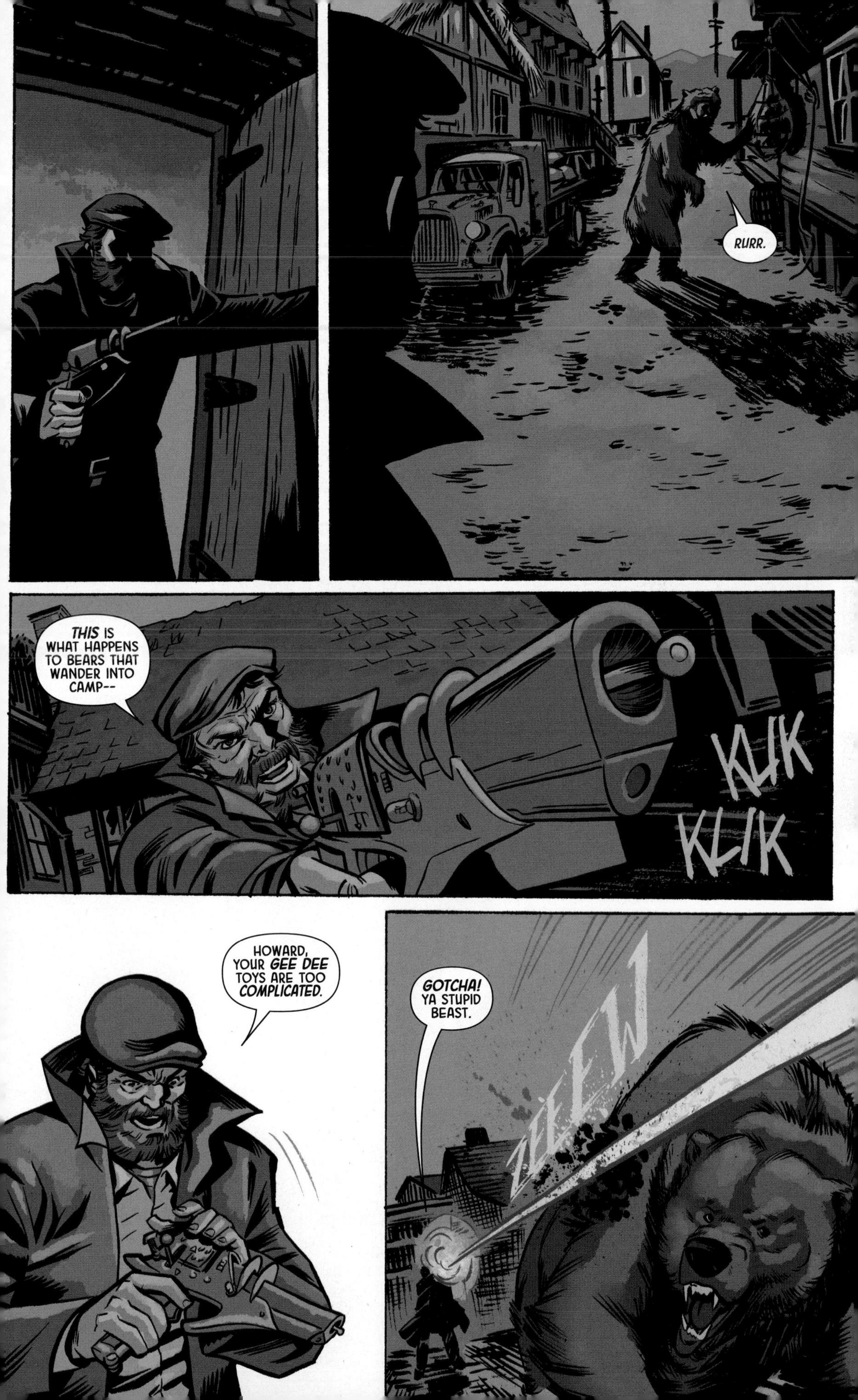
RURR.
THIS IS WHAT HAPPENS TO BEARS THAT WANDER INTO CAMP--
KLIK KLIK
HOWARD, YOUR GEE DEE TOYS ARE TOO COMPLICATED.
GOTCHA! YA STUPID BEAST.
ZEEEW

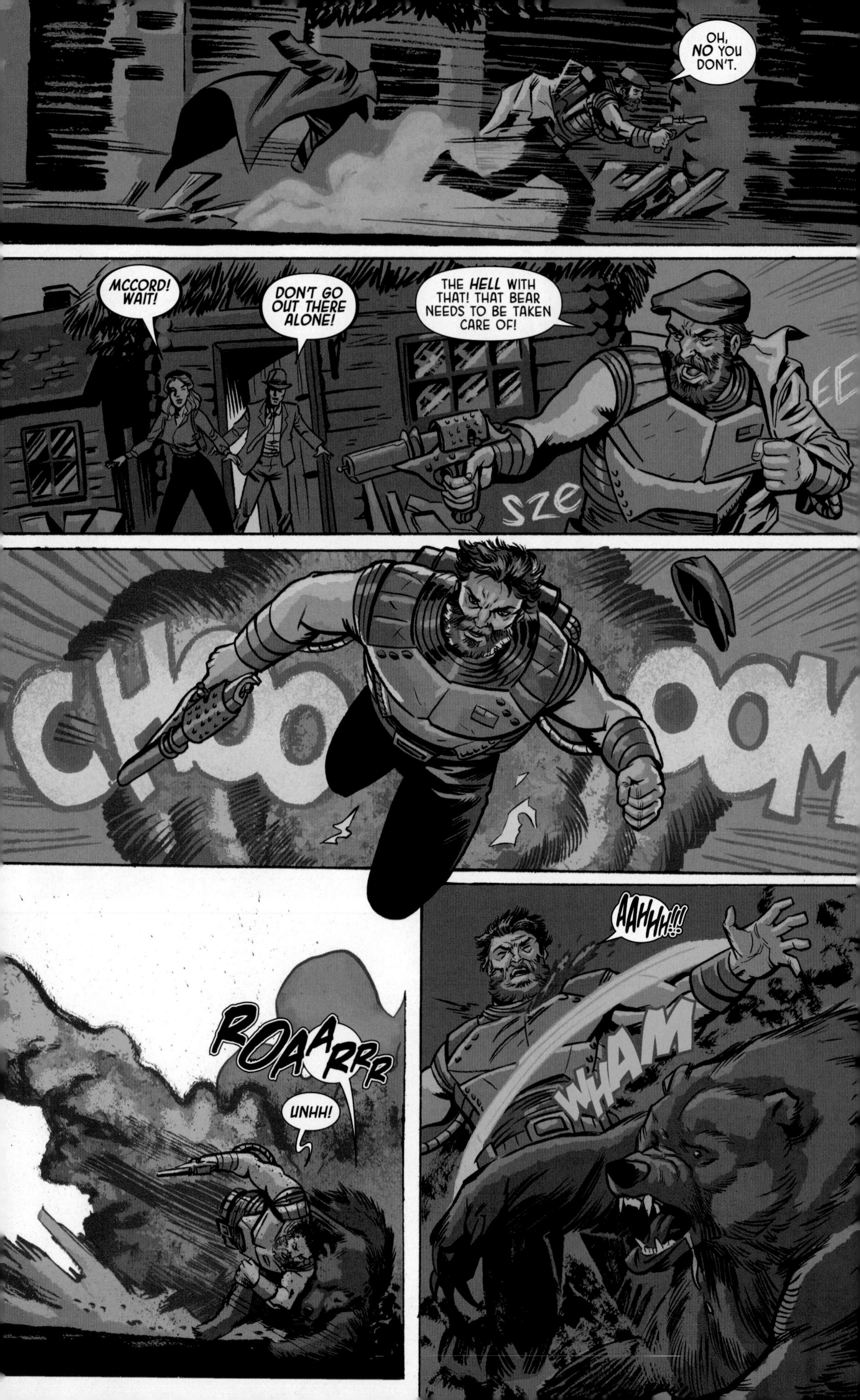

OH, NO YOU DON'T.
MCCORD! WAIT!
DON'T GO OUT THERE ALONE!
THE HELL WITH THAT! THAT BEAR NEEDS TO BE TAKEN CARE OF!
SZE
EE
CHOOOOOOM
ROAARRR
UNHH!
AAHHH!!!
WHAM

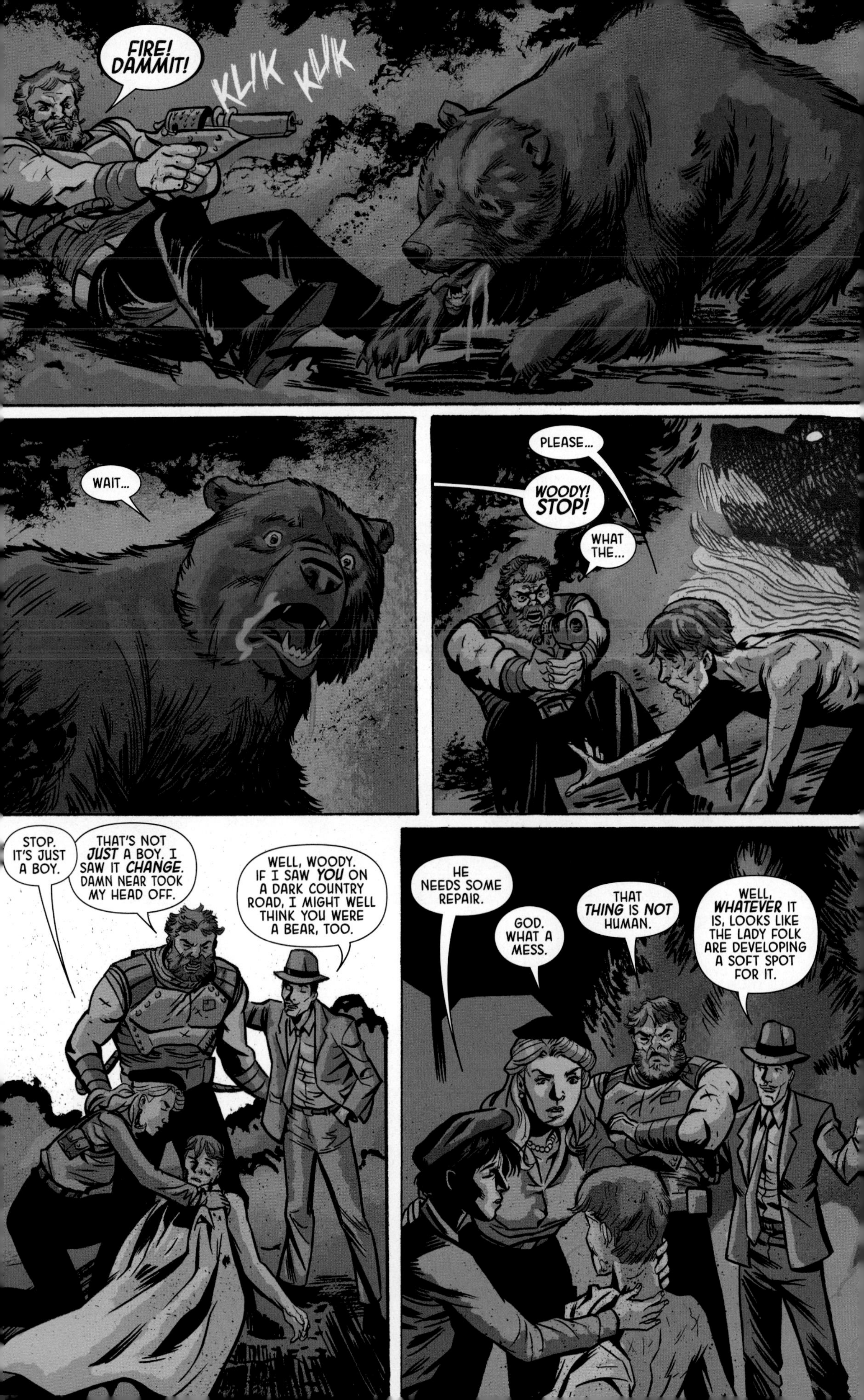

FIRE! DAMMIT!
KLIK KLIK
WAIT...
PLEASE...
WOODY! STOP!
WHAT THE...
STOP. IT'S JUST A BOY.
THAT'S NOT JUST A BOY. I SAW IT CHANGE. DAMN NEAR TOOK MY HEAD OFF.
WELL, WOODY. IF I SAW YOU ON A DARK COUNTRY ROAD, I MIGHT WELL THINK YOU WERE A BEAR, TOO.
HE NEEDS SOME REPAIR.
GOD. WHAT A MESS.
THAT THING IS NOT HUMAN.
WELL, WHATEVER IT IS, LOOKS LIKE THE LADY FOLK ARE DEVELOPING A SOFT SPOT FOR IT.

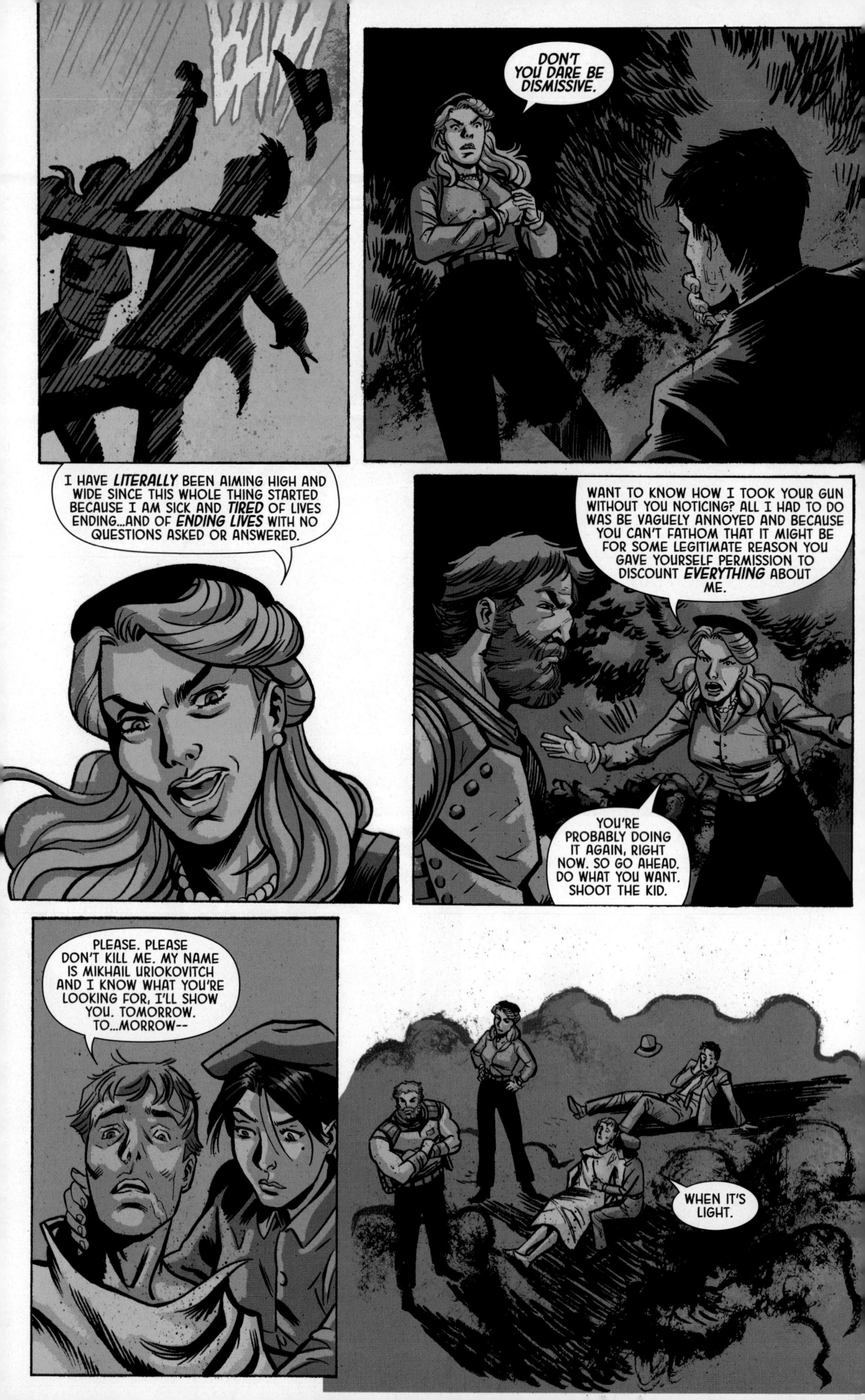

DON'T YOU DARE BE DISMISSIVE.
I HAVE LITERALLY BEEN AIMING HIGH AND WIDE SINCE THIS WHOLE THING STARTED BECAUSE I AM SICK AND TIRED OF LIVES ENDING...AND OF ENDING LIVES WITH NO QUESTIONS ASKED OR ANSWERED.
WANT TO KNOW HOW I TOOK YOUR GUN WITHOUT YOU NOTICING? ALL I HAD TO DO WAS BE VAGUELY ANNOYED AND BECAUSE YOU CAN'T FATHOM THAT IT MIGHT BE FOR SOME LEGITIMATE REASON YOU GAVE YOURSELF PERMISSION TO DISCOUNT EVERYTHING ABOUT ME.
YOU'RE PROBABLY DOING IT AGAIN, RIGHT NOW. SO GO AHEAD. DO WHAT YOU WANT. SHOOT THE KID.
PLEASE. PLEASE DON'T KILL ME. MY NAME IS MIKHAIL URIOKOVITCH AND I KNOW WHAT YOU'RE LOOKING FOR, I'LL SHOW YOU. TOMORROW. TO...MORROW--
WHEN IT'S LIGHT.

3

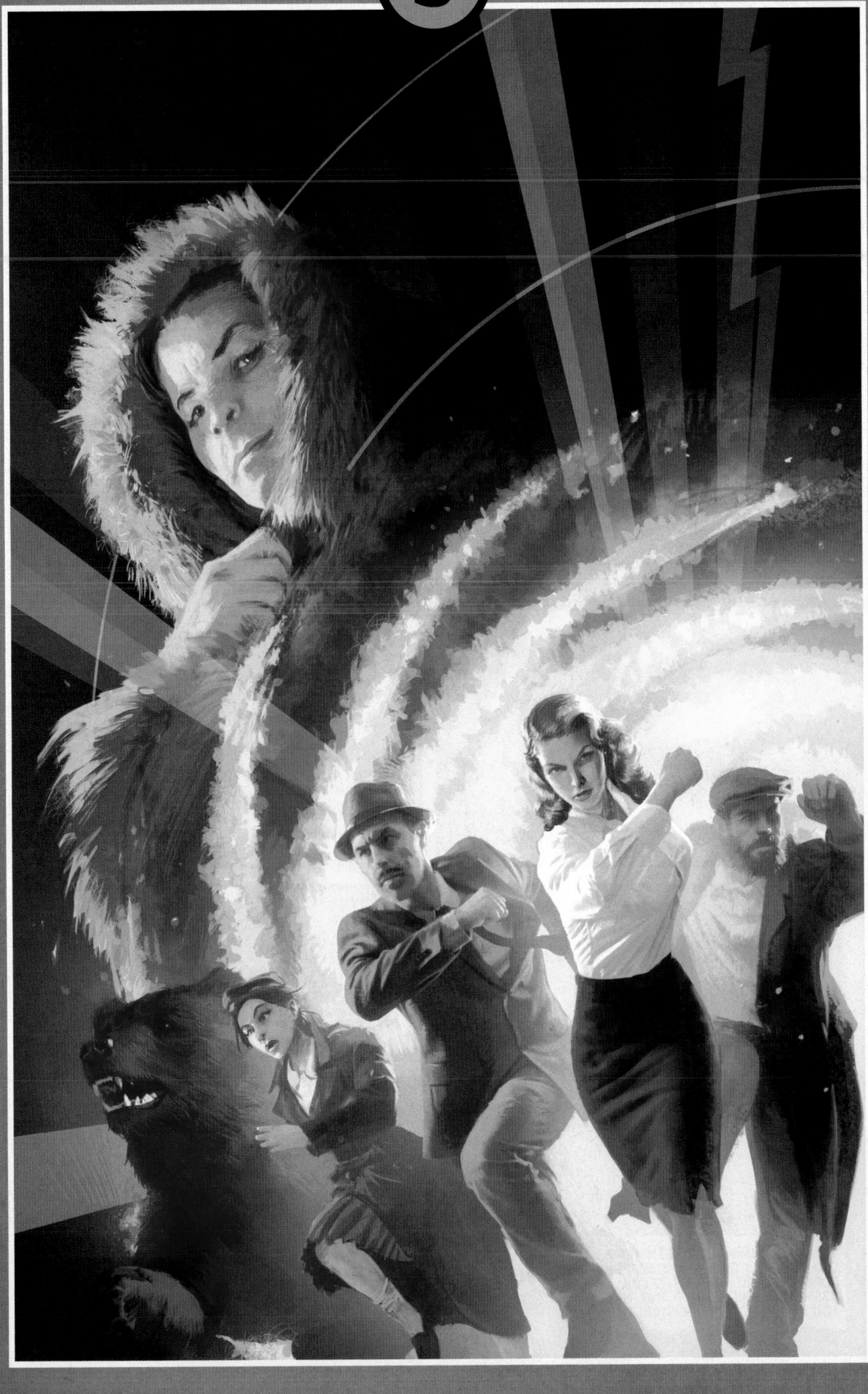

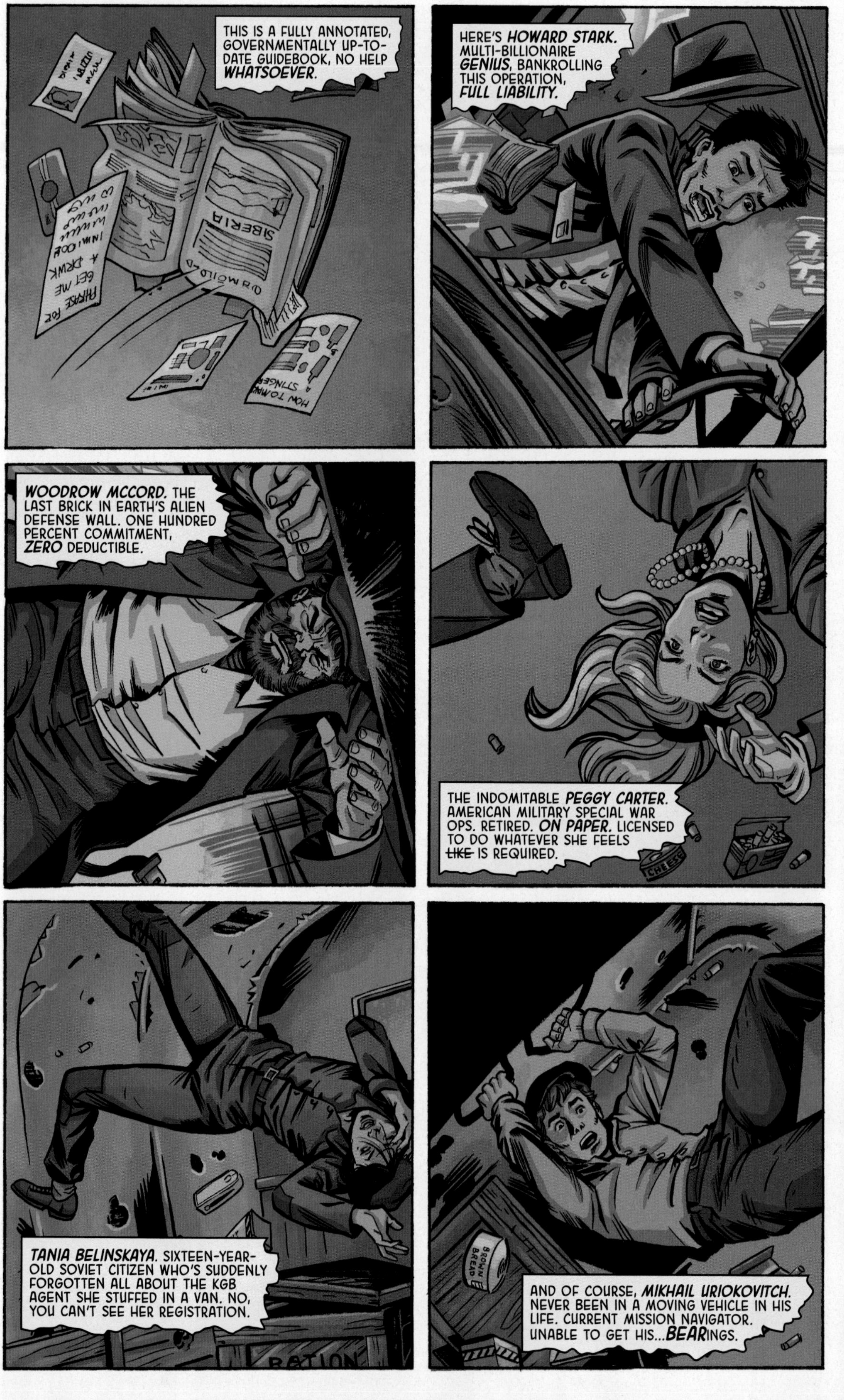
THIS IS A FULLY ANNOTATED, GOVERNMENTALLY UP-TO-DATE GUIDEBOOK, NO HELP **WHATSOEVER**.
HERE'S **HOWARD STARK.** MULTI-BILLIONAIRE **GENIUS**, BANKROLLING THIS OPERATION, **FULL LIABILITY.**
WOODROW MCCORD. THE LAST BRICK IN EARTH'S ALIEN DEFENSE WALL. ONE HUNDRED PERCENT COMMITMENT, **ZERO** DEDUCTIBLE.
THE INDOMITABLE **PEGGY CARTER**. AMERICAN MILITARY SPECIAL WAR OPS. RETIRED. **ON PAPER.** LICENSED TO DO WHATEVER SHE FEELS ~~LIKE~~ IS REQUIRED.
CHEESE
TANIA BELINSKAYA. SIXTEEN-YEAR-OLD SOVIET CITIZEN WHO'S SUDDENLY FORGOTTEN ALL ABOUT THE KGB AGENT SHE STUFFED IN A VAN. NO, YOU CAN'T SEE HER REGISTRATION.
RATION
BROWN BREAD
AND OF COURSE, **MIKHAIL URIOKOVITCH.** NEVER BEEN IN A MOVING VEHICLE IN HIS LIFE. CURRENT MISSION NAVIGATOR. UNABLE TO GET HIS...**BEAR**INGS.

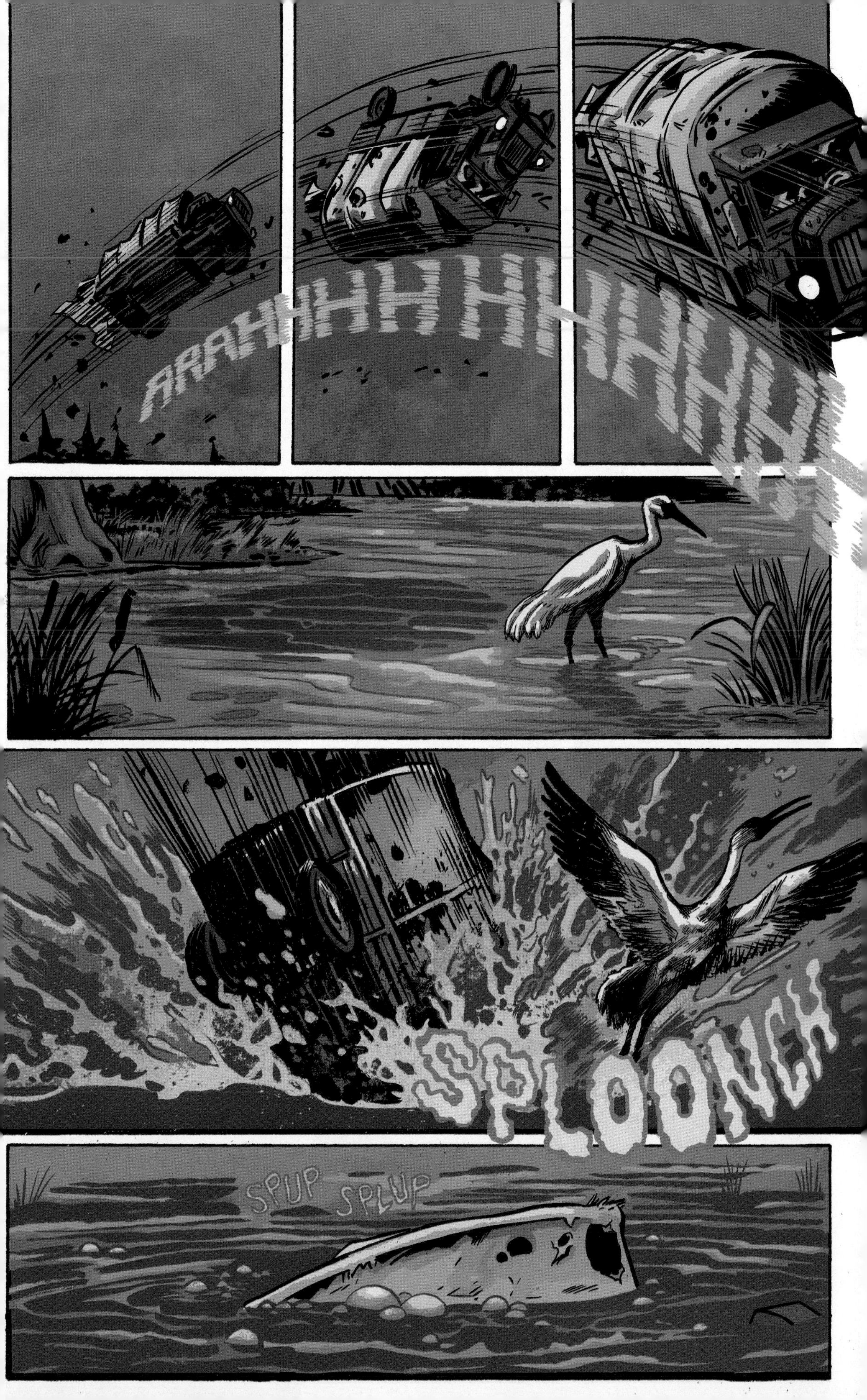
ARAHHHHHHHHHH
SPLOONCH
SPUP SPLUP

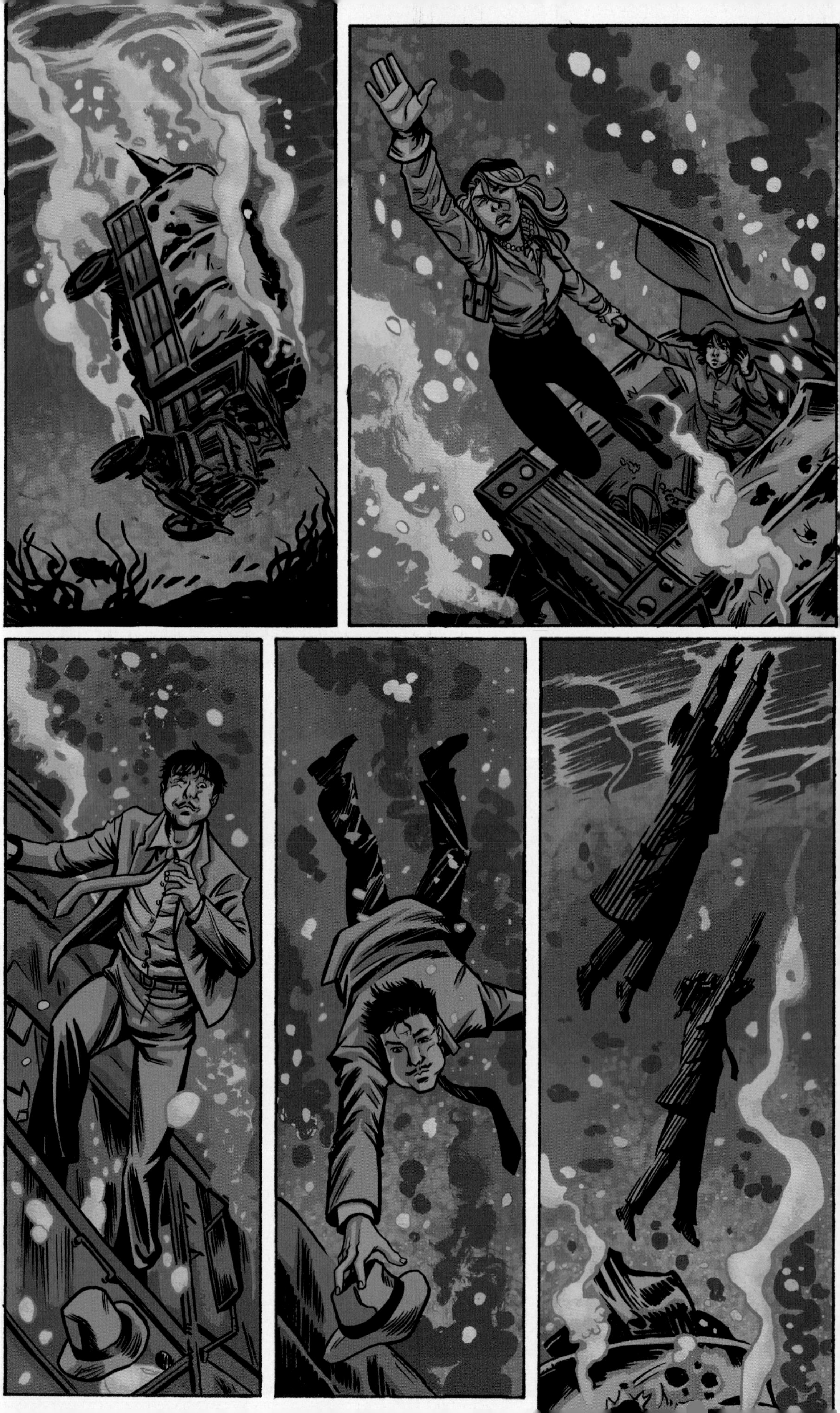

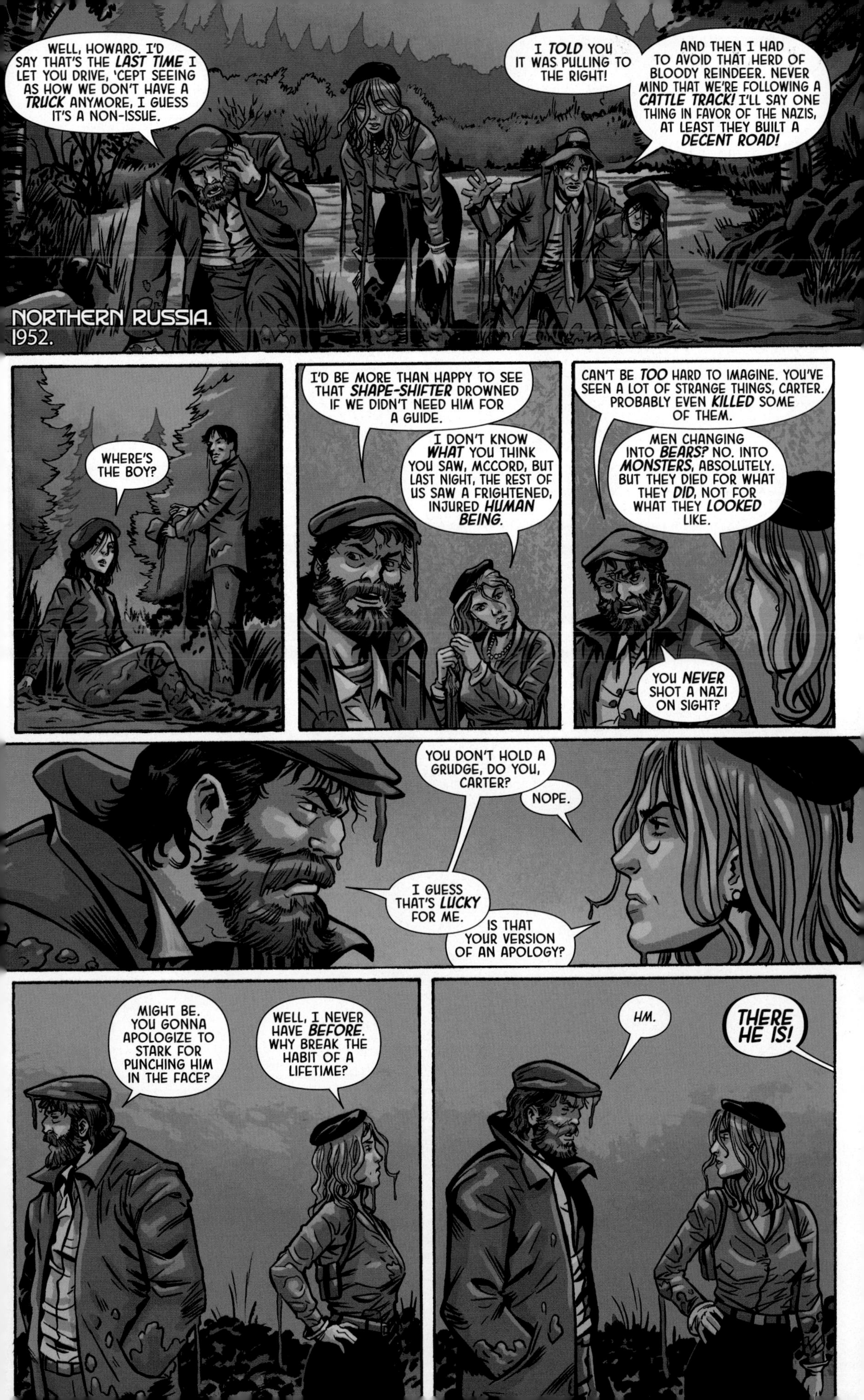
WELL, HOWARD. I'D SAY THAT'S THE LAST TIME I LET YOU DRIVE, 'CEPT SEEING AS HOW WE DON'T HAVE A TRUCK ANYMORE, I GUESS IT'S A NON-ISSUE.
I TOLD YOU IT WAS PULLING TO THE RIGHT!
AND THEN I HAD TO AVOID THAT HERD OF BLOODY REINDEER. NEVER MIND THAT WE'RE FOLLOWING A CATTLE TRACK! I'LL SAY ONE THING IN FAVOR OF THE NAZIS, AT LEAST THEY BUILT A DECENT ROAD!
NORTHERN RUSSIA. 1952.
WHERE'S THE BOY?
I'D BE MORE THAN HAPPY TO SEE THAT SHAPE-SHIFTER DROWNED IF WE DIDN'T NEED HIM FOR A GUIDE.
I DON'T KNOW WHAT YOU THINK YOU SAW, MCCORD, BUT LAST NIGHT, THE REST OF US SAW A FRIGHTENED, INJURED HUMAN BEING.
CAN'T BE TOO HARD TO IMAGINE. YOU'VE SEEN A LOT OF STRANGE THINGS, CARTER. PROBABLY EVEN KILLED SOME OF THEM.
MEN CHANGING INTO BEARS? NO. INTO MONSTERS, ABSOLUTELY. BUT THEY DIED FOR WHAT THEY DID, NOT FOR WHAT THEY LOOKED LIKE.
YOU NEVER SHOT A NAZI ON SIGHT?
YOU DON'T HOLD A GRUDGE, DO YOU, CARTER?
NOPE.
I GUESS THAT'S LUCKY FOR ME.
IS THAT YOUR VERSION OF AN APOLOGY?
MIGHT BE. YOU GONNA APOLOGIZE TO STARK FOR PUNCHING HIM IN THE FACE?
WELL, I NEVER HAVE BEFORE. WHY BREAK THE HABIT OF A LIFETIME?
HM.
THERE HE IS!

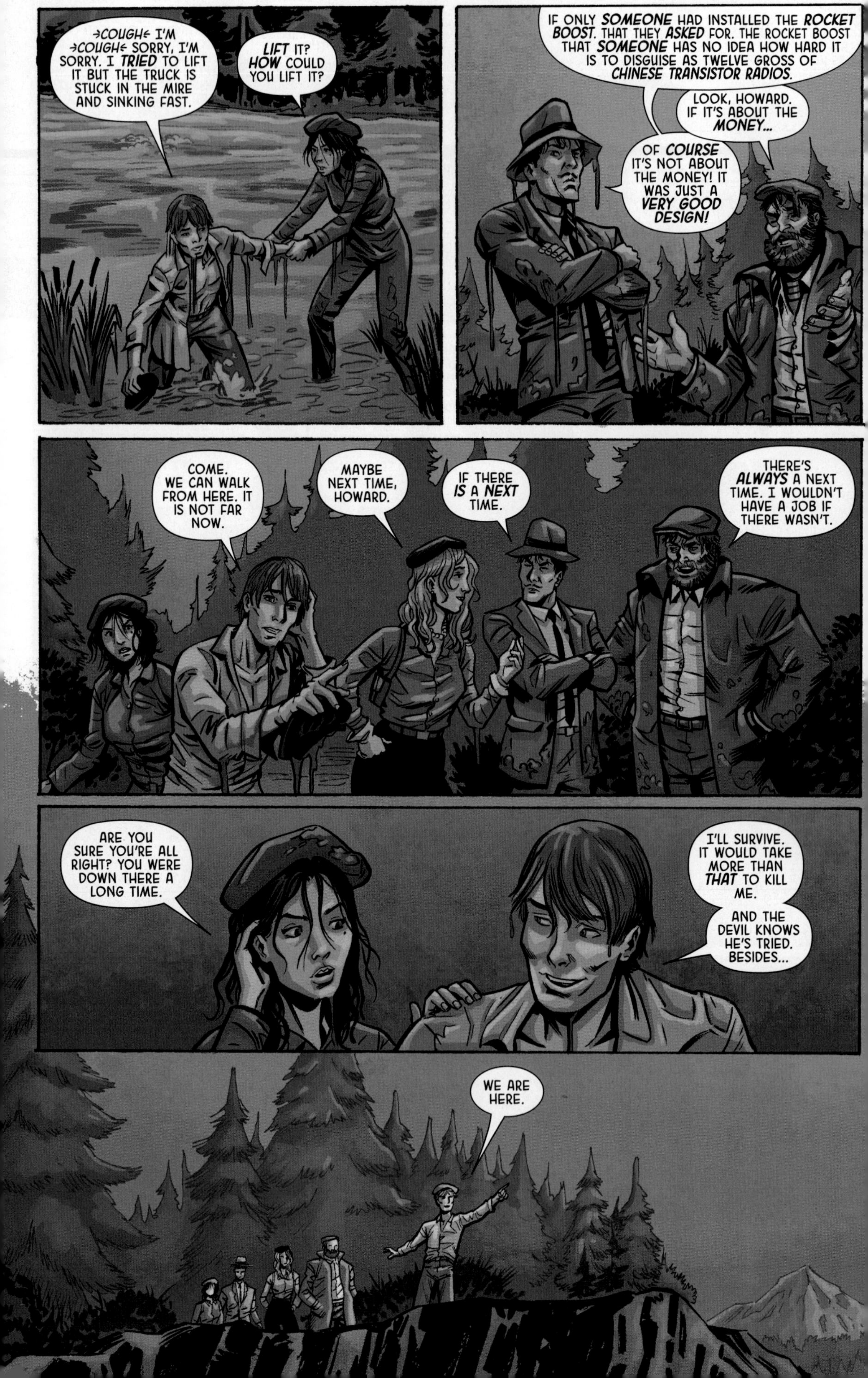

>COUGH< I'M >COUGH< SORRY, I'M SORRY. I TRIED TO LIFT IT BUT THE TRUCK IS STUCK IN THE MIRE AND SINKING FAST.
LIFT IT? HOW COULD YOU LIFT IT?
IF ONLY SOMEONE HAD INSTALLED THE ROCKET BOOST. THAT THEY ASKED FOR. THE ROCKET BOOST THAT SOMEONE HAS NO IDEA HOW HARD IT IS TO DISGUISE AS TWELVE GROSS OF CHINESE TRANSISTOR RADIOS.
LOOK, HOWARD. IF IT'S ABOUT THE MONEY...
OF COURSE IT'S NOT ABOUT THE MONEY! IT WAS JUST A VERY GOOD DESIGN!
COME. WE CAN WALK FROM HERE. IT IS NOT FAR NOW.
MAYBE NEXT TIME, HOWARD.
IF THERE IS A NEXT TIME.
THERE'S ALWAYS A NEXT TIME. I WOULDN'T HAVE A JOB IF THERE WASN'T.
ARE YOU SURE YOU'RE ALL RIGHT? YOU WERE DOWN THERE A LONG TIME.
I'LL SURVIVE. IT WOULD TAKE MORE THAN THAT TO KILL ME.
AND THE DEVIL KNOWS HE'S TRIED. BESIDES...
WE ARE HERE.

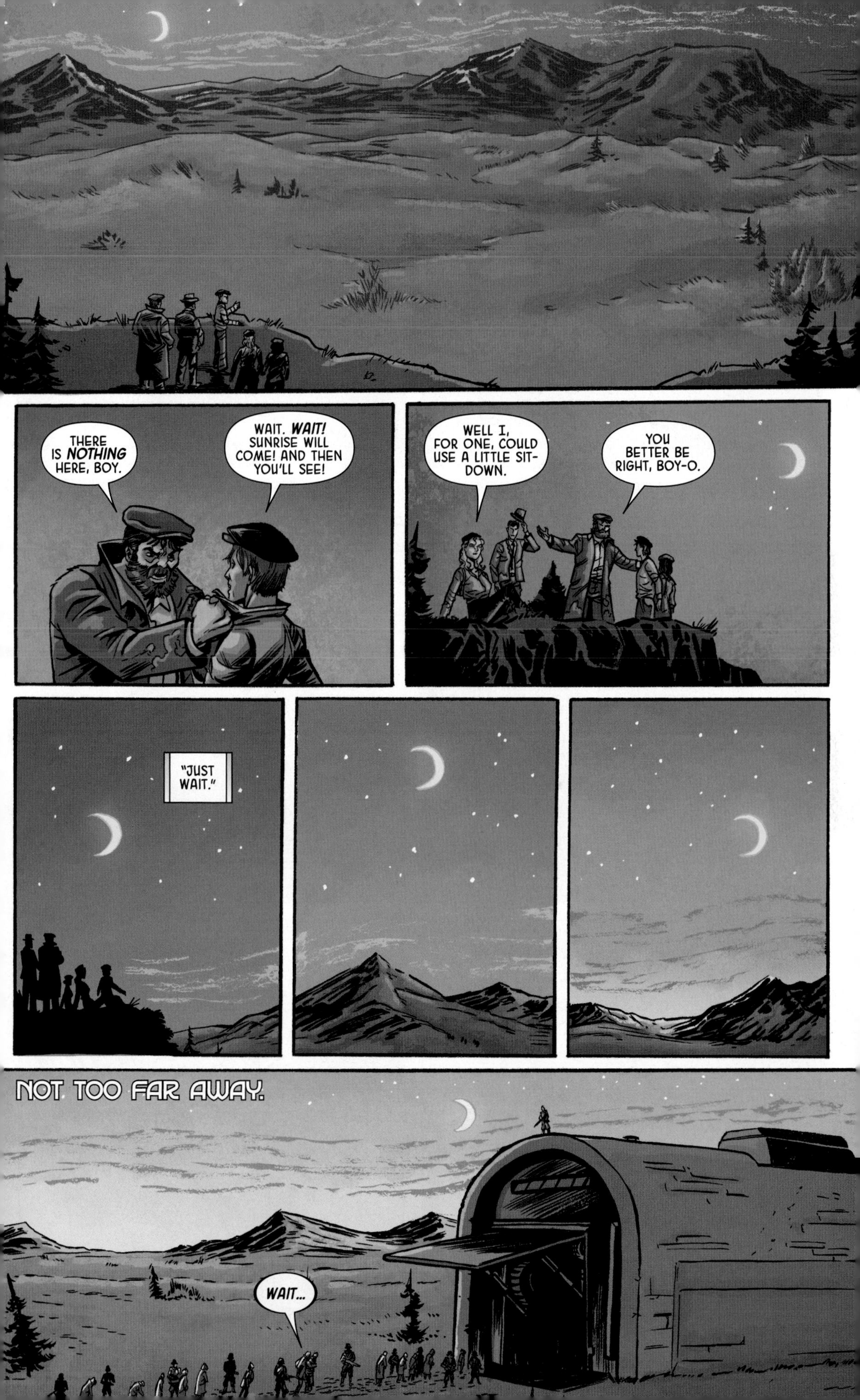
THERE IS NOTHING HERE, BOY.
WAIT. WAIT! SUNRISE WILL COME! AND THEN YOU'LL SEE!
WELL I, FOR ONE, COULD USE A LITTLE SIT-DOWN.
YOU BETTER BE RIGHT, BOY-O.
"JUST WAIT."
NOT TOO FAR AWAY.
WAIT...

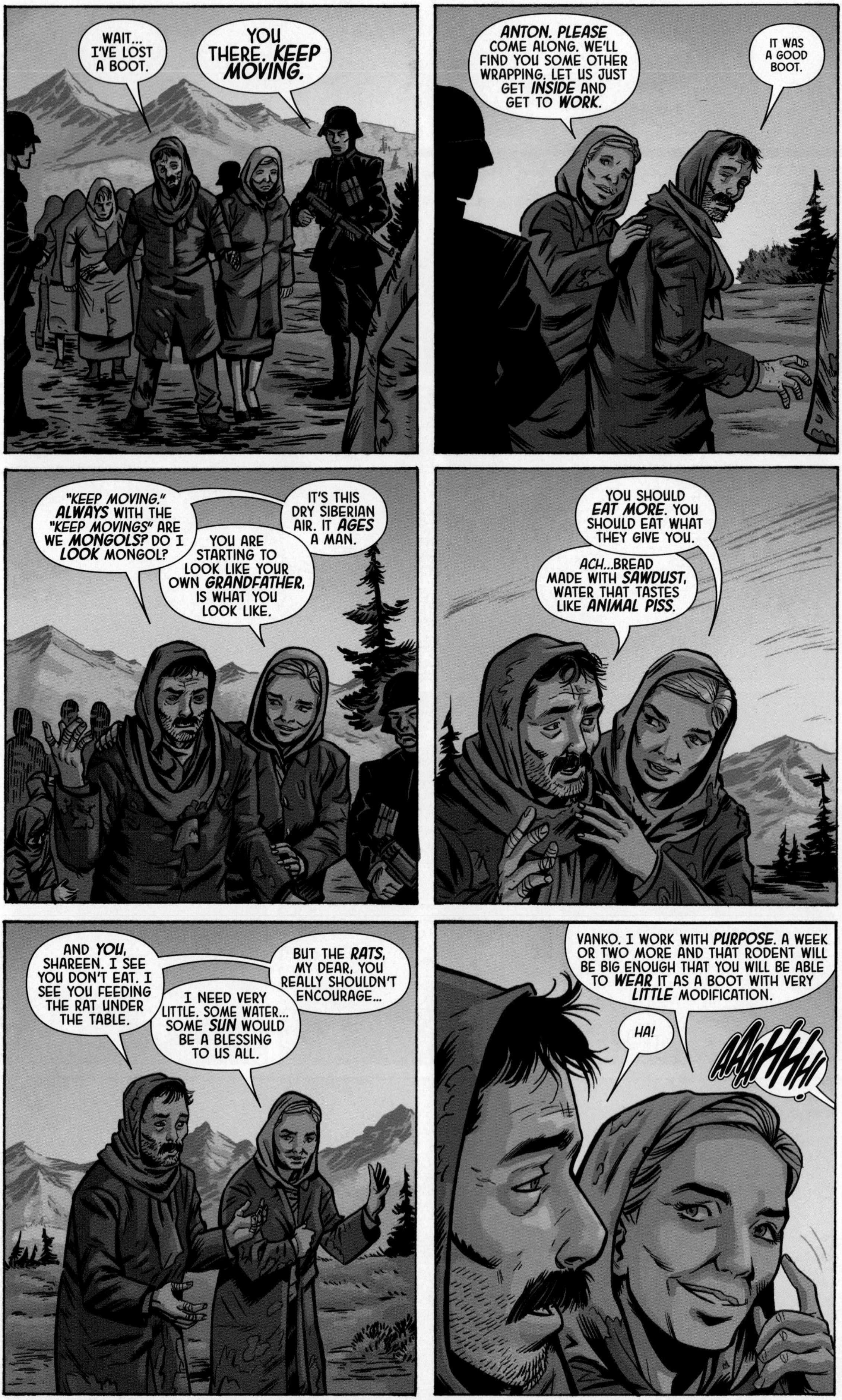
WAIT... I'VE LOST A BOOT.
YOU THERE. KEEP MOVING.
ANTON. PLEASE COME ALONG. WE'LL FIND YOU SOME OTHER WRAPPING. LET US JUST GET INSIDE AND GET TO WORK.
IT WAS A GOOD BOOT.
"KEEP MOVING." ALWAYS WITH THE "KEEP MOVINGS" ARE WE MONGOLS? DO I LOOK MONGOL?
YOU ARE STARTING TO LOOK LIKE YOUR OWN GRANDFATHER, IS WHAT YOU LOOK LIKE.
IT'S THIS DRY SIBERIAN AIR. IT AGES A MAN.
YOU SHOULD EAT MORE. YOU SHOULD EAT WHAT THEY GIVE YOU.
ACH...BREAD MADE WITH SAWDUST, WATER THAT TASTES LIKE ANIMAL PISS.
AND YOU, SHAREEN. I SEE YOU DON'T EAT. I SEE YOU FEEDING THE RAT UNDER THE TABLE.
I NEED VERY LITTLE. SOME WATER... SOME SUN WOULD BE A BLESSING TO US ALL.
BUT THE RATS, MY DEAR, YOU REALLY SHOULDN'T ENCOURAGE...
VANKO. I WORK WITH PURPOSE. A WEEK OR TWO MORE AND THAT RODENT WILL BE BIG ENOUGH THAT YOU WILL BE ABLE TO WEAR IT AS A BOOT WITH VERY LITTLE MODIFICATION.
HA!
AAAHHH!

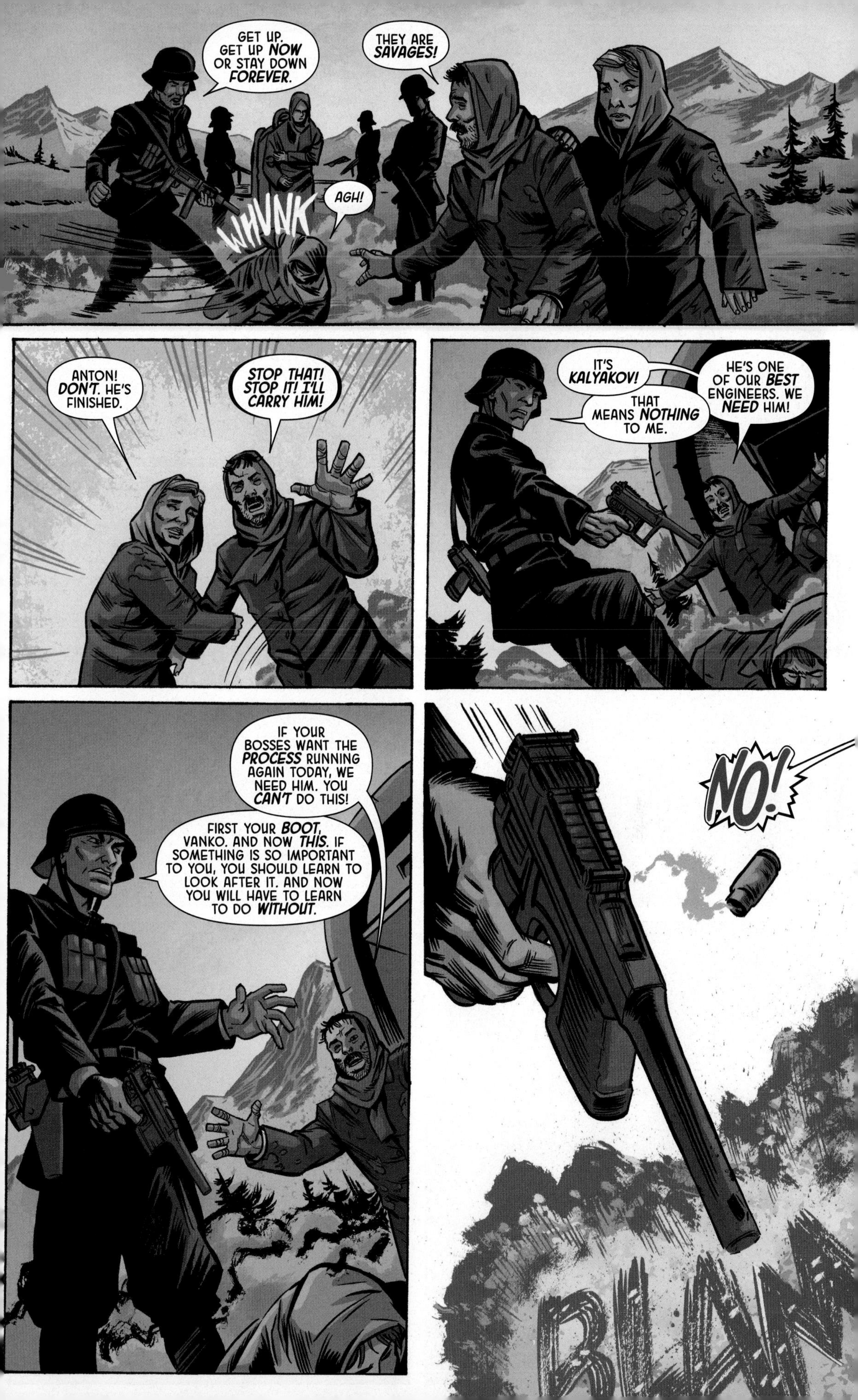
GET UP. GET UP NOW OR STAY DOWN FOREVER.
THEY ARE SAVAGES!
WHVNK
AGH!
ANTON! DON'T. HE'S FINISHED.
STOP THAT! STOP IT! I'LL CARRY HIM!
IT'S KALYAKOV!
HE'S ONE OF OUR BEST ENGINEERS. WE NEED HIM!
THAT MEANS NOTHING TO ME.
IF YOUR BOSSES WANT THE PROCESS RUNNING AGAIN TODAY, WE NEED HIM. YOU CAN'T DO THIS!
FIRST YOUR BOOT, VANKO. AND NOW THIS. IF SOMETHING IS SO IMPORTANT TO YOU, YOU SHOULD LEARN TO LOOK AFTER IT. AND NOW YOU WILL HAVE TO LEARN TO DO WITHOUT.
NO!

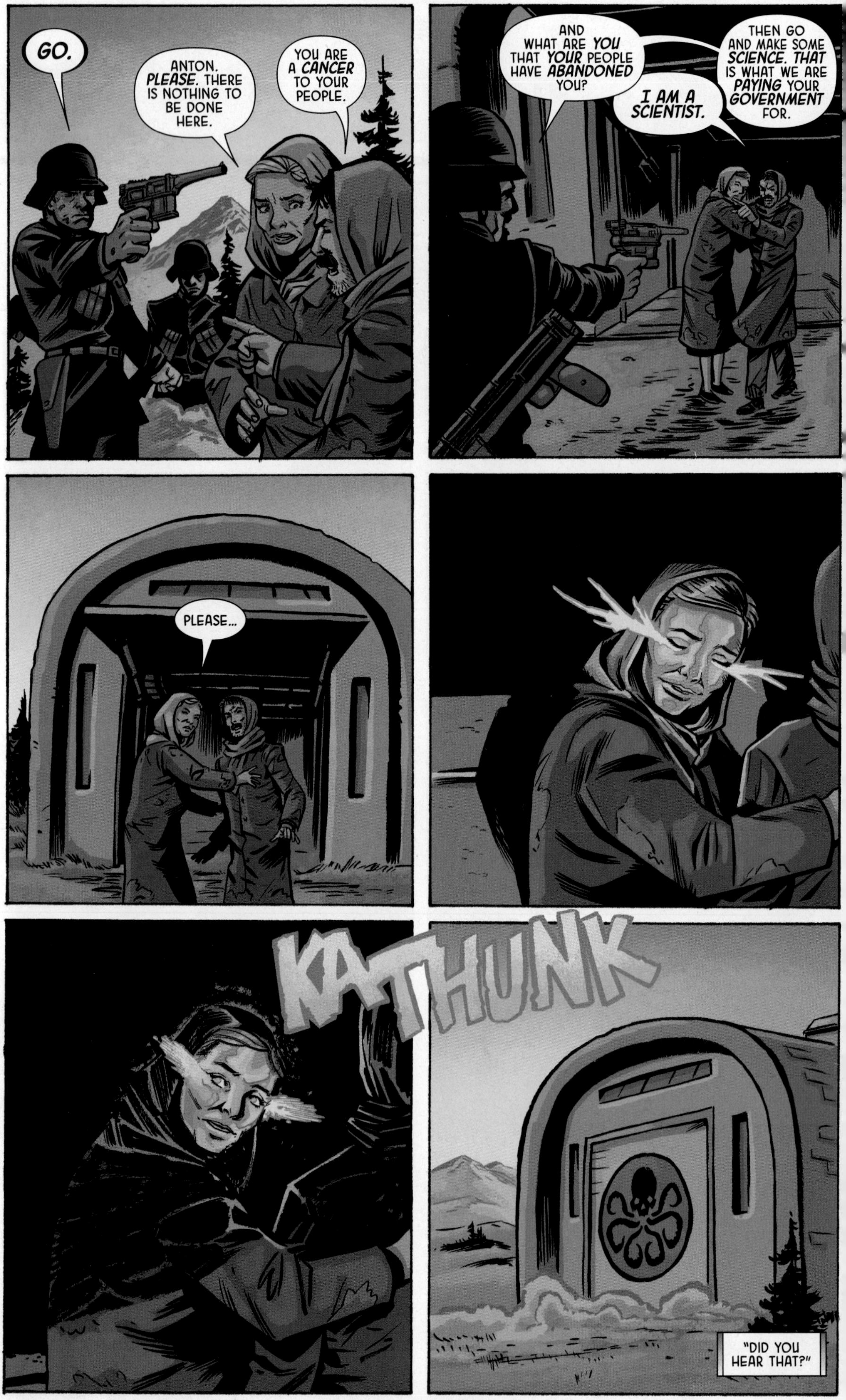
GO.
ANTON. PLEASE. THERE IS NOTHING TO BE DONE HERE.
YOU ARE A CANCER TO YOUR PEOPLE.
AND WHAT ARE YOU THAT YOUR PEOPLE HAVE ABANDONED YOU?
I AM A SCIENTIST.
THEN GO AND MAKE SOME SCIENCE. THAT IS WHAT WE ARE PAYING YOUR GOVERNMENT FOR.
PLEASE...
KATHUNK
"DID YOU HEAR THAT?"

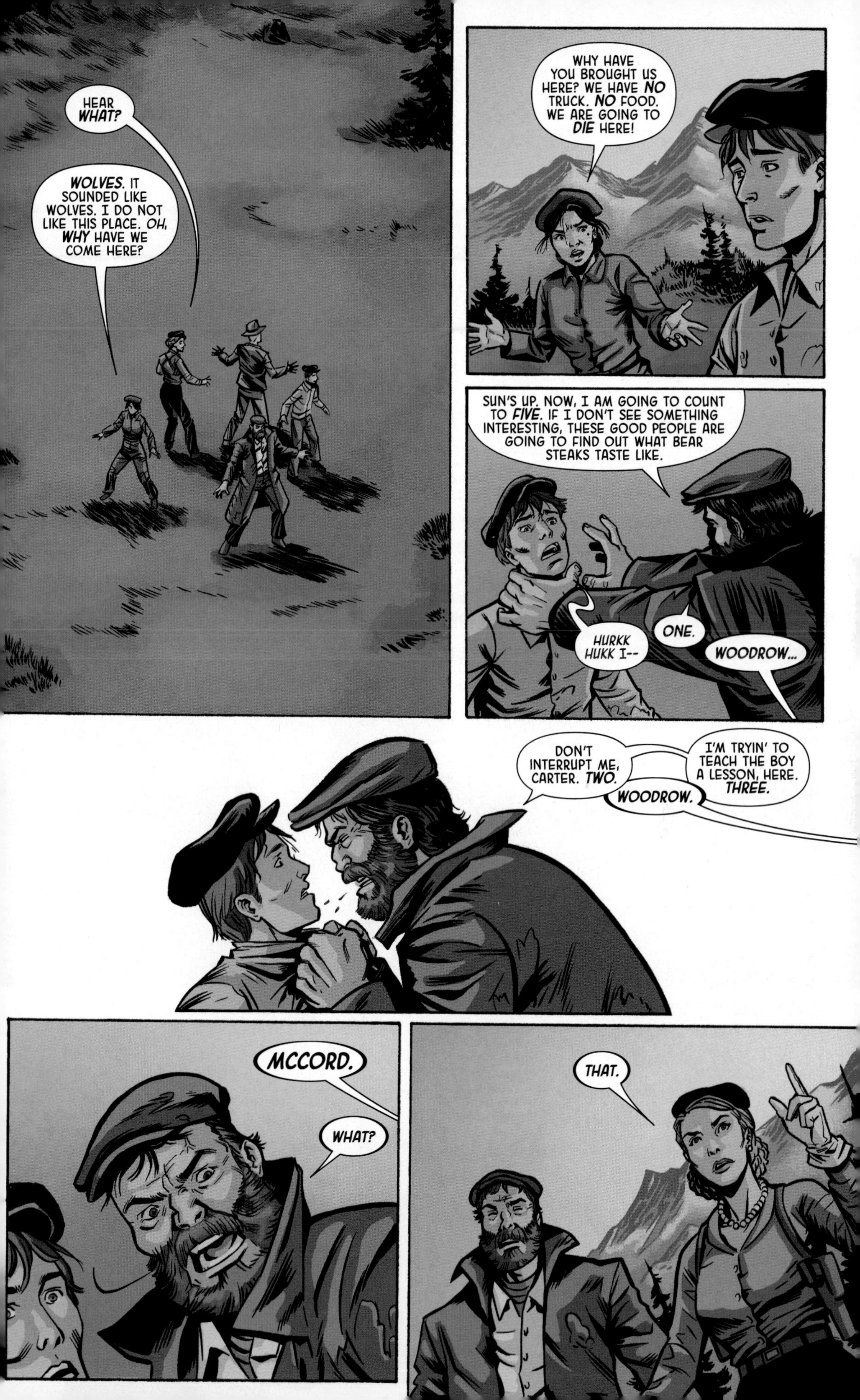
HEAR WHAT?
WOLVES. IT SOUNDED LIKE WOLVES. I DO NOT LIKE THIS PLACE. OH, WHY HAVE WE COME HERE?
WHY HAVE YOU BROUGHT US HERE? WE HAVE NO TRUCK. NO FOOD. WE ARE GOING TO DIE HERE!
SUN'S UP. NOW, I AM GOING TO COUNT TO FIVE. IF I DON'T SEE SOMETHING INTERESTING, THESE GOOD PEOPLE ARE GOING TO FIND OUT WHAT BEAR STEAKS TASTE LIKE.
HURKK HUKK I--
ONE.
WOODROW...
DON'T INTERRUPT ME, CARTER. TWO.
I'M TRYIN' TO TEACH THE BOY A LESSON, HERE. THREE.
WOODROW.
MCCORD.
WHAT?
THAT.

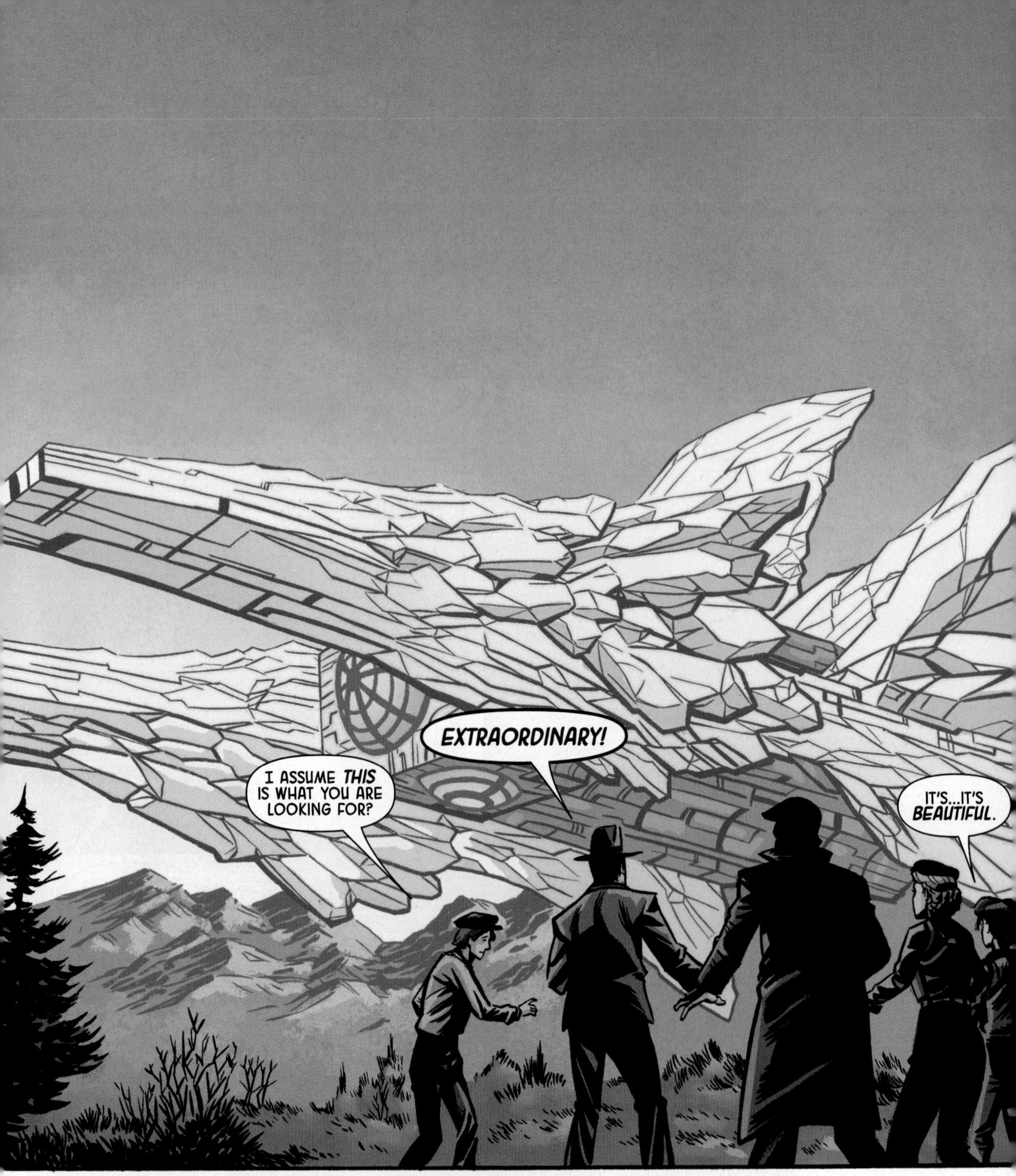
EXTRAORDINARY!
I ASSUME THIS IS WHAT YOU ARE LOOKING FOR?
IT'S...IT'S BEAUTIFUL.

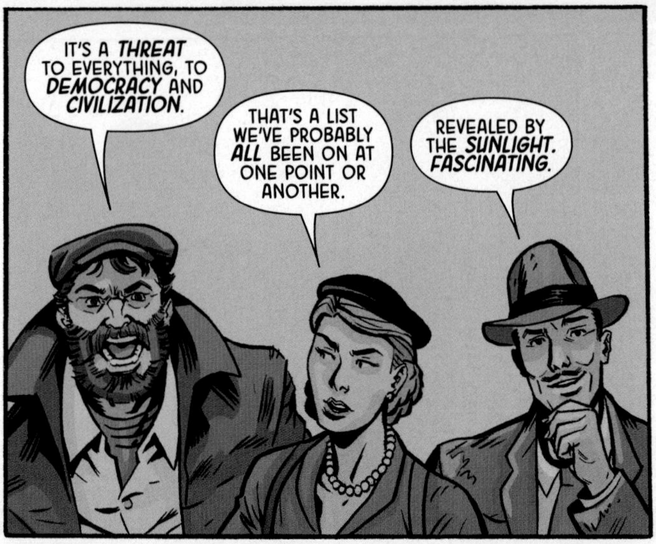
IT'S A THREAT TO EVERYTHING, TO DEMOCRACY AND CIVILIZATION.
THAT'S A LIST WE'VE PROBABLY ALL BEEN ON AT ONE POINT OR ANOTHER.
REVEALED BY THE SUNLIGHT. FASCINATING.

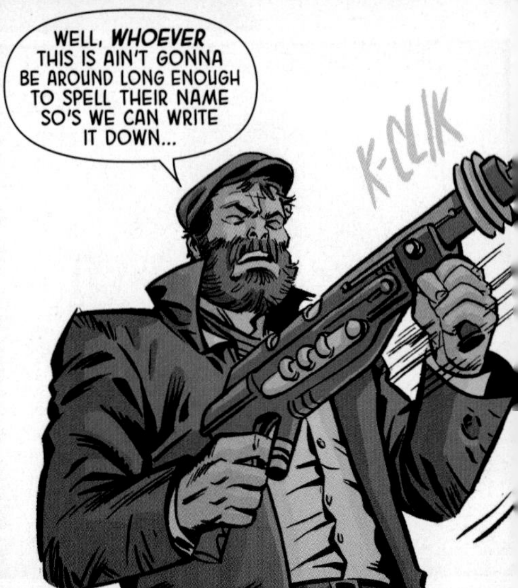
WELL, WHOEVER THIS IS AIN'T GONNA BE AROUND LONG ENOUGH TO SPELL THEIR NAME SO'S WE CAN WRITE IT DOWN...
K-CLIK

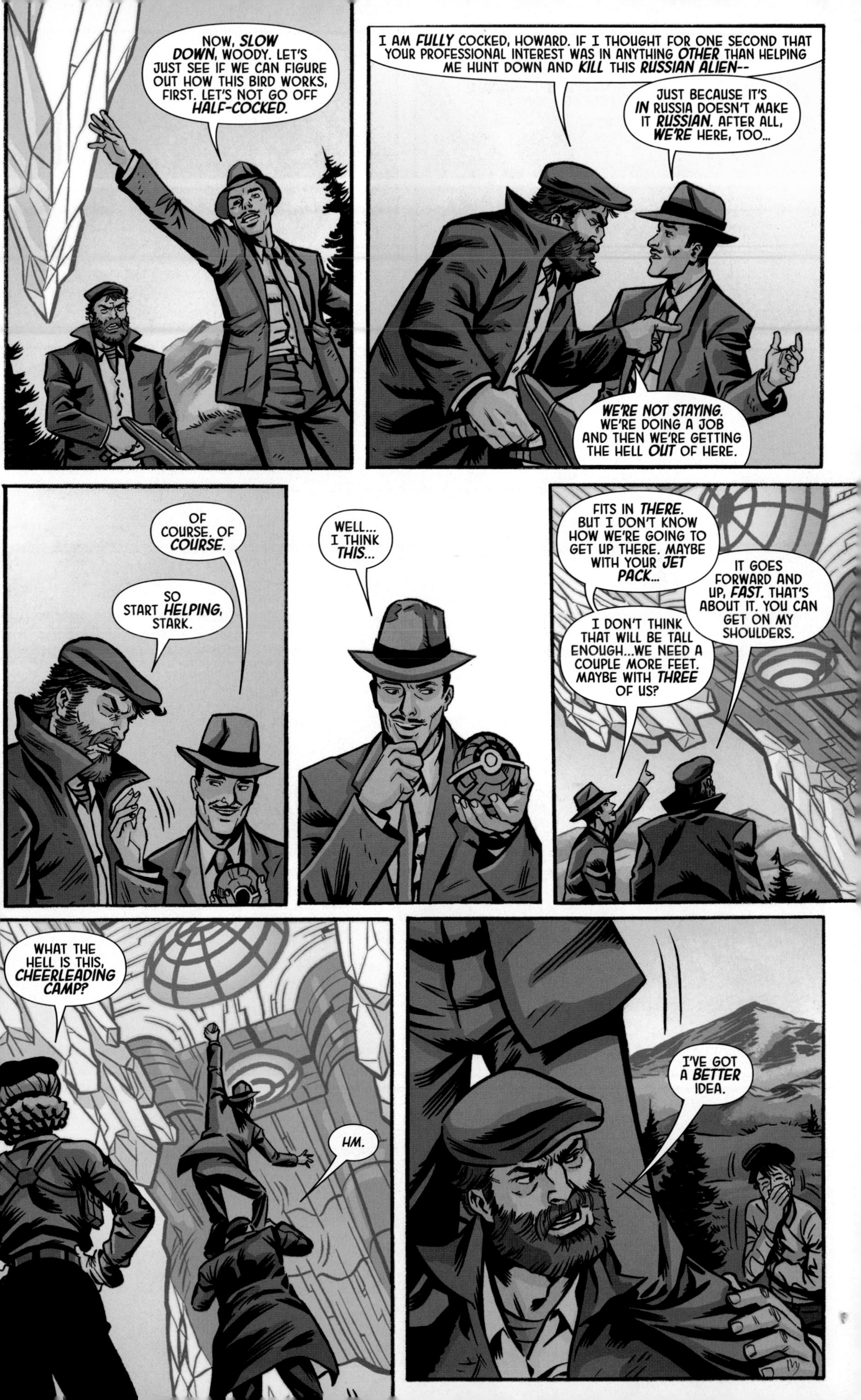
NOW, SLOW DOWN, WOODY. LET'S JUST SEE IF WE CAN FIGURE OUT HOW THIS BIRD WORKS, FIRST. LET'S NOT GO OFF HALF-COCKED.
I AM FULLY COCKED, HOWARD. IF I THOUGHT FOR ONE SECOND THAT YOUR PROFESSIONAL INTEREST WAS IN ANYTHING OTHER THAN HELPING ME HUNT DOWN AND KILL THIS RUSSIAN ALIEN--
JUST BECAUSE IT'S IN RUSSIA DOESN'T MAKE IT RUSSIAN. AFTER ALL, WE'RE HERE, TOO...
WE'RE NOT STAYING. WE'RE DOING A JOB AND THEN WE'RE GETTING THE HELL OUT OF HERE.
OF COURSE. OF COURSE.
SO START HELPING, STARK.
WELL... I THINK THIS...
FITS IN THERE. BUT I DON'T KNOW HOW WE'RE GOING TO GET UP THERE. MAYBE WITH YOUR JET PACK...
IT GOES FORWARD AND UP, FAST. THAT'S ABOUT IT. YOU CAN GET ON MY SHOULDERS.
I DON'T THINK THAT WILL BE TALL ENOUGH...WE NEED A COUPLE MORE FEET. MAYBE WITH THREE OF US?
WHAT THE HELL IS THIS, CHEERLEADING CAMP?
HM.
I'VE GOT A BETTER IDEA.

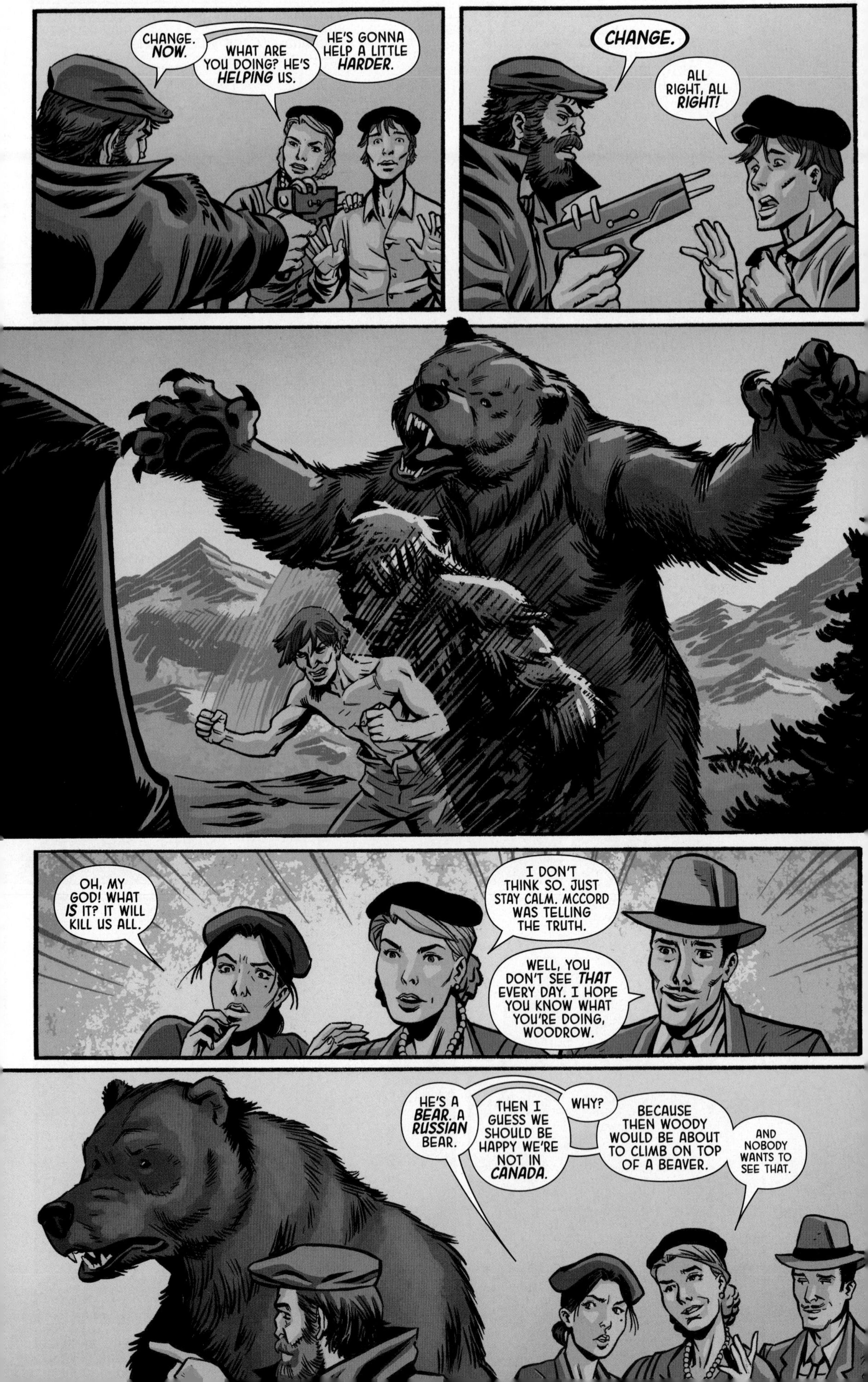
CHANGE. NOW.
WHAT ARE YOU DOING? HE'S HELPING US.
HE'S GONNA HELP A LITTLE HARDER.
CHANGE.
ALL RIGHT, ALL RIGHT!
OH, MY GOD! WHAT IS IT? IT WILL KILL US ALL.
I DON'T THINK SO. JUST STAY CALM. MCCORD WAS TELLING THE TRUTH.
WELL, YOU DON'T SEE THAT EVERY DAY. I HOPE YOU KNOW WHAT YOU'RE DOING, WOODROW.
HE'S A BEAR. A RUSSIAN BEAR.
THEN I GUESS WE SHOULD BE HAPPY WE'RE NOT IN CANADA.
WHY?
BECAUSE THEN WOODY WOULD BE ABOUT TO CLIMB ON TOP OF A BEAVER.
AND NOBODY WANTS TO SEE THAT.

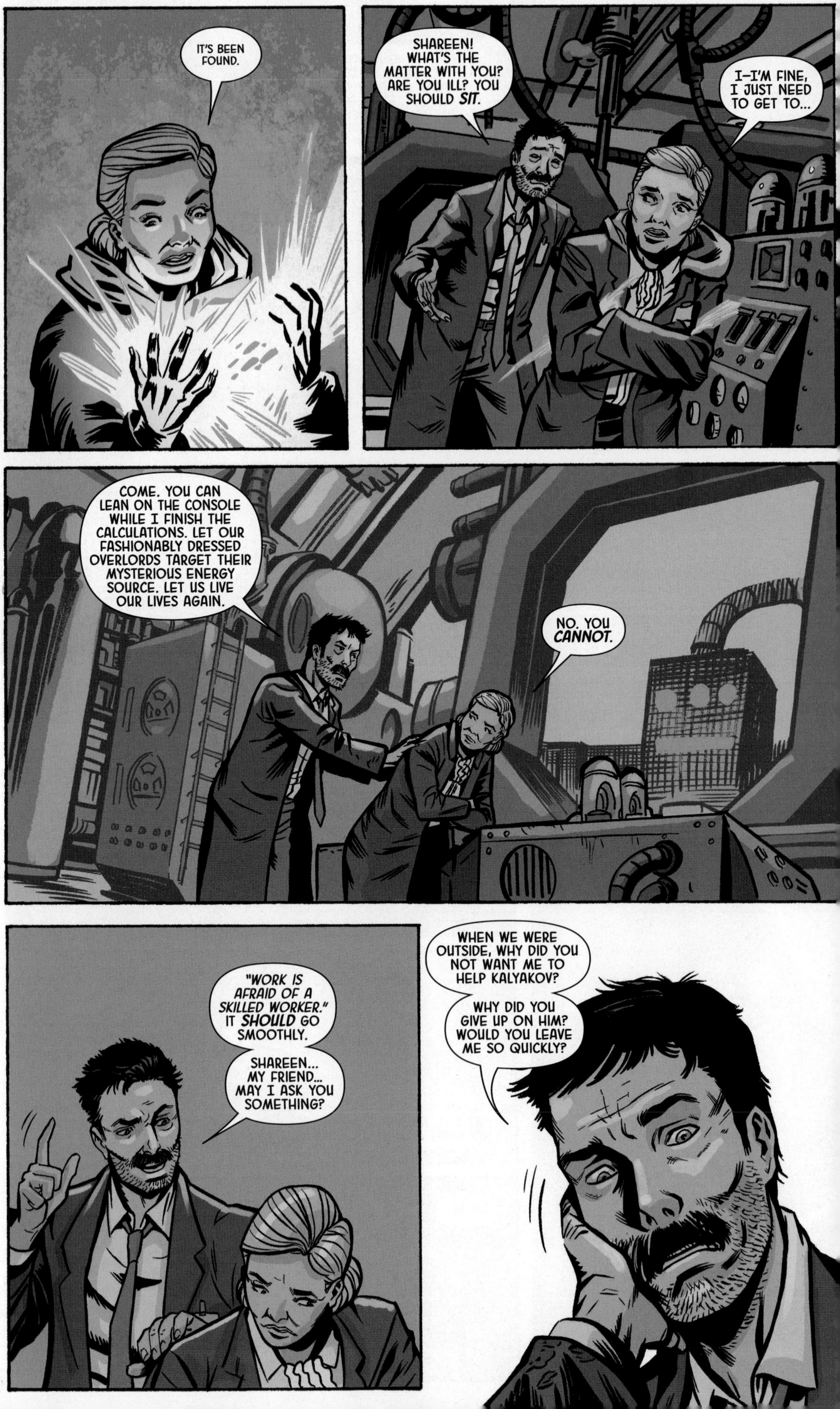
IT'S BEEN FOUND.
SHAREEN! WHAT'S THE MATTER WITH YOU? ARE YOU ILL? YOU SHOULD *SIT*.
I—I'M FINE, I JUST NEED TO GET TO...
COME. YOU CAN LEAN ON THE CONSOLE WHILE I FINISH THE CALCULATIONS. LET OUR FASHIONABLY DRESSED OVERLORDS TARGET THEIR MYSTERIOUS ENERGY SOURCE. LET US LIVE OUR LIVES AGAIN.
NO. YOU *CANNOT*.
"WORK IS AFRAID OF A SKILLED WORKER." IT *SHOULD* GO SMOOTHLY.
SHAREEN... MY FRIEND... MAY I ASK YOU SOMETHING?
WHEN WE WERE OUTSIDE, WHY DID YOU NOT WANT ME TO HELP KALYAKOV?
WHY DID YOU GIVE UP ON HIM? WOULD YOU LEAVE ME SO QUICKLY?

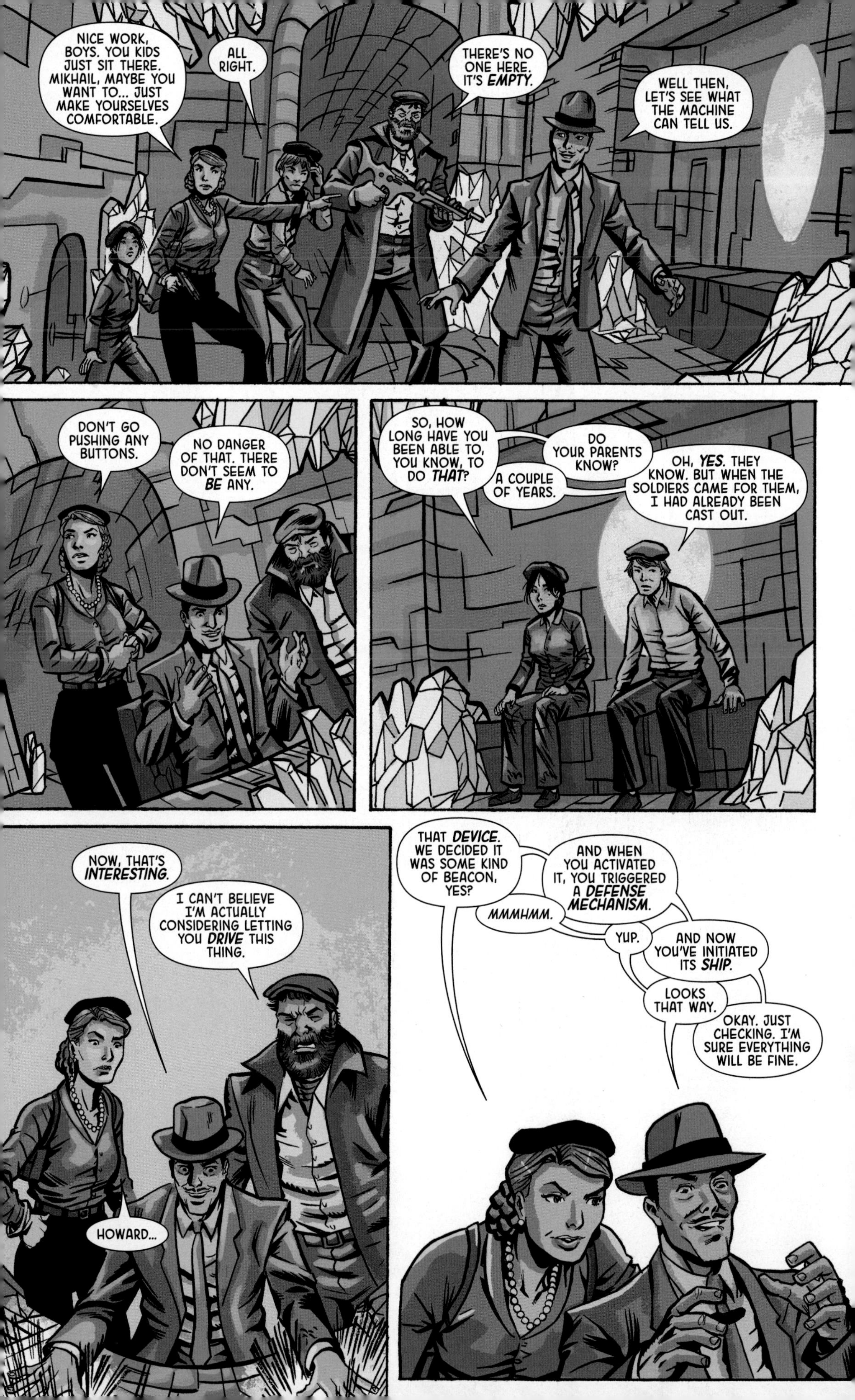
NICE WORK, BOYS. YOU KIDS JUST SIT THERE. MIKHAIL, MAYBE YOU WANT TO... JUST MAKE YOURSELVES COMFORTABLE.
ALL RIGHT.
THERE'S NO ONE HERE. IT'S *EMPTY*.
WELL THEN, LET'S SEE WHAT THE MACHINE CAN TELL US.
DON'T GO PUSHING ANY BUTTONS.
NO DANGER OF THAT. THERE DON'T SEEM TO *BE* ANY.
SO, HOW LONG HAVE YOU BEEN ABLE TO, YOU KNOW, TO DO *THAT*?
A COUPLE OF YEARS.
DO YOUR PARENTS KNOW?
OH, *YES*. THEY KNOW. BUT WHEN THE SOLDIERS CAME FOR THEM, I HAD ALREADY BEEN CAST OUT.
NOW, THAT'S *INTERESTING*.
I CAN'T BELIEVE I'M ACTUALLY CONSIDERING LETTING YOU *DRIVE* THIS THING.
HOWARD...
THAT *DEVICE*. WE DECIDED IT WAS SOME KIND OF BEACON, YES?
MMMHMM.
AND WHEN YOU ACTIVATED IT, YOU TRIGGERED A *DEFENSE MECHANISM*.
YUP.
AND NOW YOU'VE INITIATED ITS *SHIP*.
LOOKS THAT WAY.
OKAY. JUST CHECKING. I'M SURE EVERYTHING WILL BE FINE.

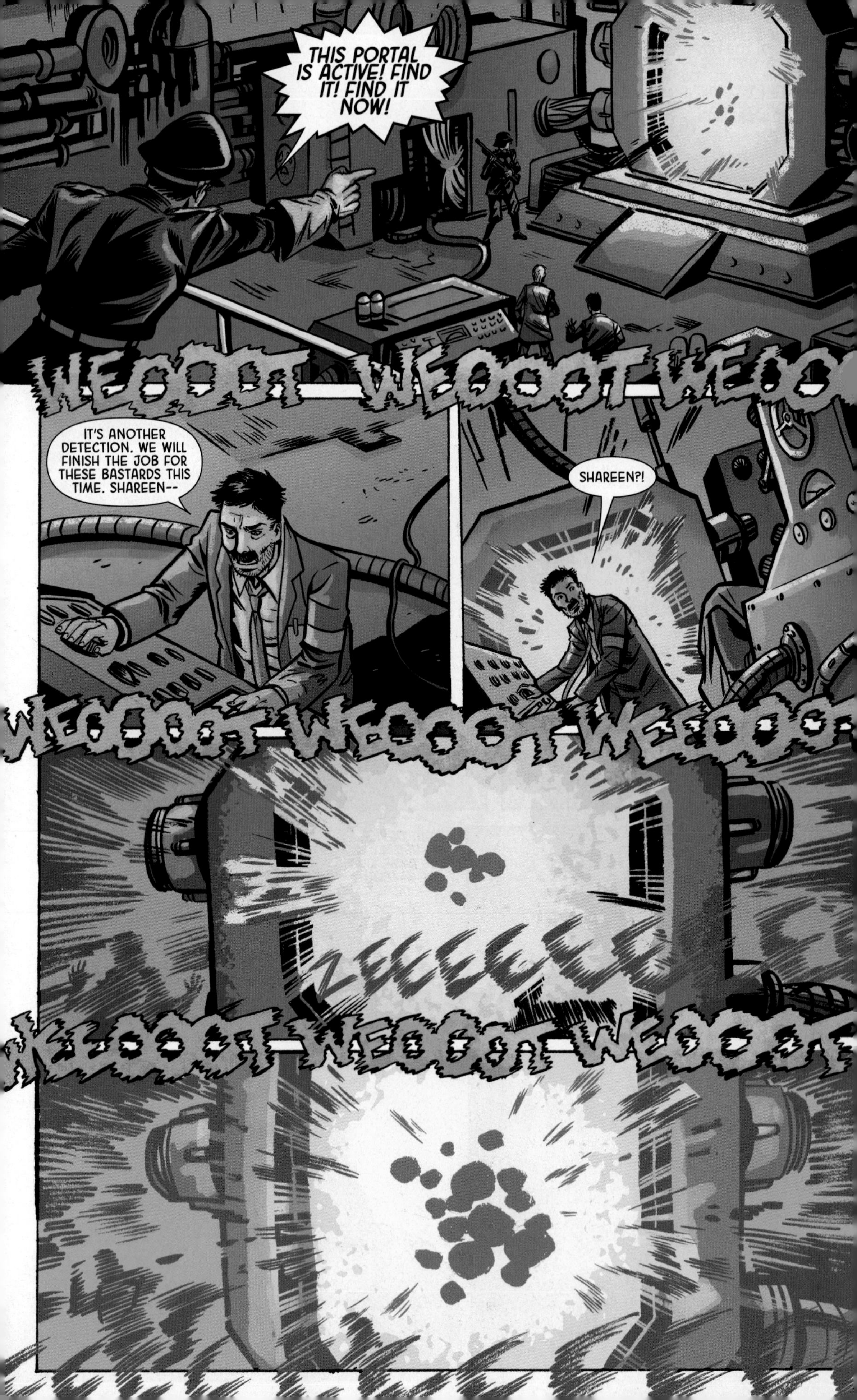
THIS PORTAL IS ACTIVE! FIND IT! FIND IT NOW!
WEOOOT WEOOOT
IT'S ANOTHER DETECTION. WE WILL FINISH THE JOB FOR THESE BASTARDS THIS TIME. SHAREEN--
SHAREEN?!
WEOOOT WEOOOT

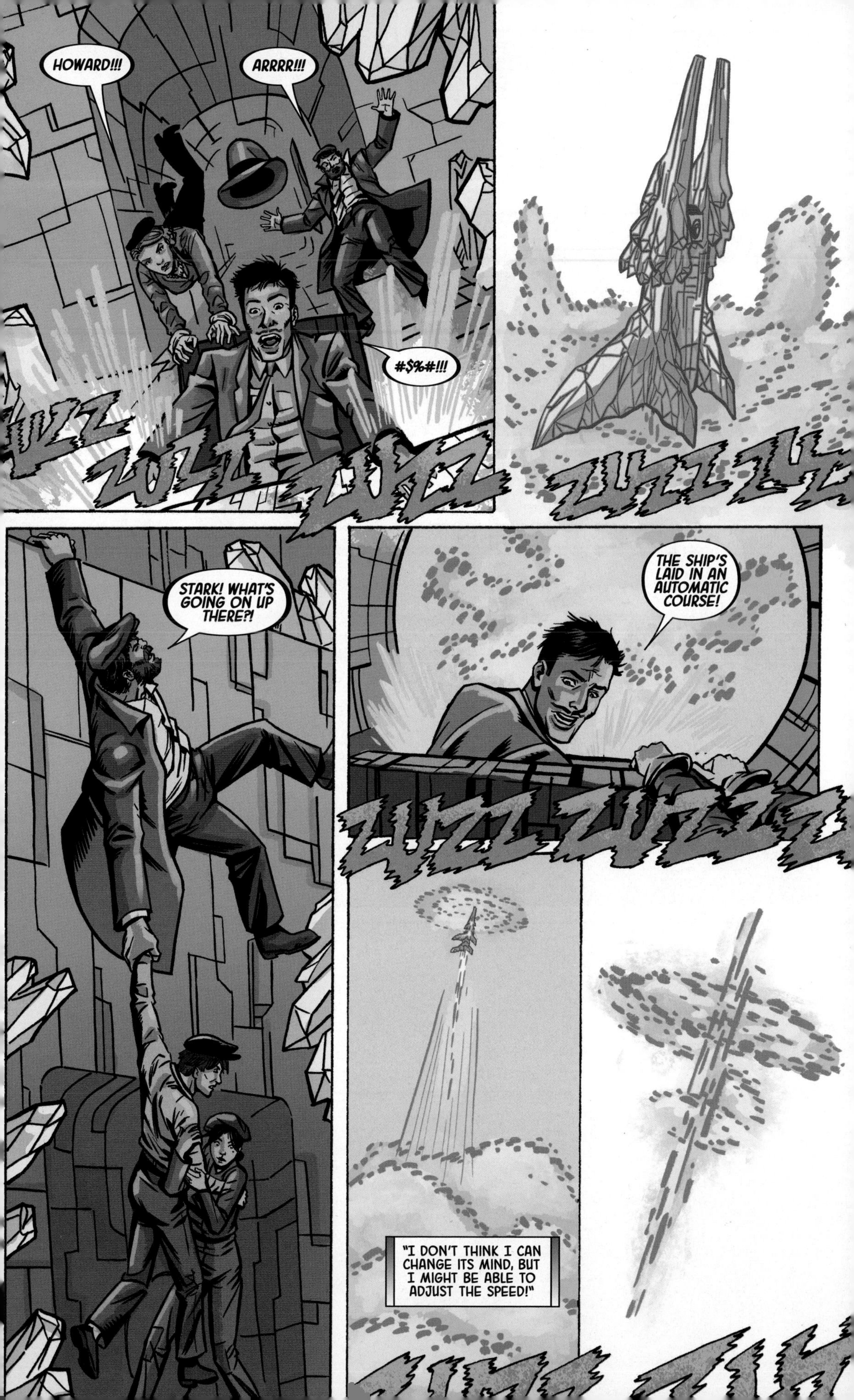
HOWARD!!!
ARRRR!!!
#$%#!!!
ZUZZ ZUZZ ZUZZ ZUZZ
STARK! WHAT'S GOING ON UP THERE?!
THE SHIP'S LAID IN AN AUTOMATIC COURSE!
ZUZZ ZUZZ
"I DON'T THINK I CAN CHANGE ITS MIND, BUT I MIGHT BE ABLE TO ADJUST THE SPEED!"

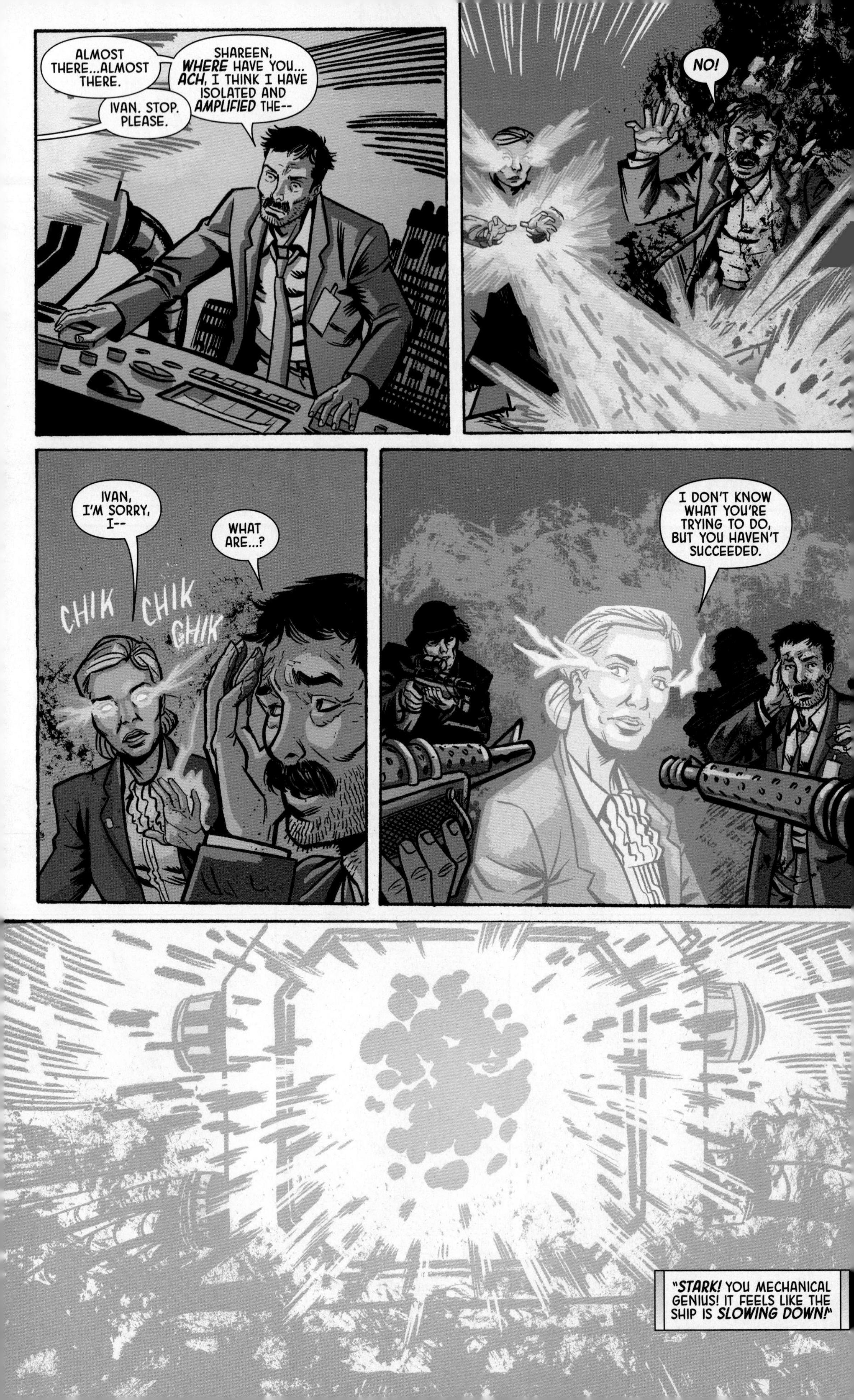
ALMOST THERE...ALMOST THERE.
SHAREEN, WHERE HAVE YOU... ACH, I THINK I HAVE ISOLATED AND AMPLIFIED THE--
IVAN. STOP. PLEASE.
NO!
IVAN, I'M SORRY, I--
WHAT ARE...?
CHIK CHIK CHIK
I DON'T KNOW WHAT YOU'RE TRYING TO DO, BUT YOU HAVEN'T SUCCEEDED.
"STARK! YOU MECHANICAL GENIUS! IT FEELS LIKE THE SHIP IS SLOWING DOWN!"

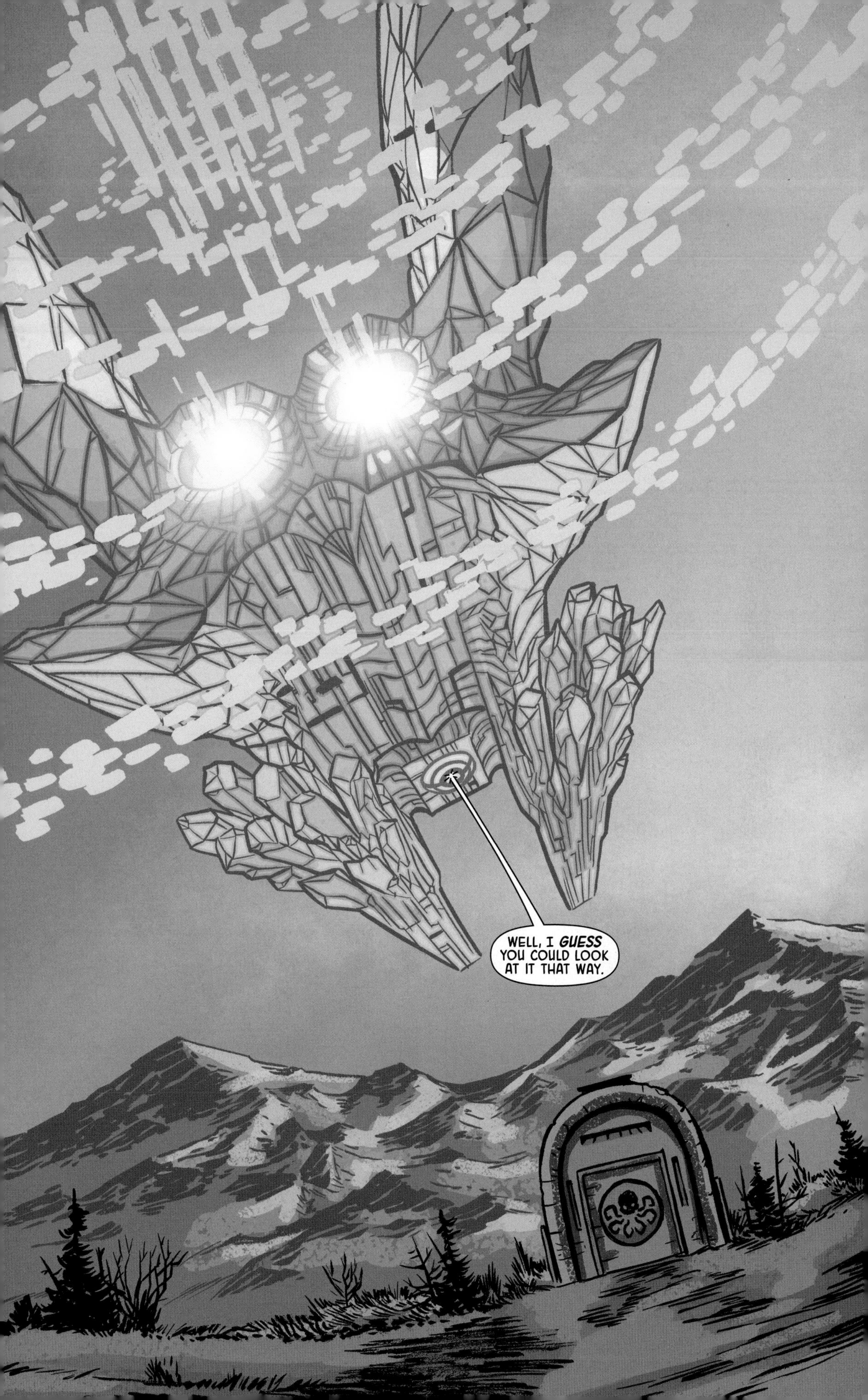
WELL, I GUESS YOU COULD LOOK AT IT THAT WAY.

4

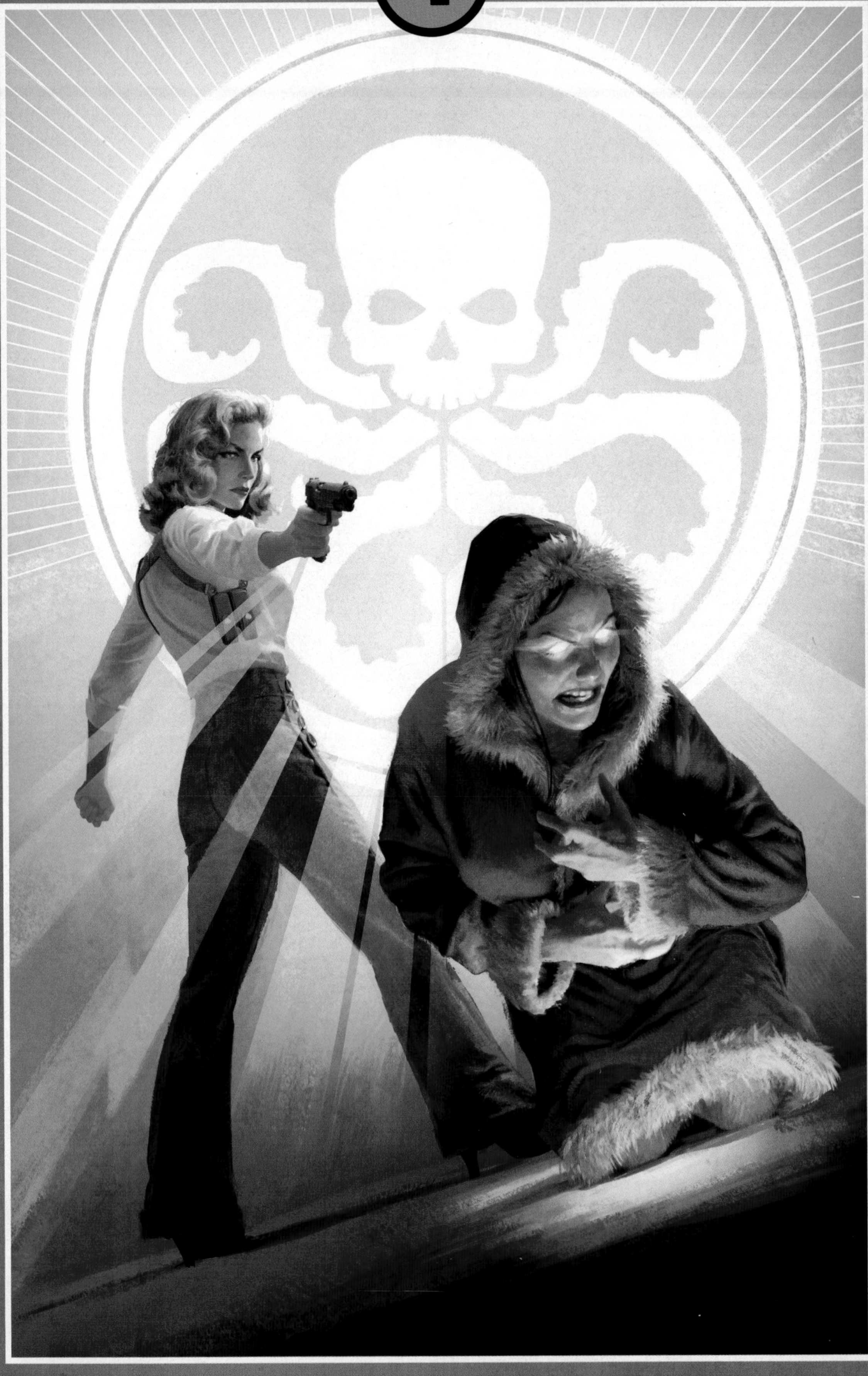

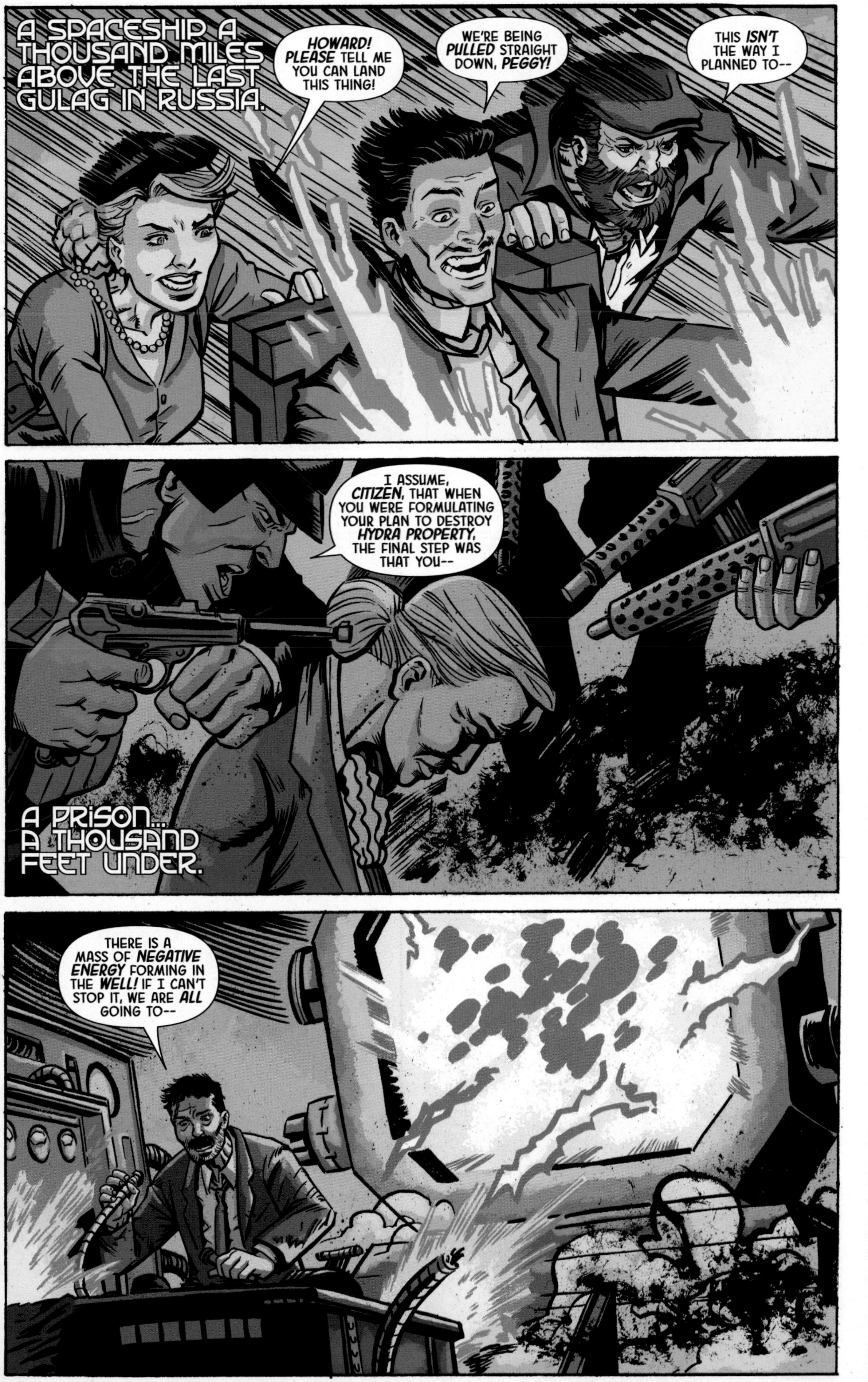
A SPACESHIP A THOUSAND MILES ABOVE THE LAST GULAG IN RUSSIA.
HOWARD! PLEASE TELL ME YOU CAN LAND THIS THING!
WE'RE BEING PULLED STRAIGHT DOWN, PEGGY!
THIS ISN'T THE WAY I PLANNED TO--
I ASSUME, CITIZEN, THAT WHEN YOU WERE FORMULATING YOUR PLAN TO DESTROY HYDRA PROPERTY, THE FINAL STEP WAS THAT YOU--
A PRISON... A THOUSAND FEET UNDER.
THERE IS A MASS OF NEGATIVE ENERGY FORMING IN THE WELL! IF I CAN'T STOP IT, WE ARE ALL GOING TO--

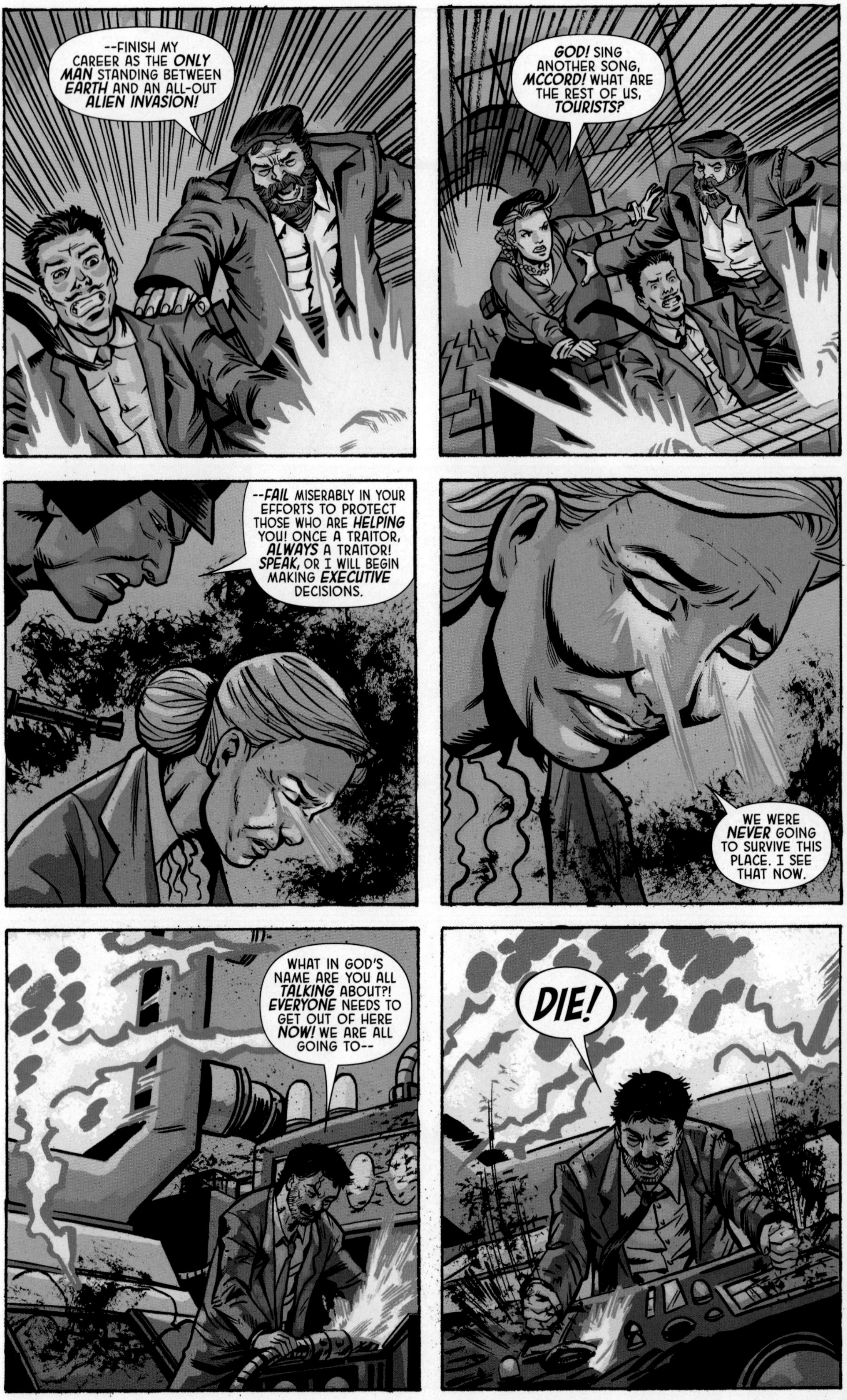
--FINISH MY CAREER AS THE ONLY MAN STANDING BETWEEN EARTH AND AN ALL-OUT ALIEN INVASION!
GOD! SING ANOTHER SONG, MCCORD! WHAT ARE THE REST OF US, TOURISTS?
--FAIL MISERABLY IN YOUR EFFORTS TO PROTECT THOSE WHO ARE HELPING YOU! ONCE A TRAITOR, ALWAYS A TRAITOR! SPEAK, OR I WILL BEGIN MAKING EXECUTIVE DECISIONS.
WE WERE NEVER GOING TO SURVIVE THIS PLACE. I SEE THAT NOW.
WHAT IN GOD'S NAME ARE YOU ALL TALKING ABOUT?! EVERYONE NEEDS TO GET OUT OF HERE NOW! WE ARE ALL GOING TO--
DIE!

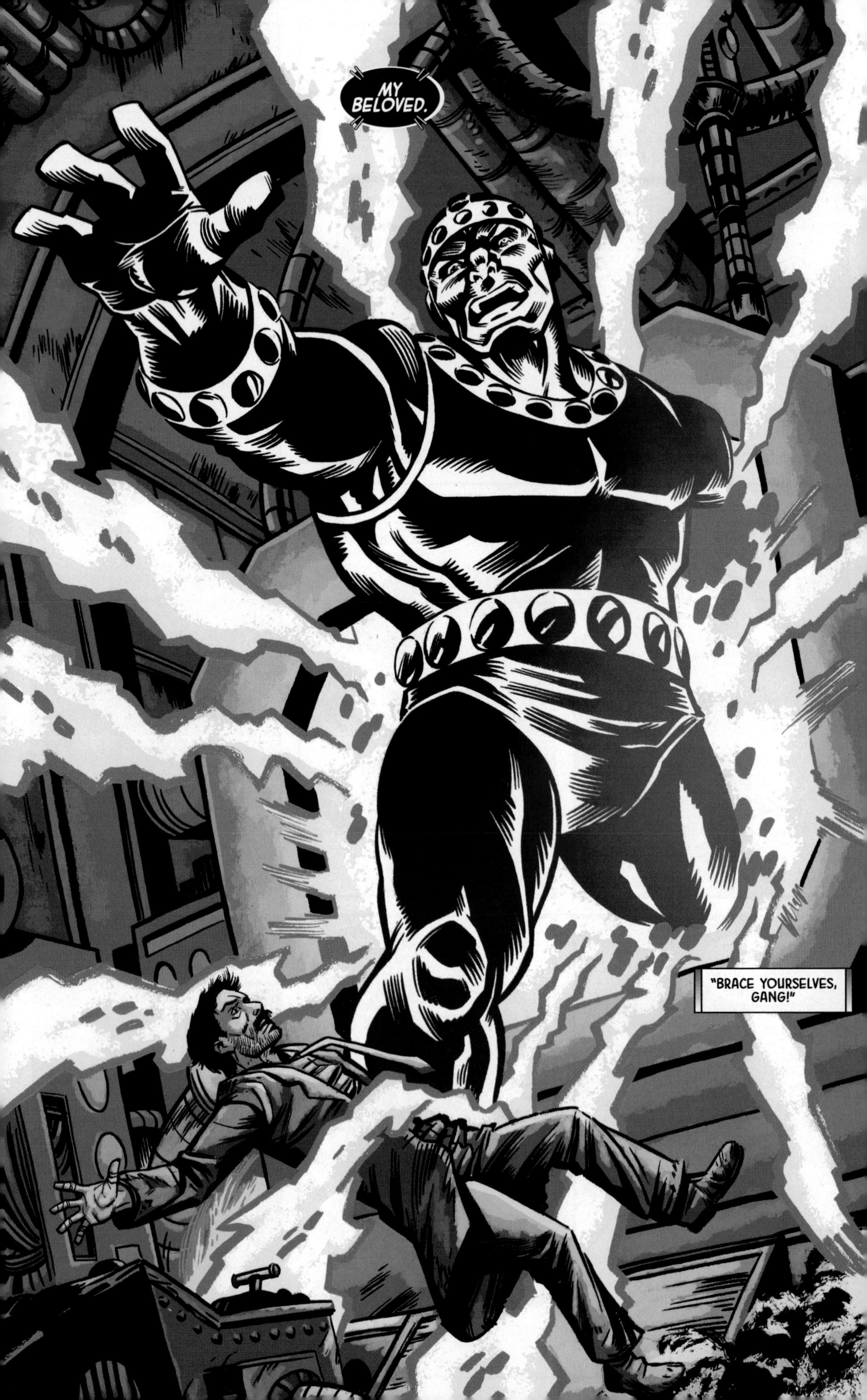
MY BELOVED.
"BRACE YOURSELVES, GANG!"

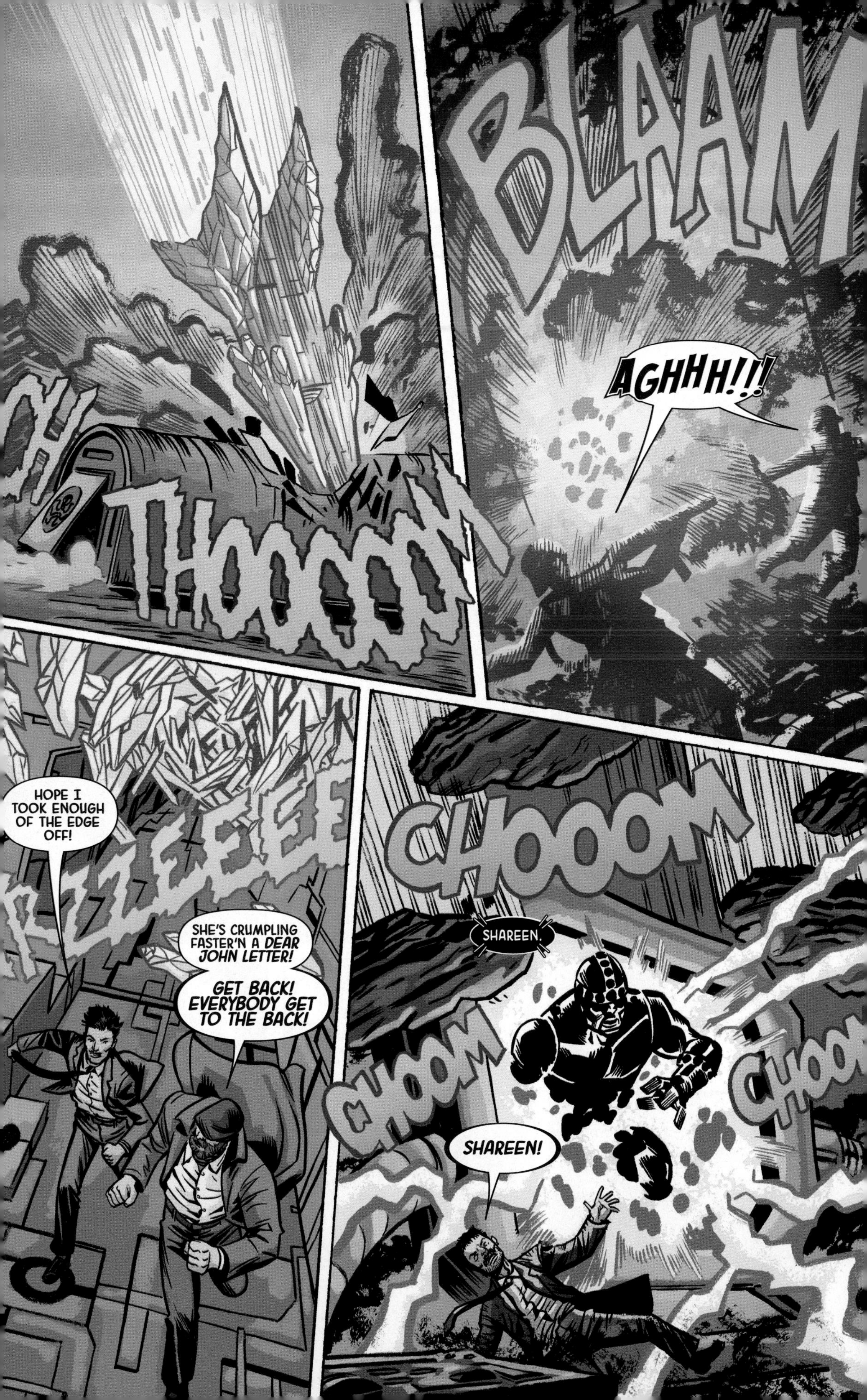
THOOOOM
BLAAM
AGHHH!!!
HOPE I TOOK ENOUGH OF THE EDGE OFF!
SHE'S CRUMPLING FASTER'N A DEAR JOHN LETTER!
GET BACK! EVERYBODY GET TO THE BACK!
CHOOOM
SHAREEN.
CHOOM
SHAREEN!

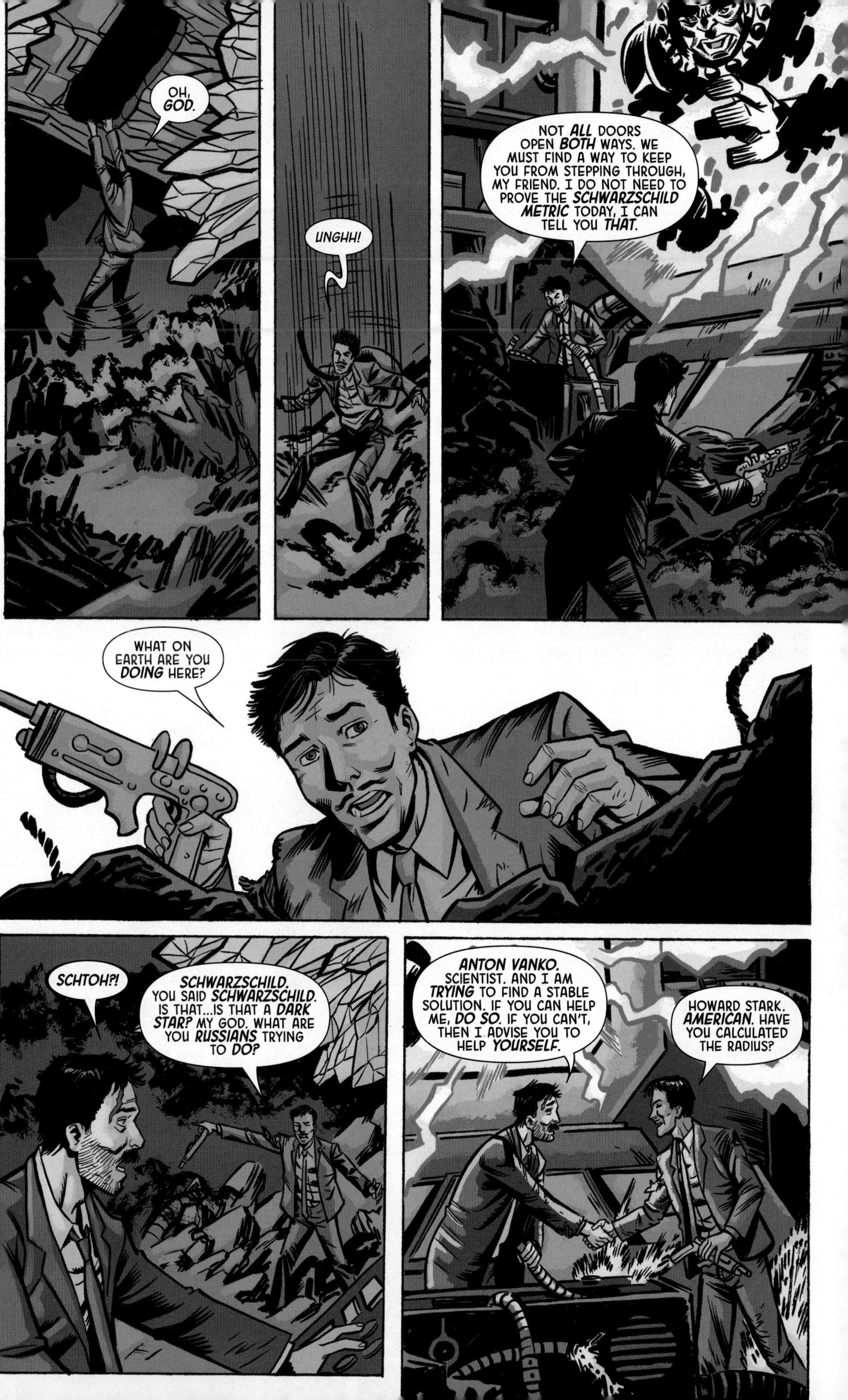
OH, GOD.
UNGHH!
NOT ALL DOORS OPEN BOTH WAYS. WE MUST FIND A WAY TO KEEP YOU FROM STEPPING THROUGH, MY FRIEND. I DO NOT NEED TO PROVE THE SCHWARZSCHILD METRIC TODAY, I CAN TELL YOU THAT.
WHAT ON EARTH ARE YOU DOING HERE?
SCHTOH?!
SCHWARZSCHILD. YOU SAID SCHWARZSCHILD. IS THAT...IS THAT A DARK STAR? MY GOD. WHAT ARE YOU RUSSIANS TRYING TO DO?
ANTON VANKO. SCIENTIST. AND I AM TRYING TO FIND A STABLE SOLUTION. IF YOU CAN HELP ME, DO SO. IF YOU CAN'T, THEN I ADVISE YOU TO HELP YOURSELF.
HOWARD STARK. AMERICAN. HAVE YOU CALCULATED THE RADIUS?

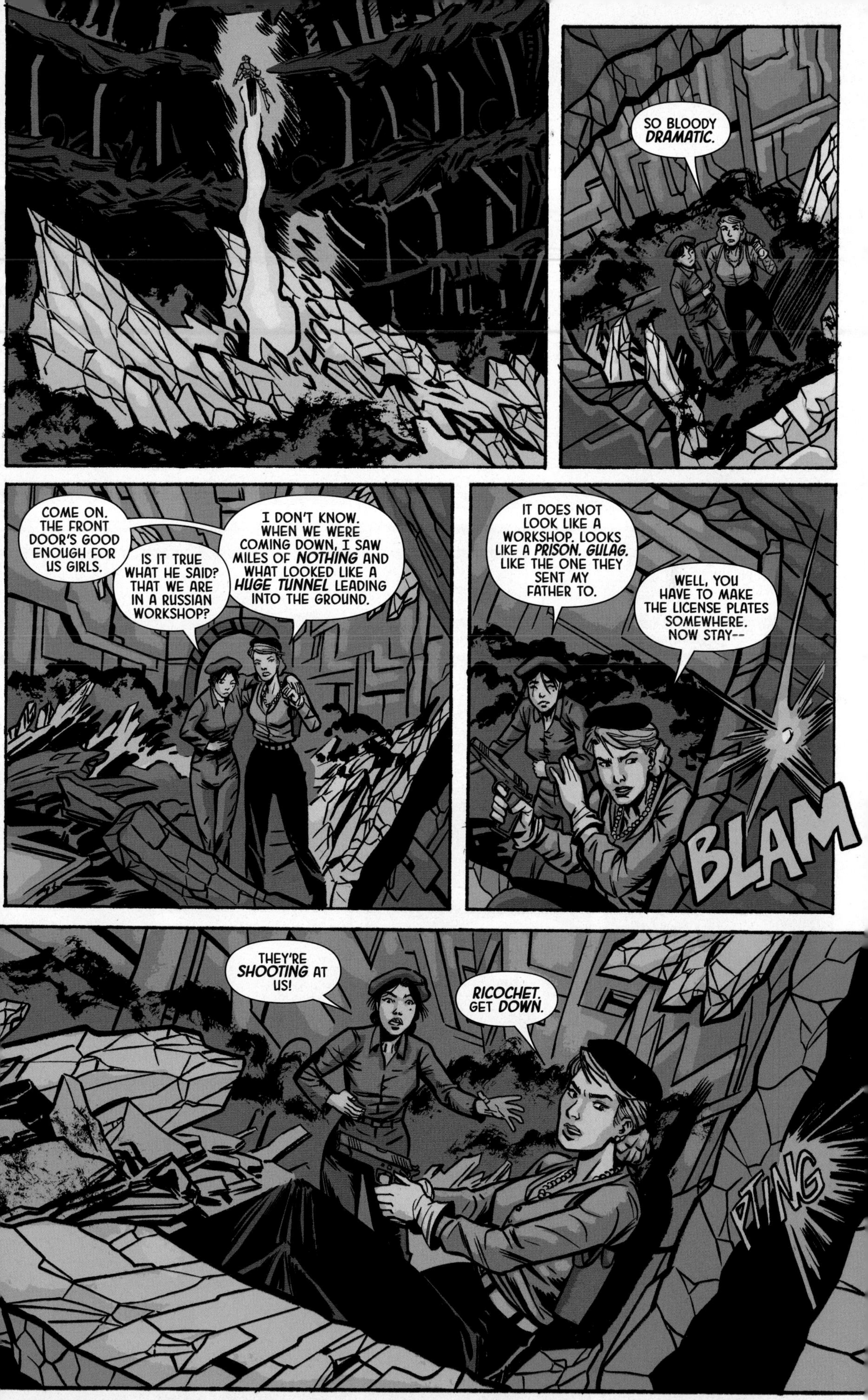
SO BLOODY *DRAMATIC*.
COME ON. THE FRONT DOOR'S GOOD ENOUGH FOR US GIRLS.
IS IT TRUE WHAT HE SAID? THAT WE ARE IN A RUSSIAN WORKSHOP?
I DON'T KNOW. WHEN WE WERE COMING DOWN, I SAW MILES OF *NOTHING* AND WHAT LOOKED LIKE A *HUGE TUNNEL* LEADING INTO THE GROUND.
IT DOES NOT LOOK LIKE A WORKSHOP. LOOKS LIKE A *PRISON. GULAG.* LIKE THE ONE THEY SENT MY FATHER TO.
WELL, YOU HAVE TO MAKE THE LICENSE PLATES SOMEWHERE. NOW STAY--
BLAM
THEY'RE *SHOOTING* AT US!
RICOCHET. GET *DOWN*.
PTING

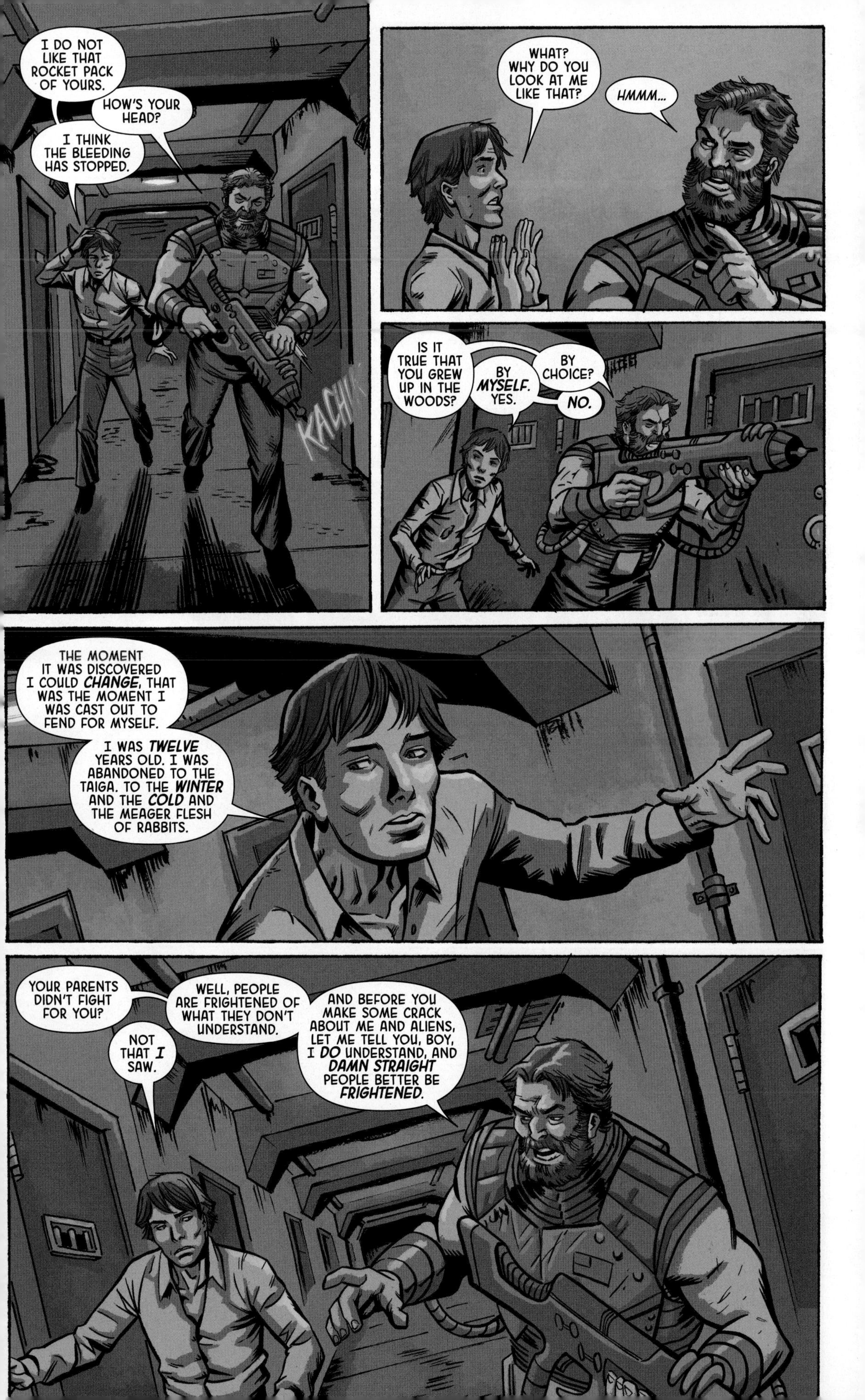

I DO NOT LIKE THAT ROCKET PACK OF YOURS.
HOW'S YOUR HEAD?
I THINK THE BLEEDING HAS STOPPED.
KACHIK
WHAT? WHY DO YOU LOOK AT ME LIKE THAT?
HMMM...
IS IT TRUE THAT YOU GREW UP IN THE WOODS?
BY *MYSELF*. YES.
BY CHOICE?
NO.
THE MOMENT IT WAS DISCOVERED I COULD *CHANGE*, THAT WAS THE MOMENT I WAS CAST OUT TO FEND FOR MYSELF.
I WAS *TWELVE* YEARS OLD. I WAS ABANDONED TO THE TAIGA. TO THE *WINTER* AND THE *COLD* AND THE MEAGER FLESH OF RABBITS.
YOUR PARENTS DIDN'T FIGHT FOR YOU?
NOT THAT *I* SAW.
WELL, PEOPLE ARE FRIGHTENED OF WHAT THEY DON'T UNDERSTAND.
AND BEFORE YOU MAKE SOME CRACK ABOUT ME AND ALIENS, LET ME TELL YOU, BOY, I *DO* UNDERSTAND, AND *DAMN STRAIGHT* PEOPLE BETTER BE *FRIGHTENED*.

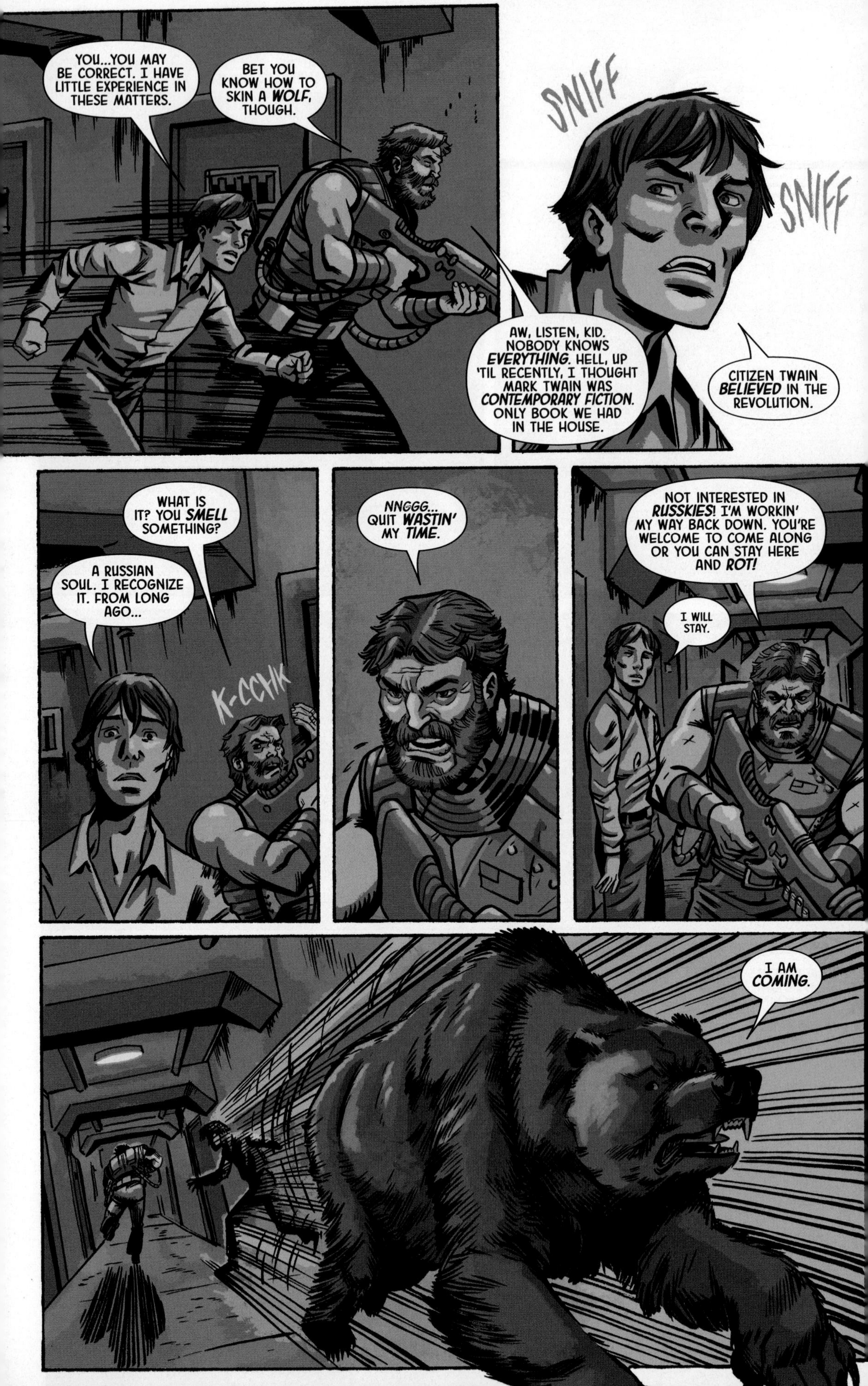
YOU...YOU MAY BE CORRECT. I HAVE LITTLE EXPERIENCE IN THESE MATTERS.
BET YOU KNOW HOW TO SKIN A *WOLF*, THOUGH.
SNIFF
SNIFF
AW, LISTEN, KID. NOBODY KNOWS *EVERYTHING*. HELL, UP 'TIL RECENTLY, I THOUGHT MARK TWAIN WAS *CONTEMPORARY FICTION*. ONLY BOOK WE HAD IN THE HOUSE.
CITIZEN TWAIN *BELIEVED* IN THE REVOLUTION.
WHAT IS IT? YOU *SMELL* SOMETHING?
A RUSSIAN SOUL. I RECOGNIZE IT. FROM LONG AGO...
K-CCHK
NNGGG... QUIT *WASTIN'* MY *TIME*.
NOT INTERESTED IN *RUSSKIES*! I'M WORKIN' MY WAY BACK DOWN. YOU'RE WELCOME TO COME ALONG OR YOU CAN STAY HERE AND *ROT*!
I WILL STAY.
I AM *COMING*.

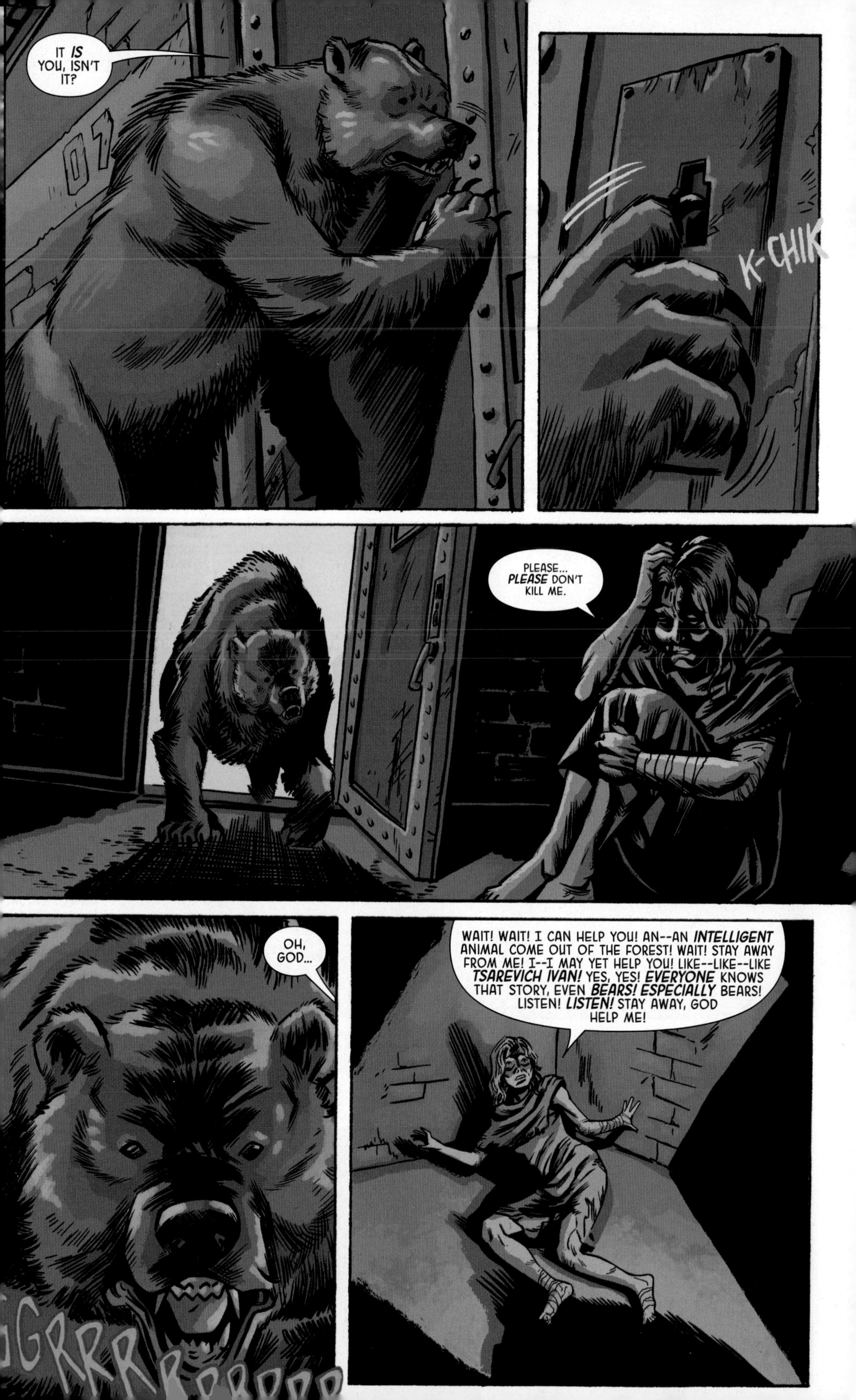
IT *IS* YOU, ISN'T IT?
K-CHIK
PLEASE... *PLEASE* DON'T KILL ME.
OH, GOD...
GRRRRRRRRR
WAIT! WAIT! I CAN HELP YOU! AN--AN *INTELLIGENT* ANIMAL COME OUT OF THE FOREST! WAIT! STAY AWAY FROM ME! I--I MAY YET HELP YOU! LIKE--LIKE--LIKE *TSAREVICH IVAN!* YES, YES! *EVERYONE* KNOWS THAT STORY, EVEN *BEARS! ESPECIALLY* BEARS! LISTEN! *LISTEN!* STAY AWAY, GOD HELP ME!

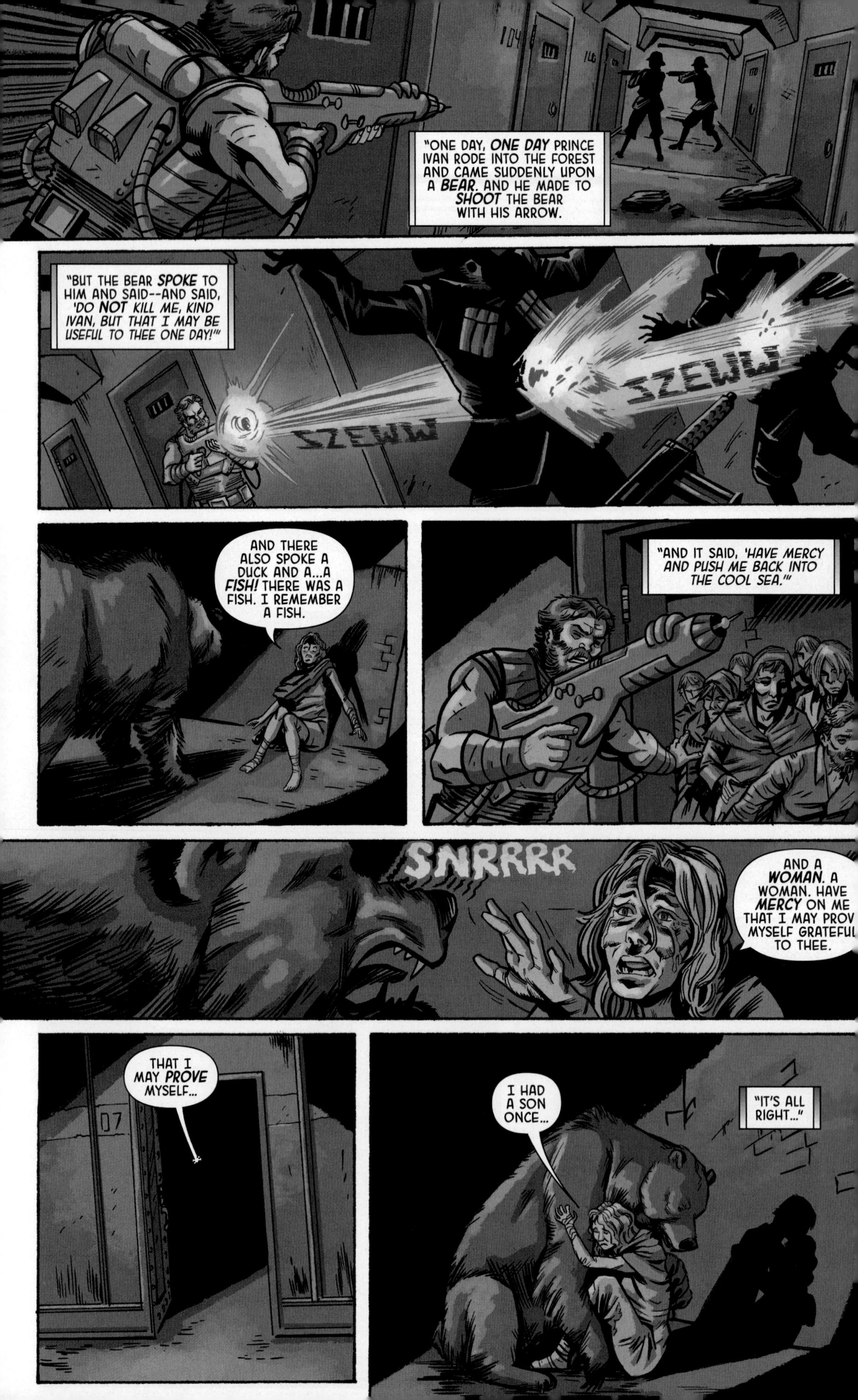
"ONE DAY, ONE DAY PRINCE IVAN RODE INTO THE FOREST AND CAME SUDDENLY UPON A BEAR. AND HE MADE TO SHOOT THE BEAR WITH HIS ARROW.
"BUT THE BEAR SPOKE TO HIM AND SAID--AND SAID, 'DO NOT KILL ME, KIND IVAN, BUT THAT I MAY BE USEFUL TO THEE ONE DAY!'"
SZEWW
SZEWW
AND THERE ALSO SPOKE A DUCK AND A...A FISH! THERE WAS A FISH. I REMEMBER A FISH.
"AND IT SAID, 'HAVE MERCY AND PUSH ME BACK INTO THE COOL SEA.'"
SNRRRR
AND A WOMAN. A WOMAN. HAVE MERCY ON ME THAT I MAY PROV MYSELF GRATEFUL TO THEE.
THAT I MAY PROVE MYSELF...
I HAD A SON ONCE...
"IT'S ALL RIGHT..."

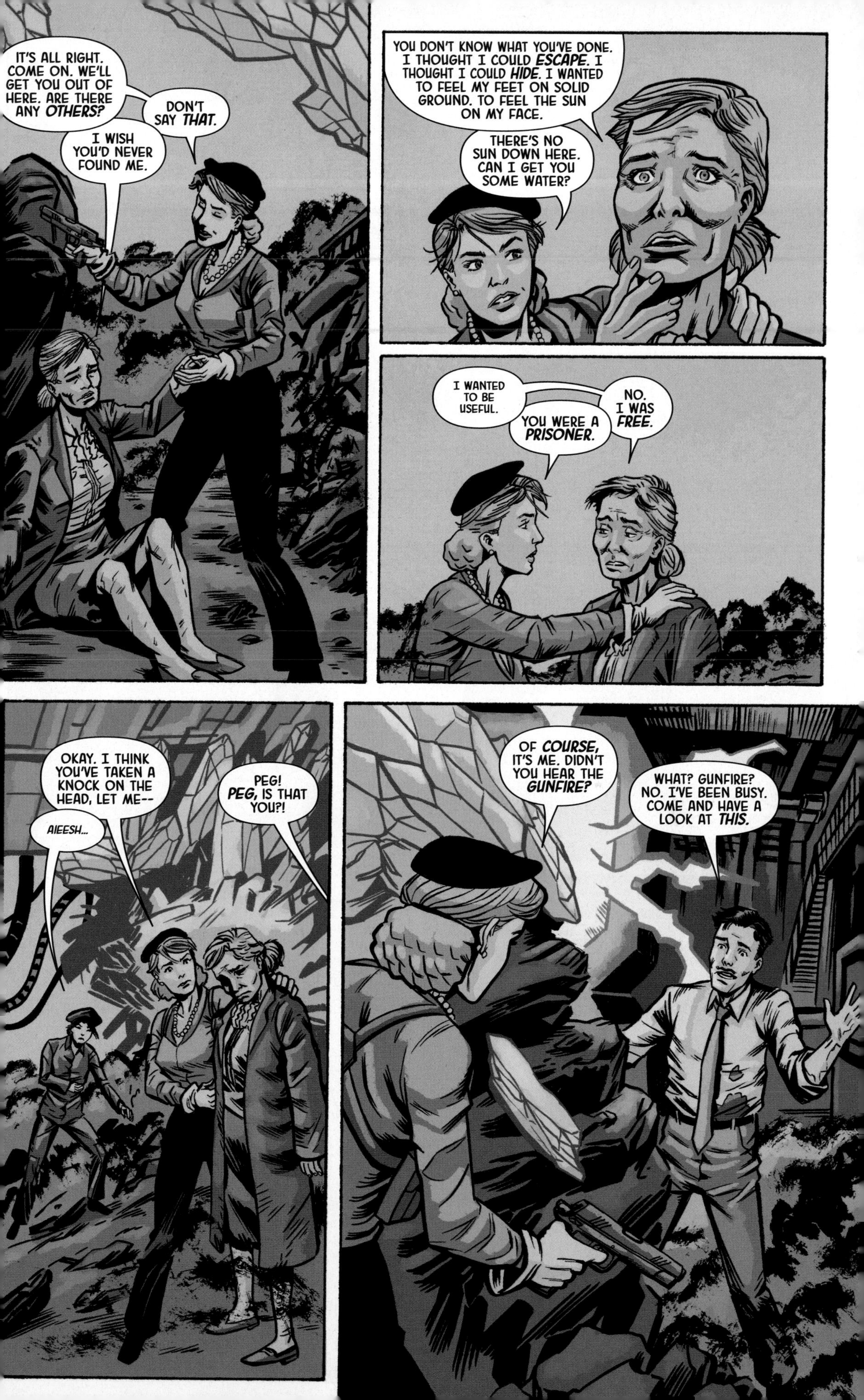
IT'S ALL RIGHT. COME ON. WE'LL GET YOU OUT OF HERE. ARE THERE ANY OTHERS?
I WISH YOU'D NEVER FOUND ME.
DON'T SAY THAT.
YOU DON'T KNOW WHAT YOU'VE DONE. I THOUGHT I COULD ESCAPE. I THOUGHT I COULD HIDE. I WANTED TO FEEL MY FEET ON SOLID GROUND. TO FEEL THE SUN ON MY FACE.
THERE'S NO SUN DOWN HERE. CAN I GET YOU SOME WATER?
I WANTED TO BE USEFUL.
YOU WERE A PRISONER.
NO. I WAS FREE.
OKAY. I THINK YOU'VE TAKEN A KNOCK ON THE HEAD, LET ME--
AIEESH...
PEG! PEG, IS THAT YOU?!
OF COURSE, IT'S ME. DIDN'T YOU HEAR THE GUNFIRE?
WHAT? GUNFIRE? NO. I'VE BEEN BUSY. COME AND HAVE A LOOK AT THIS.

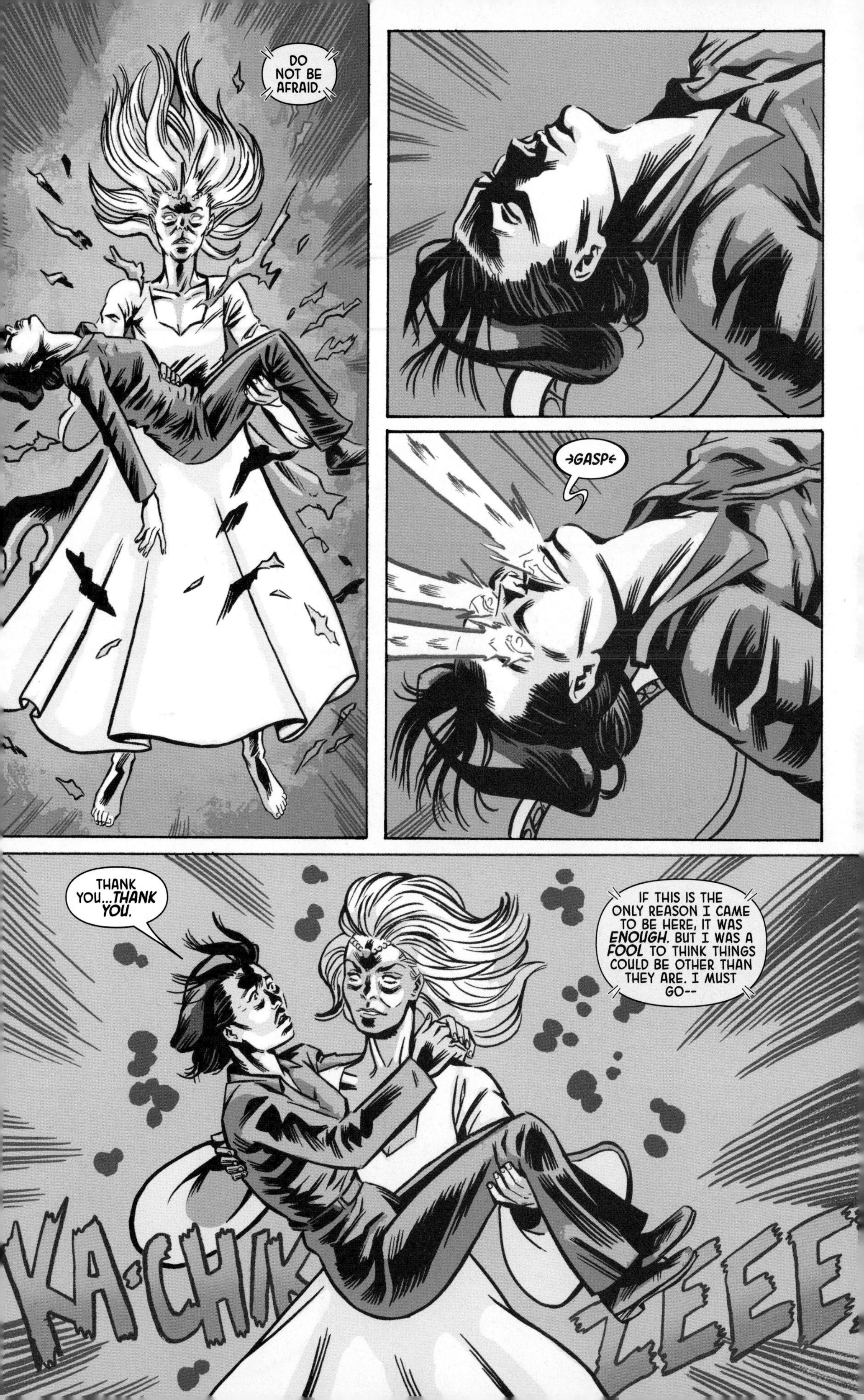
DO NOT BE AFRAID.
GASP
THANK YOU...THANK YOU.
IF THIS IS THE ONLY REASON I CAME TO BE HERE, IT WAS ENOUGH. BUT I WAS A FOOL TO THINK THINGS COULD BE OTHER THAN THEY ARE. I MUST GO--
KA-CHK
ZEEE

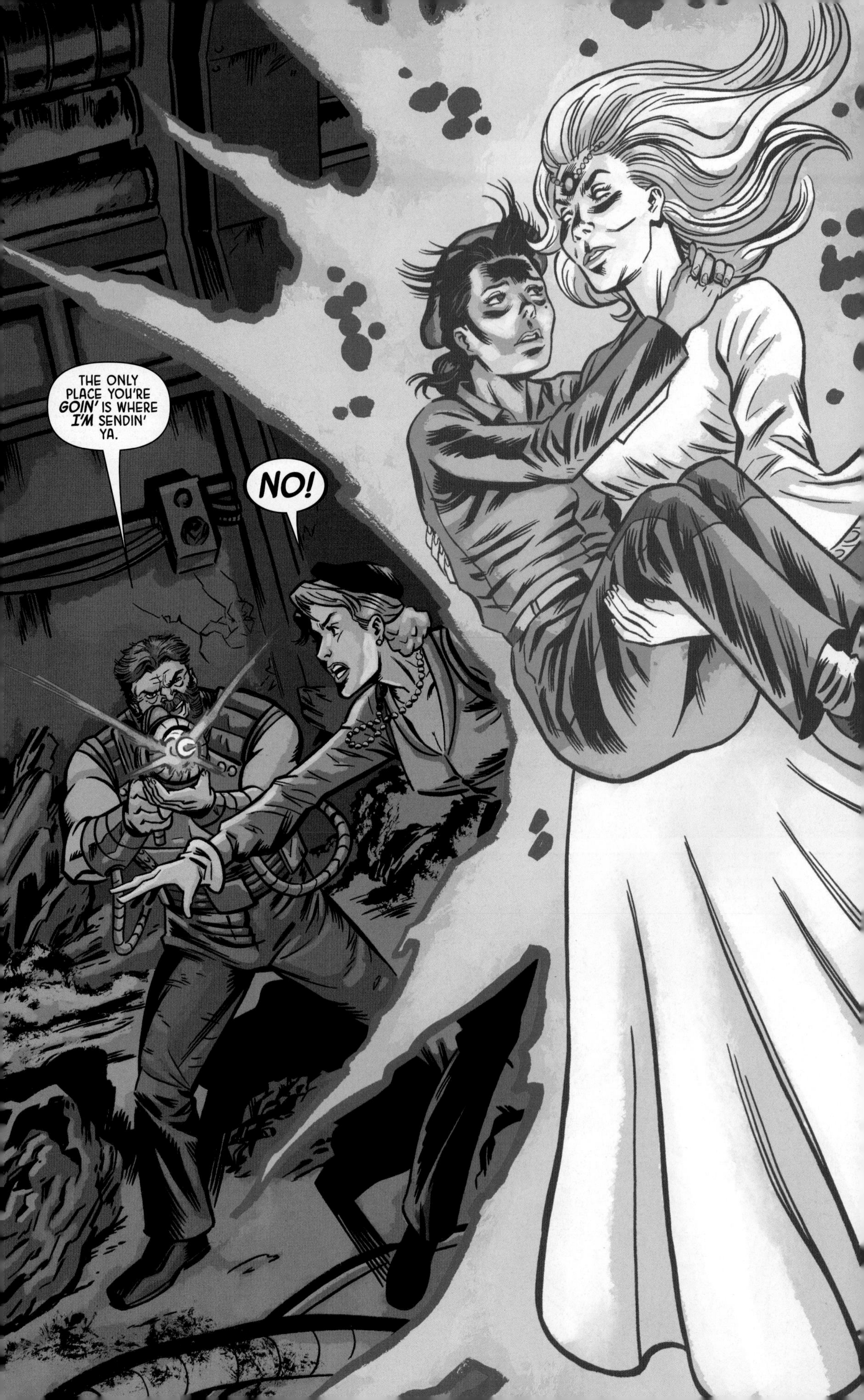
THE ONLY PLACE YOU'RE *GOIN'* IS WHERE *I'M* SENDIN' YA.
NO!

5

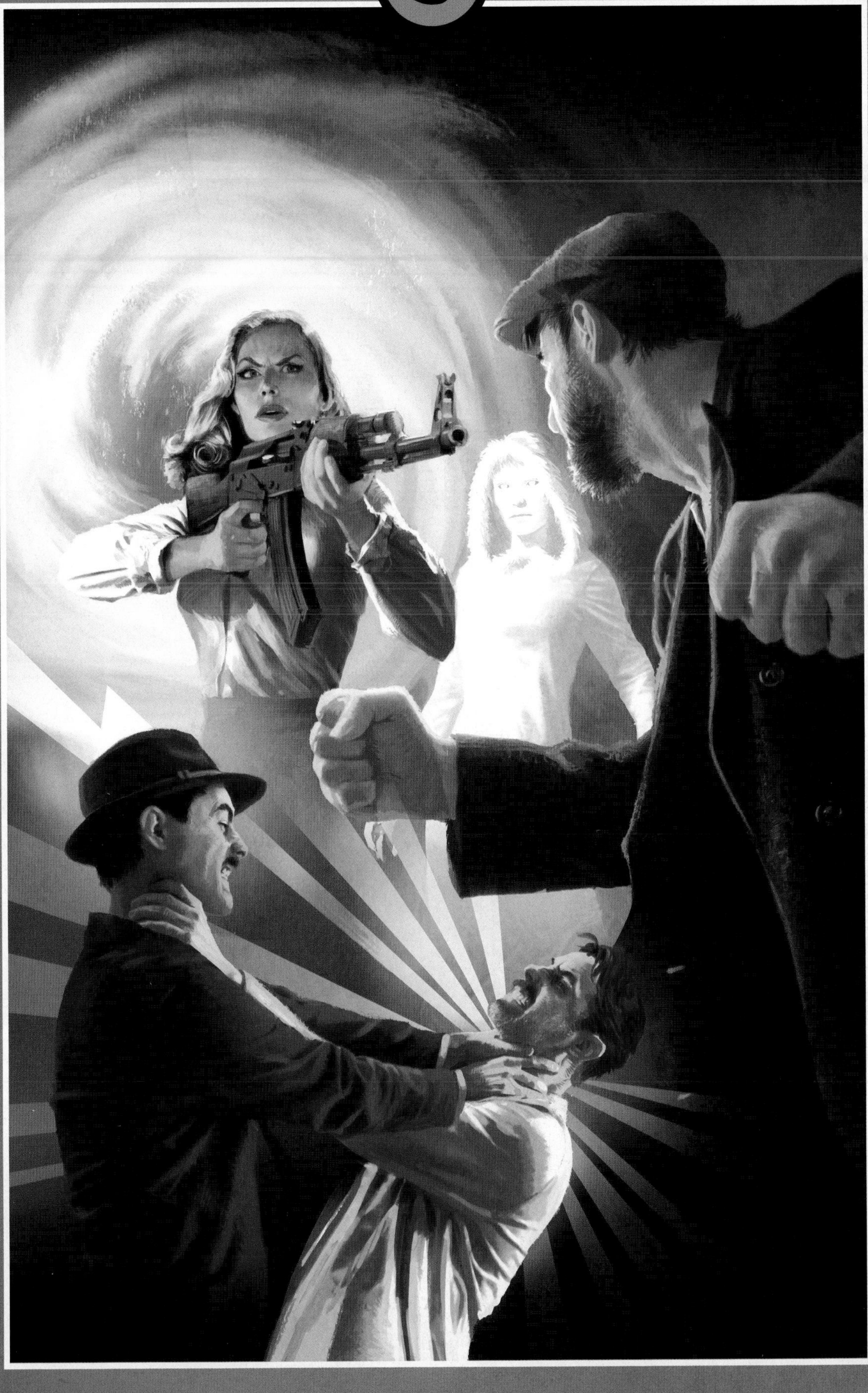

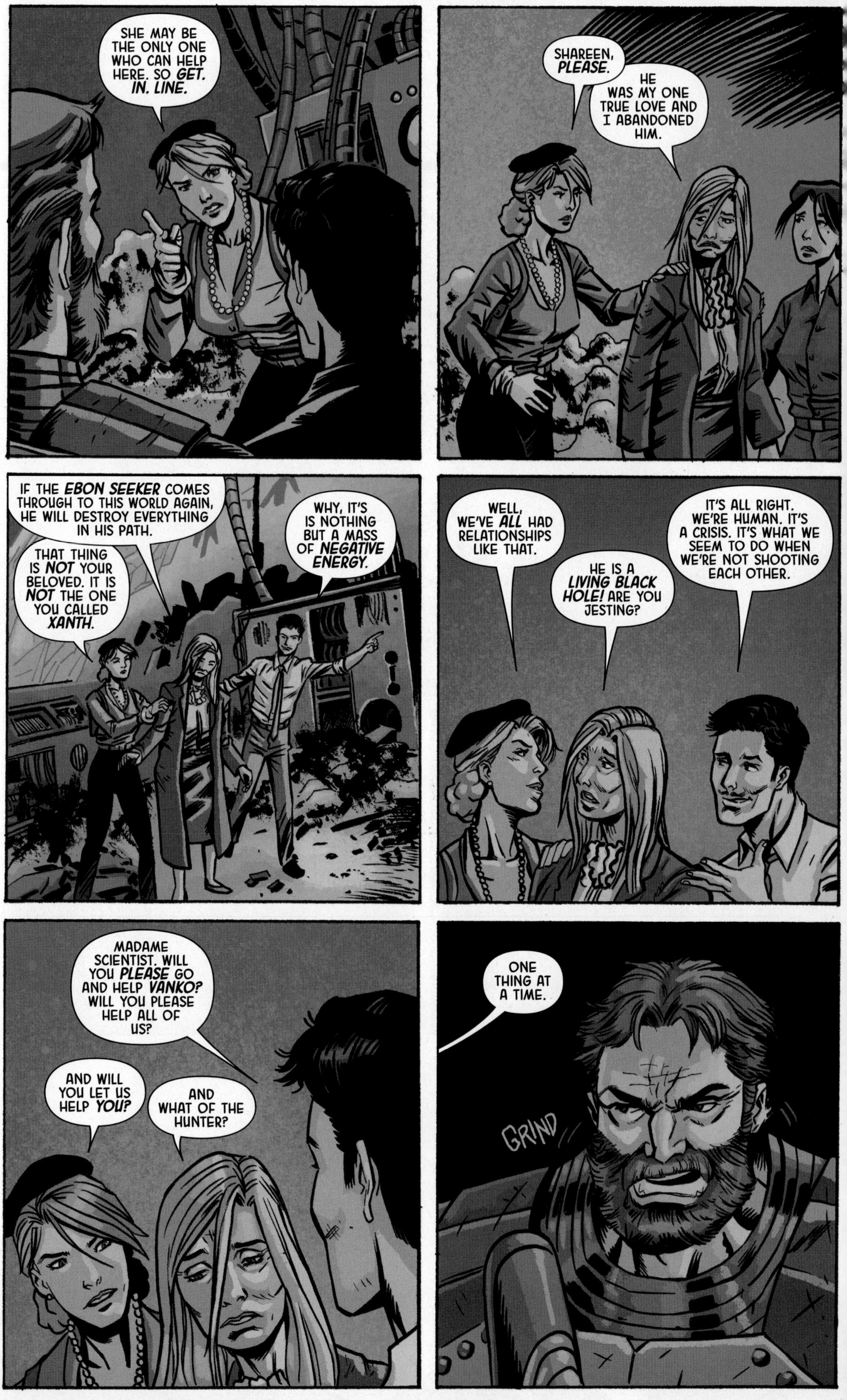
SHE MAY BE THE ONLY ONE WHO CAN HELP HERE. SO GET. IN. LINE.
SHAREEN, PLEASE.
HE WAS MY ONE TRUE LOVE AND I ABANDONED HIM.
IF THE EBON SEEKER COMES THROUGH TO THIS WORLD AGAIN, HE WILL DESTROY EVERYTHING IN HIS PATH.
THAT THING IS NOT YOUR BELOVED. IT IS NOT THE ONE YOU CALLED XANTH.
WHY, IT'S IS NOTHING BUT A MASS OF NEGATIVE ENERGY.
WELL, WE'VE ALL HAD RELATIONSHIPS LIKE THAT.
HE IS A LIVING BLACK HOLE! ARE YOU JESTING?
IT'S ALL RIGHT. WE'RE HUMAN. IT'S A CRISIS. IT'S WHAT WE SEEM TO DO WHEN WE'RE NOT SHOOTING EACH OTHER.
MADAME SCIENTIST. WILL YOU PLEASE GO AND HELP VANKO? WILL YOU PLEASE HELP ALL OF US?
AND WILL YOU LET US HELP YOU?
AND WHAT OF THE HUNTER?
ONE THING AT A TIME.
GRIND

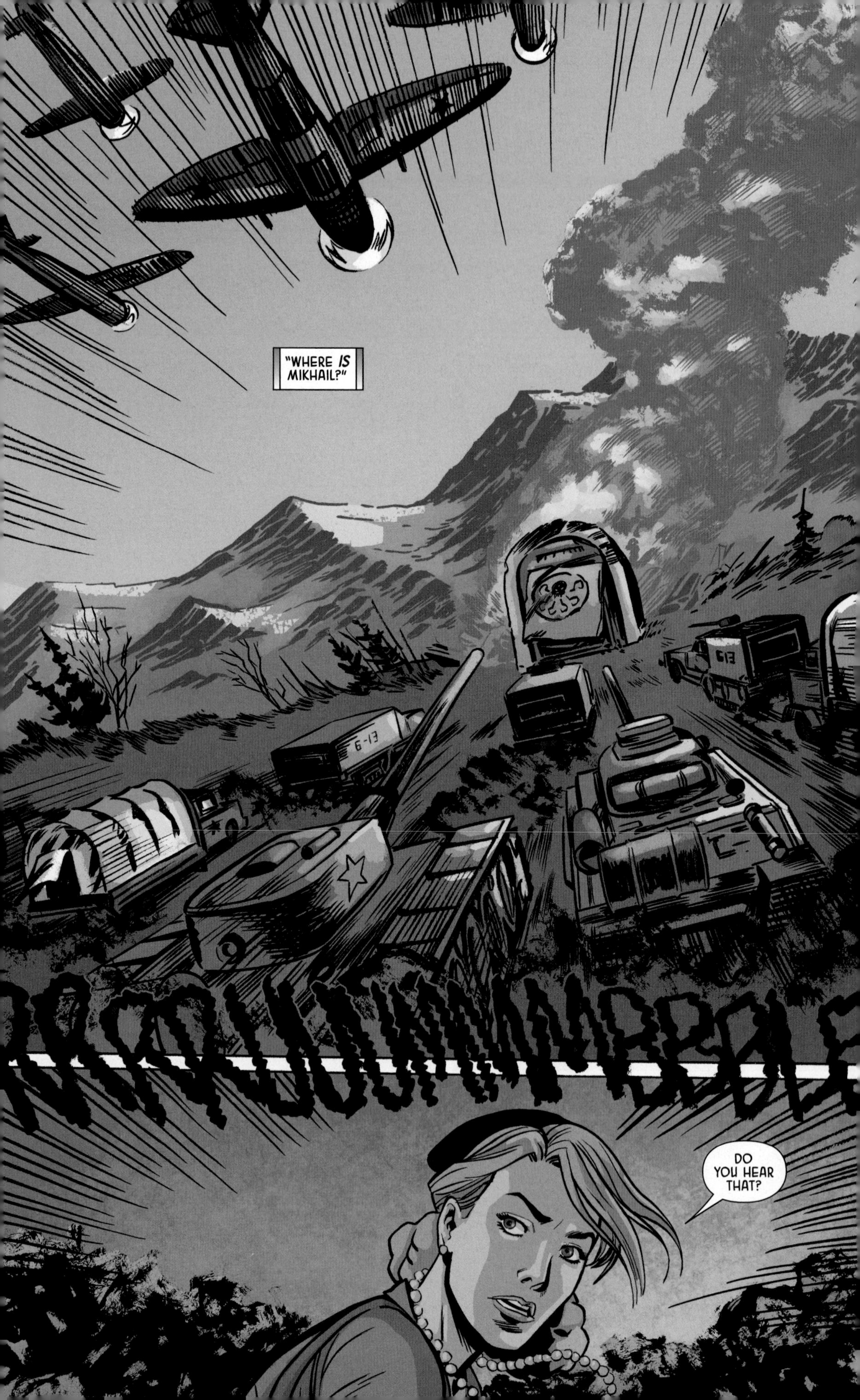

"WHERE IS MIKHAIL?"
RRRUUUMMMBBLE
DO YOU HEAR THAT?

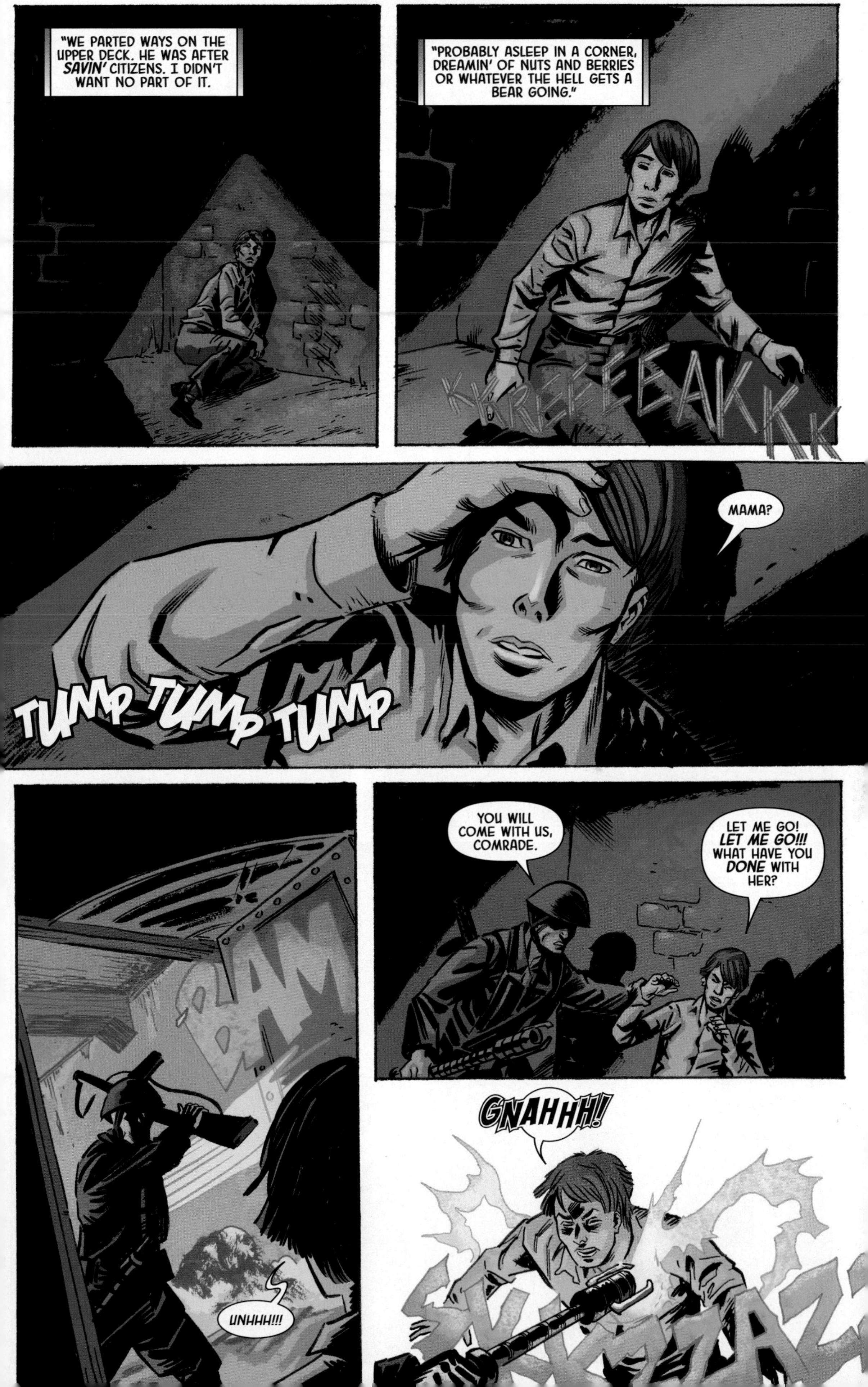
"WE PARTED WAYS ON THE UPPER DECK. HE WAS AFTER *SAVIN'* CITIZENS. I DIDN'T WANT NO PART OF IT.
"PROBABLY ASLEEP IN A CORNER, DREAMIN' OF NUTS AND BERRIES OR WHATEVER THE HELL GETS A BEAR GOING."
KKREEEEAKKKk
MAMA?
TUMP TUMP TUMP
BAM
UNHHH!!!
YOU WILL COME WITH US, COMRADE.
LET ME GO! *LET ME GO!!!* WHAT HAVE YOU *DONE* WITH HER?
GNAHHH!

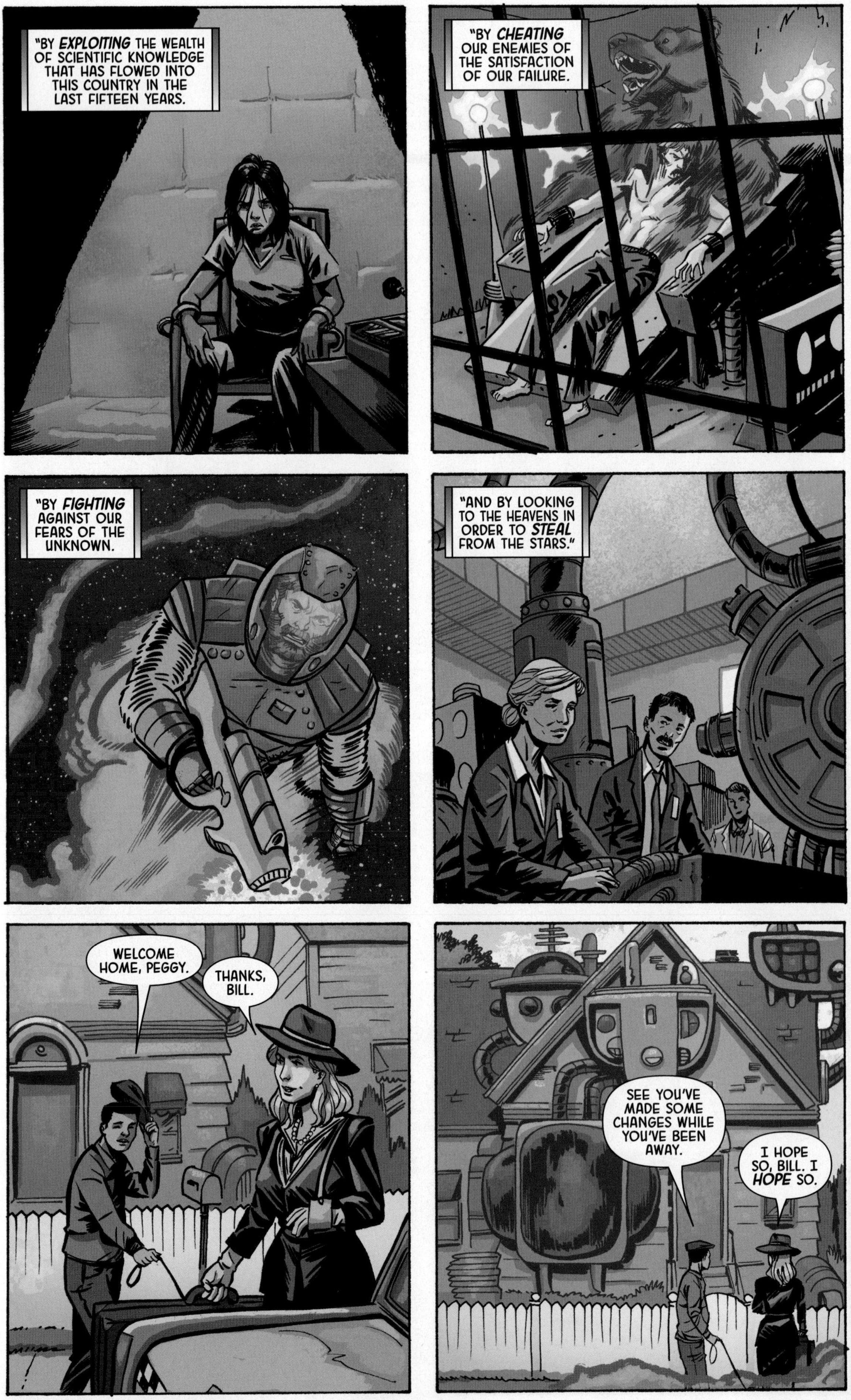
"BY EXPLOITING THE WEALTH OF SCIENTIFIC KNOWLEDGE THAT HAS FLOWED INTO THIS COUNTRY IN THE LAST FIFTEEN YEARS.
"BY CHEATING OUR ENEMIES OF THE SATISFACTION OF OUR FAILURE.
"BY FIGHTING AGAINST OUR FEARS OF THE UNKNOWN.
"AND BY LOOKING TO THE HEAVENS IN ORDER TO STEAL FROM THE STARS."
WELCOME HOME, PEGGY.
THANKS, BILL.
SEE YOU'VE MADE SOME CHANGES WHILE YOU'VE BEEN AWAY.
I HOPE SO, BILL. I HOPE SO.

"GENTLEMEN, STARK INDUSTRIES WILL NOT BE FRIGHTENED BACK TO THE *DARK AGES* BECAUSE OF SCIENTIFIC WORK USED FOR *UNSCIENTIFIC* PURPOSES."

"WE WILL *LITERALLY* SHED LIGHT ON THE DARKNESS."

PORT OF ORIGIN?

VOSTOCHNY.

RIGHT. OKAY. ALL CREW REMAINS ON BOARD AND WELCOME TO RED HOOK.

"WE WILL DO IT *QUICKLY*--

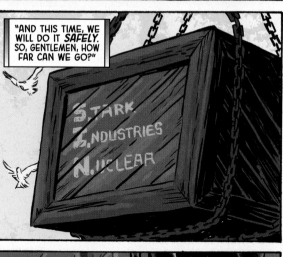

"AND THIS TIME, WE WILL DO IT *SAFELY*. SO, GENTLEMEN, HOW FAR CAN WE GO?"

S.TARK. I.NDUSTRIES N.UCLEAR

AS FAR AS WE *WANT*.

THE END.

OPERATION S.I.N.
APRIL 1952
SUBJECT: After Action Report
TO: Commanding Officer Moisan

Kathryn: So, Rich. Are you sad it's over? I should get out my thesaurus. Bump up the rhetoric. Hang on a sec...So, Rich, are you feeling atrabilious that we're done here?

Rich: My god yes, finishing the final issue felt like saying goodbye to my friends at the end of summer camp. We spent six months with Peggy and her goofy bunch of weirdos, and I had way too much fun.
　　I knew I loved Peggy after prepping for the series, but I didn't know that I would get so attached to Woody and the younger cast. Was there anything that really took you by surprise as the series played out?

K: It happens every time, right? You think you know where your affections and loyalties lie and then someone just kind of sneaks up on you. Howard and his general worldview can probably still take a hike but Woody turned out to embody some real tragedy for me...trying to do the right thing in a world where it's increasingly difficult to know what that is. I guess that really goes for all of them. I'd love to somehow revisit Tania/Red Guardian after having done this series.
　　I'll tell you what didn't take me by surprise, the fact that you've got "will draw bears for money" at the top of your resume. Ursa Major picking that lock with a claw was an office-wide delight. Everything, really. Moments big and small. I know it's ridiculous, after all the effort that went in, to pick out such a small thing, but you didn't let anything go. Your attention to detail was only outshone by your ability to keep track of the big picture. You're the Michael Mann of comics.
　　I know we've both got things that we geek out for relative to this series and time period. I've had a huge fascination with Sergei Korolev, Energomash, and Stalin's idiotic tunnel-to-Japan plan for ages. How did the research go for you?

R: To be honest the research was nothing but fun. You did most of the heavy lifting for a lot of the key set-pieces, so all I had to really worry about was fashion, cars, and props. I always end up researching those no matter what story I'm doing. The most notable fun for me was that everything designed in the '50s is way more fun to draw than modern design.
　　One of the things I love about this book was how you weaved some genuinely funny moments into the action. That and the fact that from page one, it was clear that your deep understanding of Peggy meant that she wasn't just a serious badass, but a compassionate and complex person. I could go on at length about my favorite moments, let's just say I really enjoyed getting to draw Howard getting punched. So, in the interest of talking about things we both liked, how much did you love having Jordan coloring the book?

K: Aw, hell. Thanks so much for the words about Peggy. I love her and I love the way you draw her. From the very first sketches, your Peg looked so solid. Her feet just seemed so firmly planted on the ground, literally and figuratively, and I tried to write to what you'd drawn. I think she's a serious person with a lot of internal conflict. I think she's trying to be happy but it doesn't come easily.
　　As to Mr. Boyd, what a great match for you on this book. I really believe that the art sells the book but the color gets it to the cash register. We've probably seen more advancement in color in the last decade than in any other aspect of comics and Jordan is able to deploy the practically infinite number of tools with subtlety and control. There was a little bit of throwback quality to everything that all of us did and it wouldn't have been possible without him. Her final outfit made me a little weepy. Thanks a lot (jerks).
One more question. Maybe it's just me, because I'm a child, but do you reward yourself when you're done with a project? And if so, how?

R: You know what, I don't always, but since this was my first big-two miniseries, I absolutely did. I bought myself a fancy knife-sharpening system that I've been ogling for a couple years. Writing it out, that sounds very silly, but I'm a bit of a knife/gear nerd, so I was tickled pink. I also took about a week off and finally let myself play a Dragon Age. I'm curious to know what your version looks like...?

K: Well, if we're confessing, this time it was something small that starts with an "A." ends with "lexander McQueen." I feel like we've both just gone Christmas shopping for Peg.
　　Rich, it's been a distinct pleasure getting to know Peggy Carter with you, thank you to Jon for shepherding the gang (on and off the page) and thank you so much to everyone who rode alongside us. I felt like we were driving a '57 Lincoln...room for all, everybody in the front seat. Let's do it again!

R: Thank you, Kathryn, I couldn't agree more, and I couldn't have said it better myself. So, in closing, I'll steal a line from you, Semper Peg!

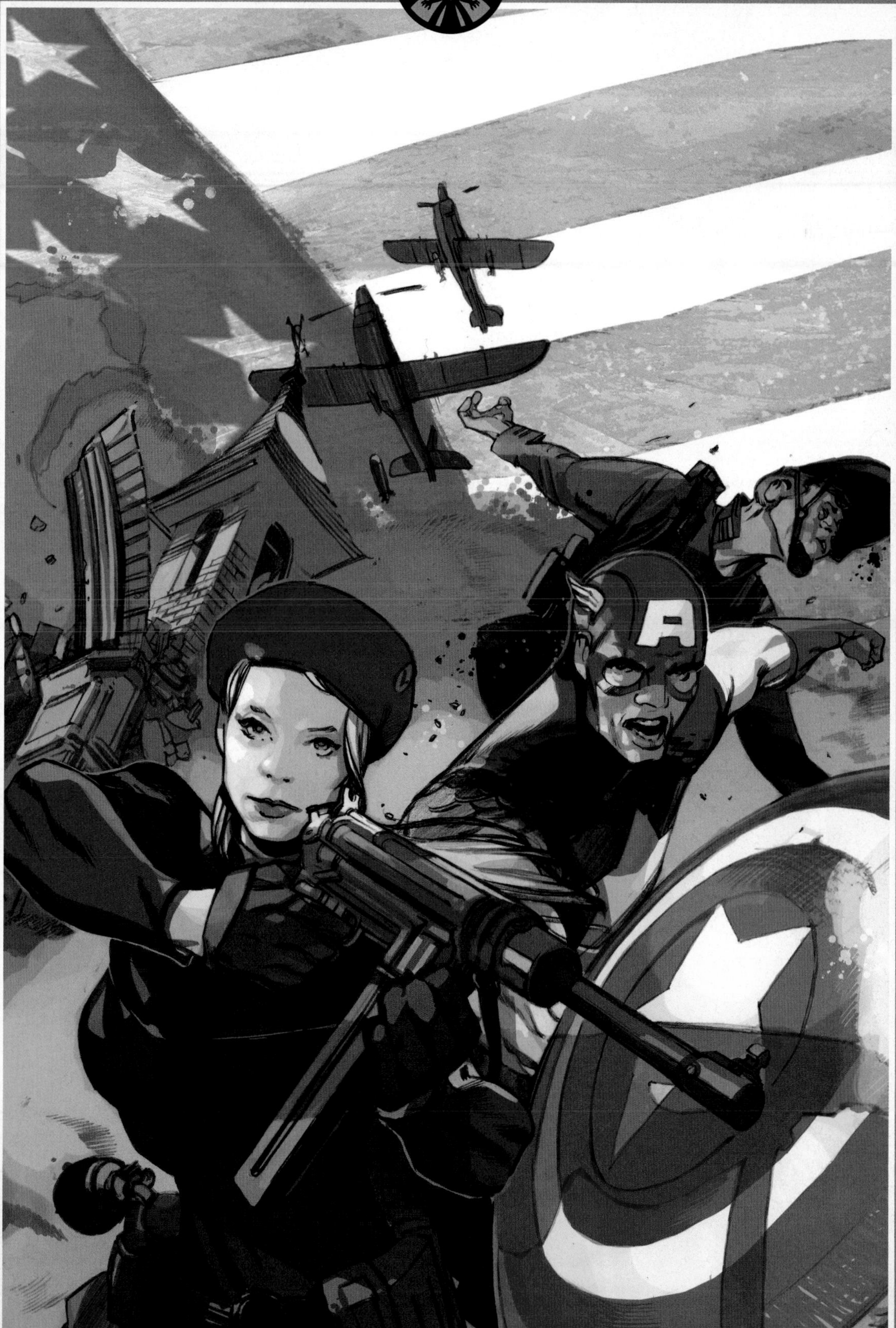
A

Captain America and the First Thirteen #1

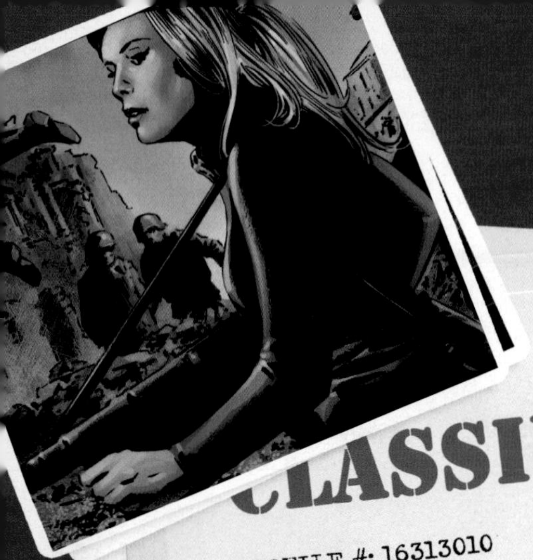

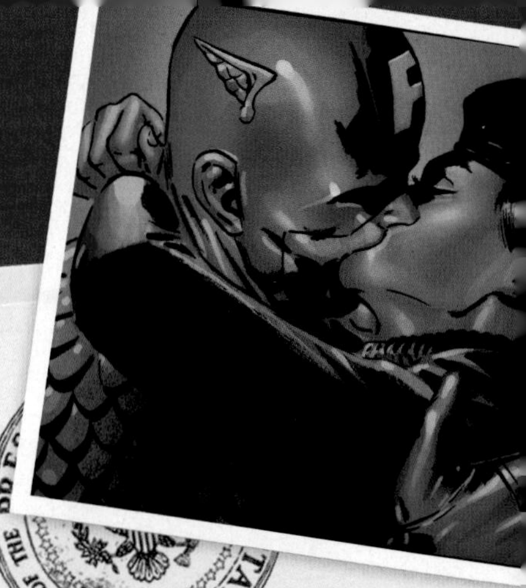

CLASSIFIED

PROFILE #: 16313010
REAL NAME: Margaret Carter
AKA: Agent 13

Margaret "Peggy" Carter was born to a wealthy American family during simpler times. When war broke out in Europe, she was not content to idly stand by and watch as the Nazis invaded the continent. Peggy left her comfortable American life to join the French Resistance and soon became one their bravest and best-trained members.

It was while fighting for their country overseas that she first encountered Captain America. Though their wartime strategies and combat tactics often differed, they were drawn together by a common purpose of service and justice. This bond between the two heroes ultimately blossomed into romance that struggled to endure the war.

Following her service, Peggy became ensconced in the international security agency S.H.I.E.L.D. and furthered her adventures championing for peace and inspiring a new generation of heroes!

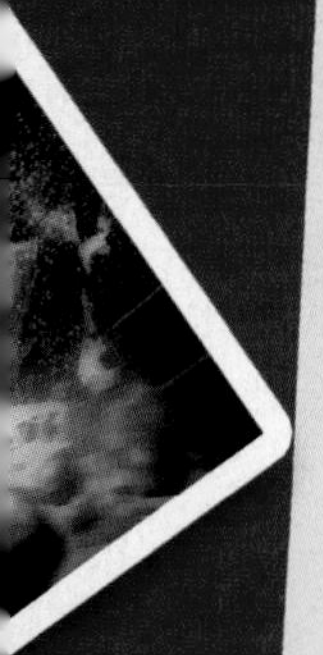

"Cherchez La Femme!"

Writer
Kathryn Immonen

Artist
Ramon Perez

Colorist
John Rauch

Letters
Jared K. Fletcher

Cover Artist
Greg Tocchini

Production
Damien Lucchese

Editor
Rachel Pinnelas

Supervising Editor
Tom Brevoort

Editor in Chief
Axel Alonso

Chief Creative Officer
Joe Quesada

Publisher
Dan Buckley

Exec. Producer
Alan Fine

Captain America created by Joe Simon and Jack Kirby

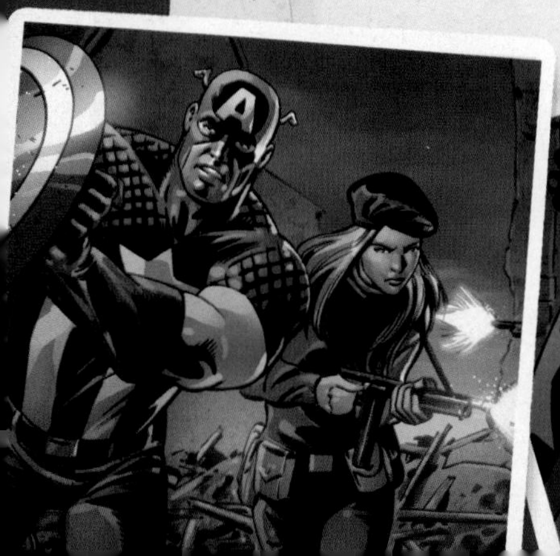

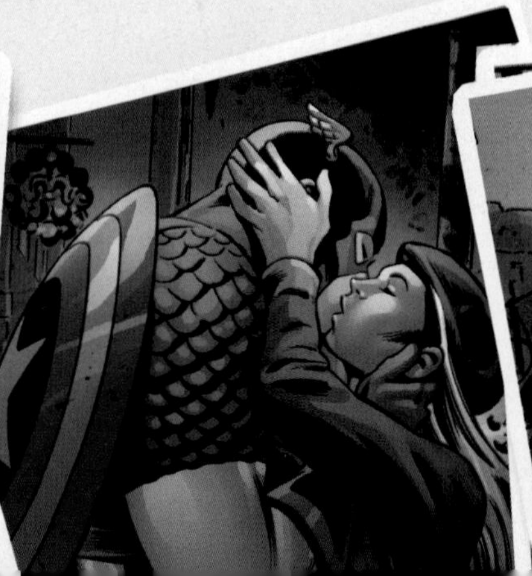

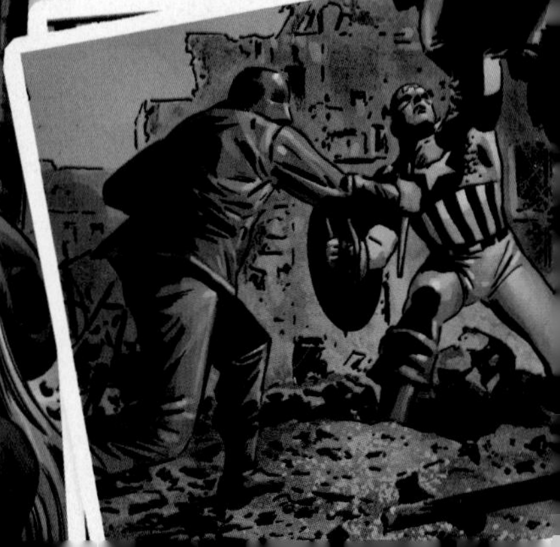

FRANCE. 1943.

SECRET AGENT PEGGY CARTER IN...

"Cherchez La Femme!"

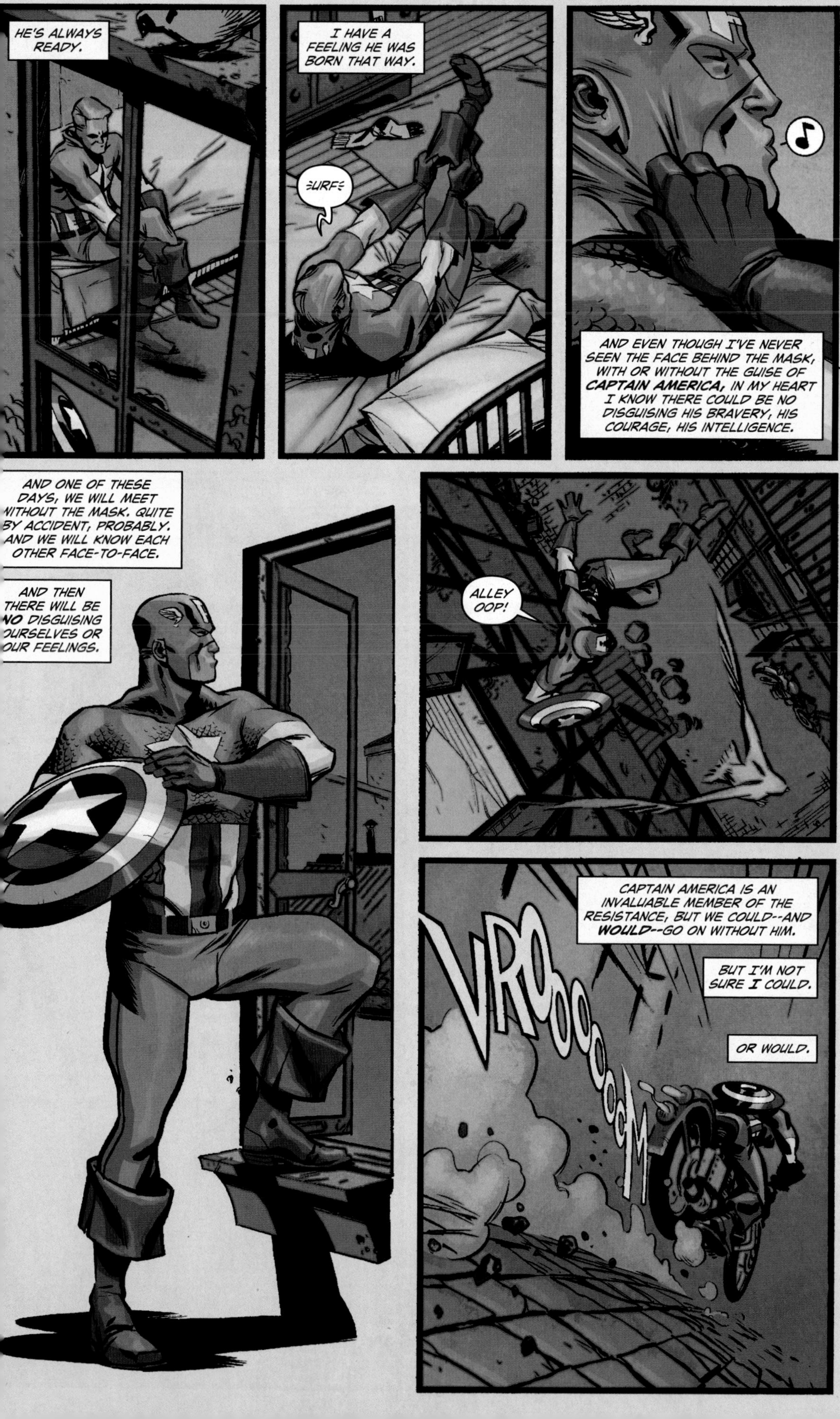
HE'S ALWAYS READY.
I HAVE A FEELING HE WAS BORN THAT WAY.
URF
AND EVEN THOUGH I'VE NEVER SEEN THE FACE BEHIND THE MASK, WITH OR WITHOUT THE GUISE OF CAPTAIN AMERICA, IN MY HEART I KNOW THERE COULD BE NO DISGUISING HIS BRAVERY, HIS COURAGE, HIS INTELLIGENCE.
AND ONE OF THESE DAYS, WE WILL MEET WITHOUT THE MASK. QUITE BY ACCIDENT, PROBABLY. AND WE WILL KNOW EACH OTHER FACE-TO-FACE.
AND THEN THERE WILL BE NO DISGUISING OURSELVES OR OUR FEELINGS.
ALLEY OOP!
CAPTAIN AMERICA IS AN INVALUABLE MEMBER OF THE RESISTANCE, BUT WE COULD--AND WOULD--GO ON WITHOUT HIM.
VROOOOOOOM
BUT I'M NOT SURE I COULD.
OR WOULD.

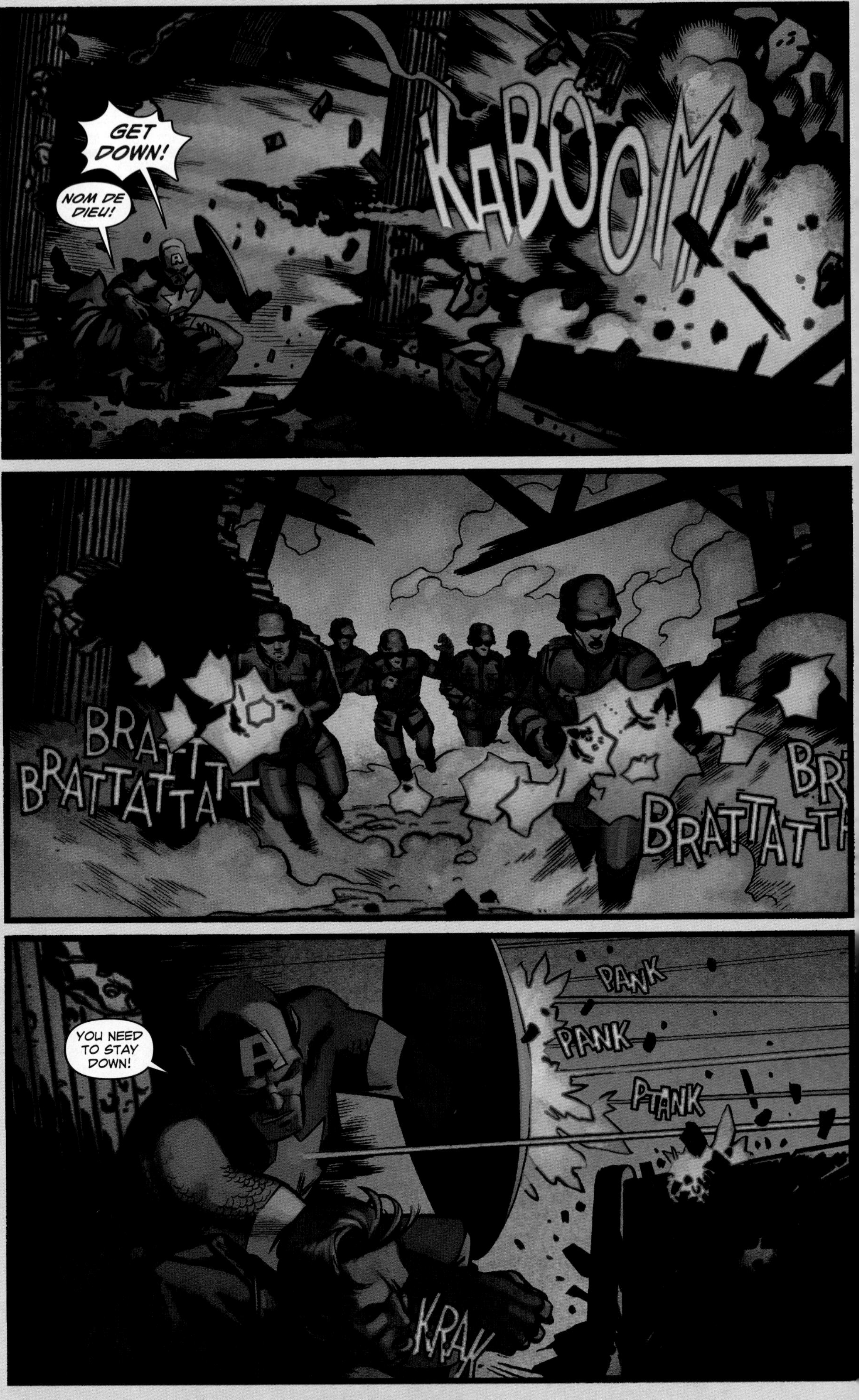
GET DOWN!
NOM DE DIEU!
KABOOM
BRATTTT
BRATTATTATT
BR
BRATTATTA
PANK
PANK
PTANK
YOU NEED TO STAY DOWN!
KRAK

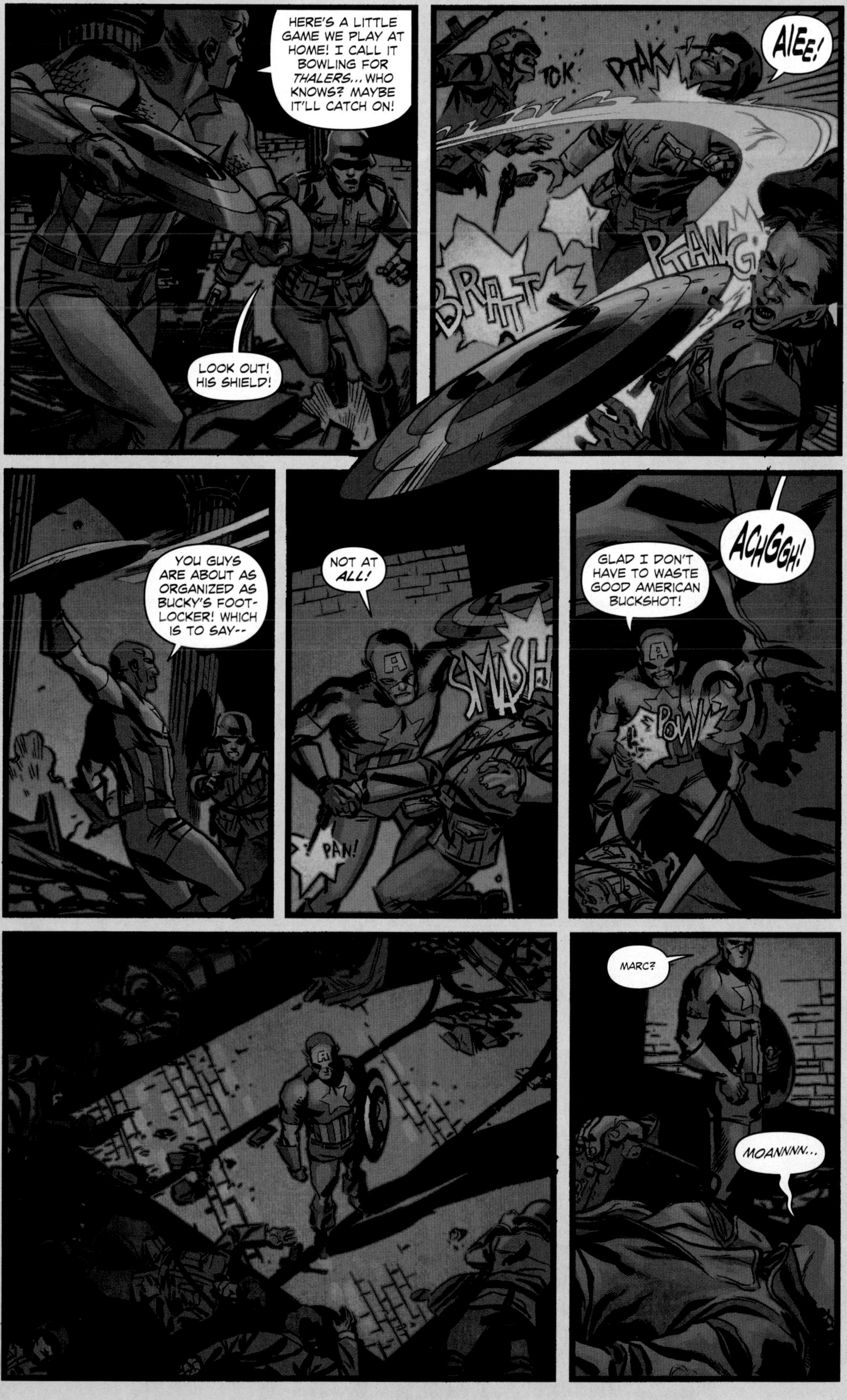
HERE'S A LITTLE GAME WE PLAY AT HOME! I CALL IT BOWLING FOR *THALERS*... WHO KNOWS? MAYBE IT'LL CATCH ON!
LOOK OUT! HIS SHIELD!
TOK
PTAK
AIEE!
BRAAT
PTANG!
YOU GUYS ARE ABOUT AS ORGANIZED AS BUCKY'S FOOT-LOCKER! WHICH IS TO SAY--
NOT AT *ALL!*
SMASH
PAN!
ACHGGH!
GLAD I DON'T HAVE TO WASTE GOOD AMERICAN BUCKSHOT!
POW
MARC?
MOANNNN...

SKAATCH

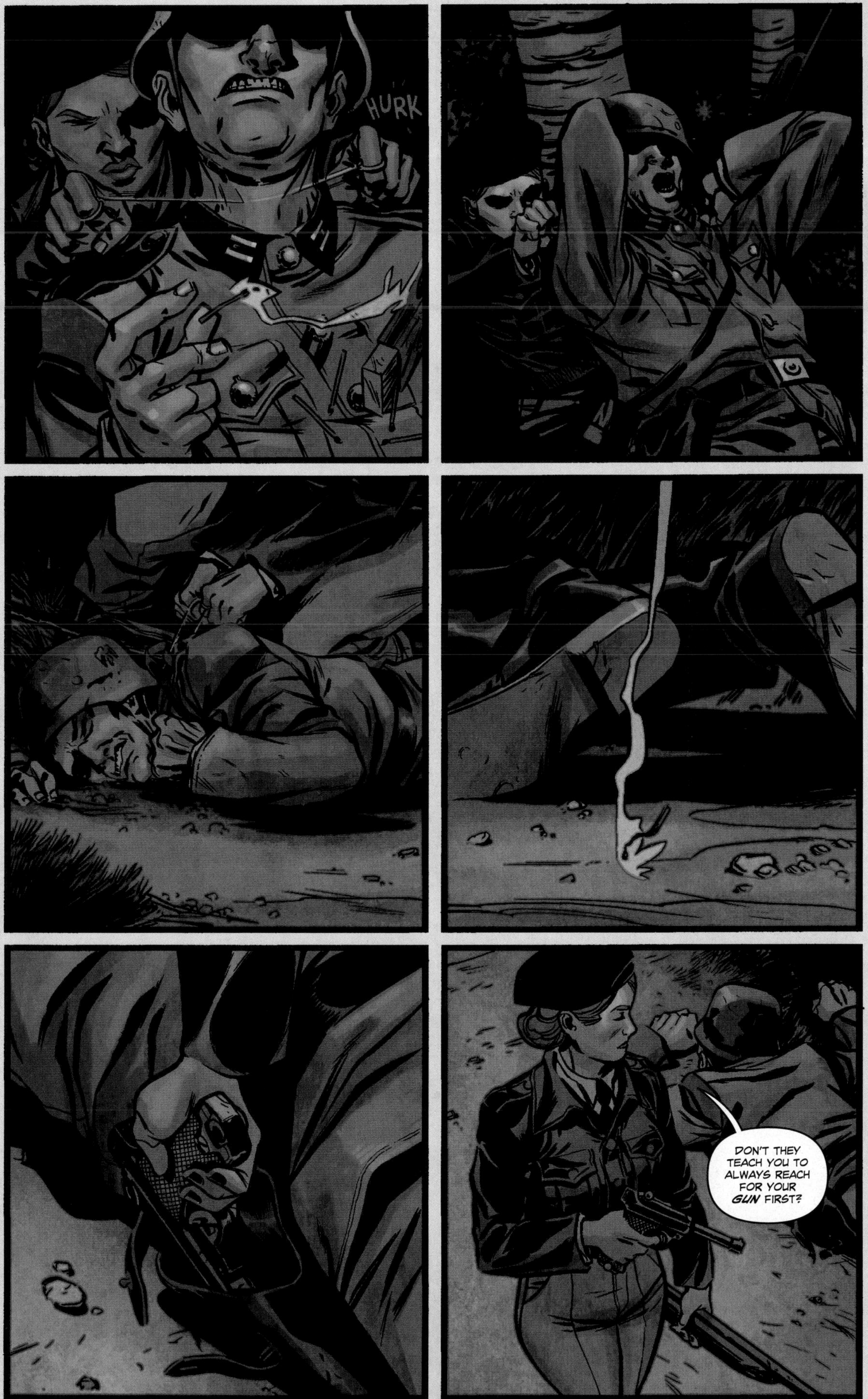
HURK
DON'T THEY TEACH YOU TO ALWAYS REACH FOR YOUR GUN FIRST?

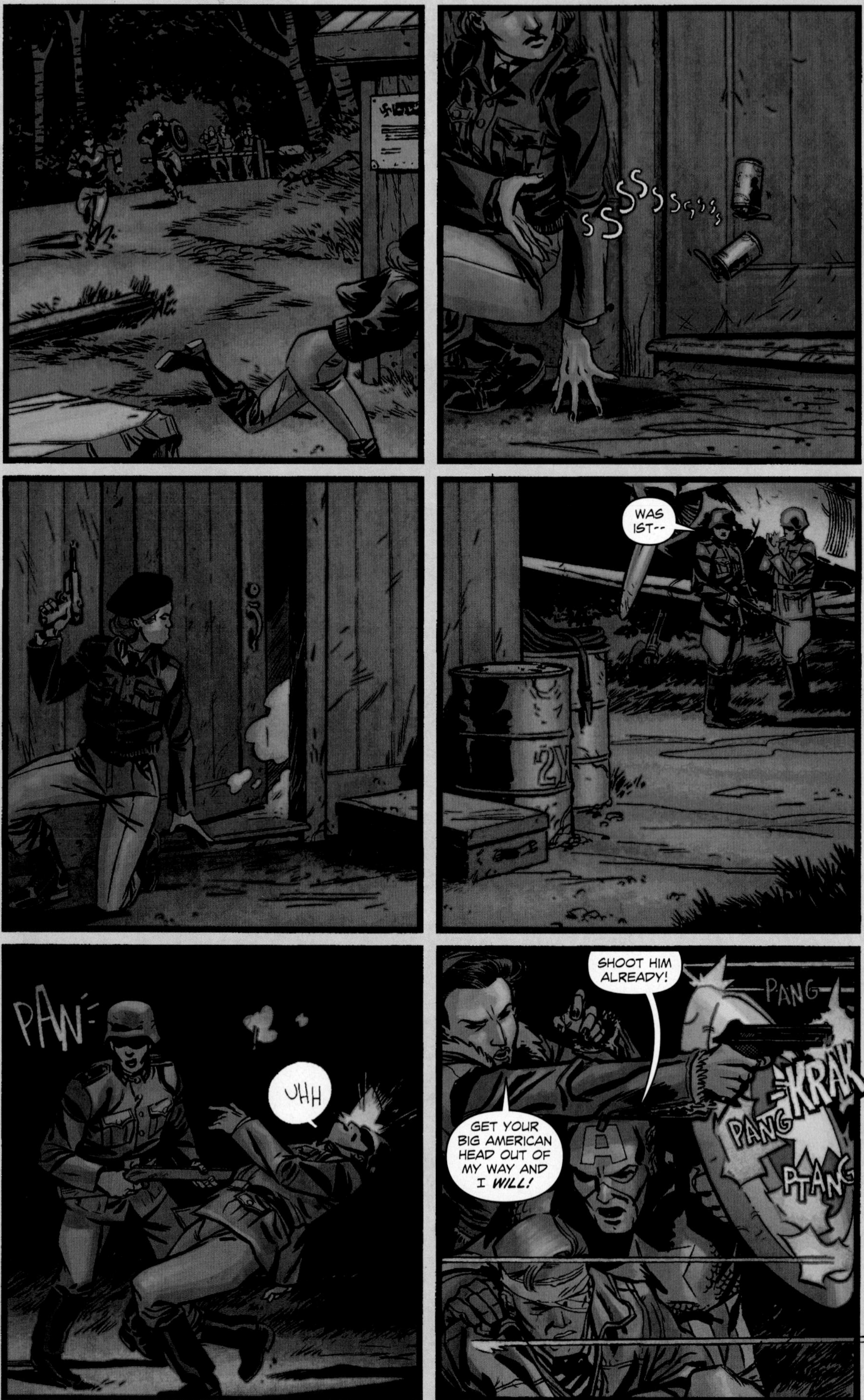
SSSSSSsssss
WAS IST--
PAW
UHH
SHOOT HIM ALREADY!
GET YOUR BIG AMERICAN HEAD OUT OF MY WAY AND I WILL!
PANG
KRAK
PANG
PTANG

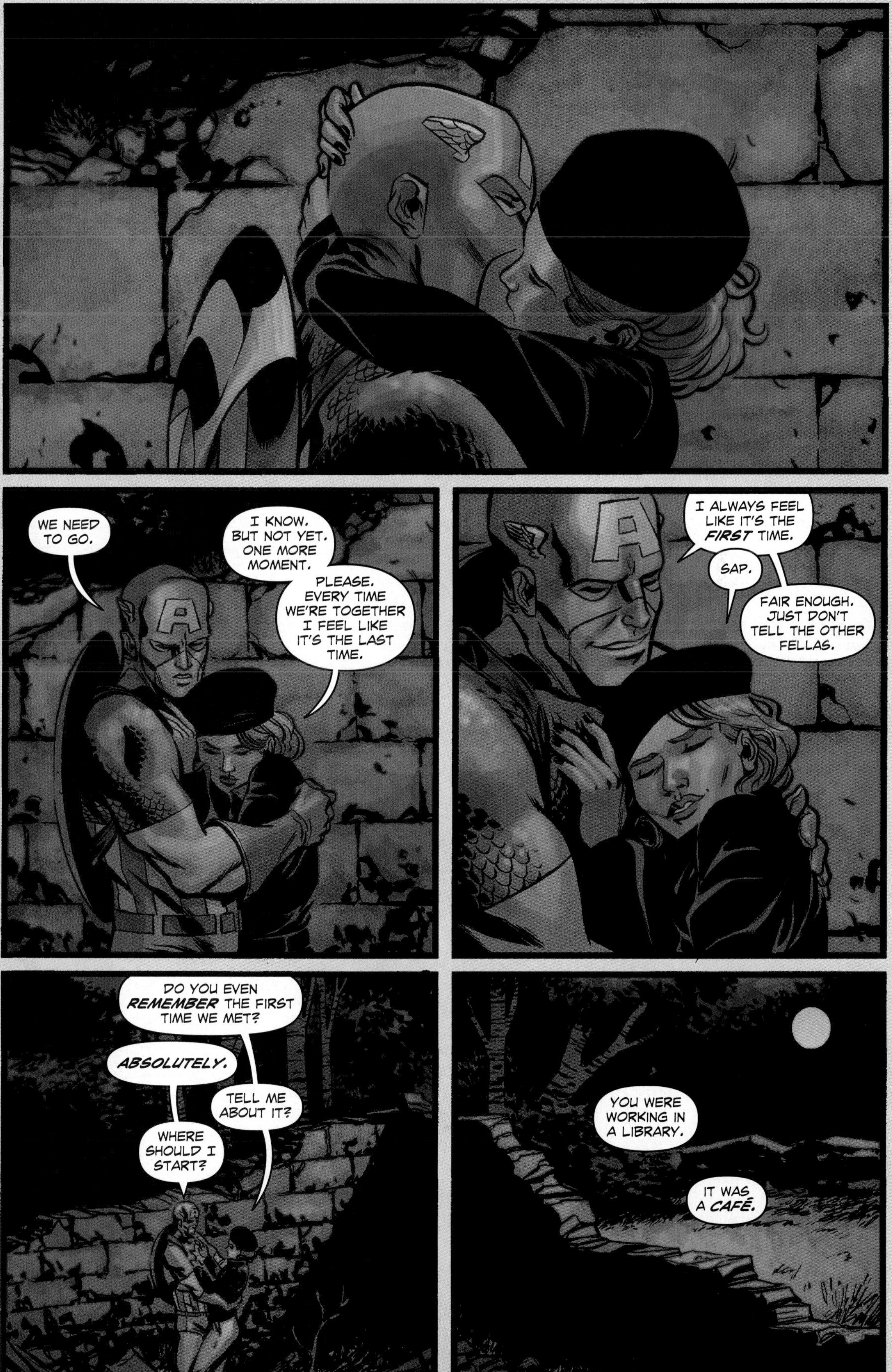
WE NEED TO GO.
I KNOW. BUT NOT YET. ONE MORE MOMENT.
PLEASE. EVERY TIME WE'RE TOGETHER I FEEL LIKE IT'S THE LAST TIME.
I ALWAYS FEEL LIKE IT'S THE *FIRST* TIME.
SAP.
FAIR ENOUGH. JUST DON'T TELL THE OTHER FELLAS.
DO YOU EVEN *REMEMBER* THE FIRST TIME WE MET?
ABSOLUTELY.
TELL ME ABOUT IT?
WHERE SHOULD I START?
YOU WERE WORKING IN A LIBRARY.
IT WAS A *CAFÉ.*

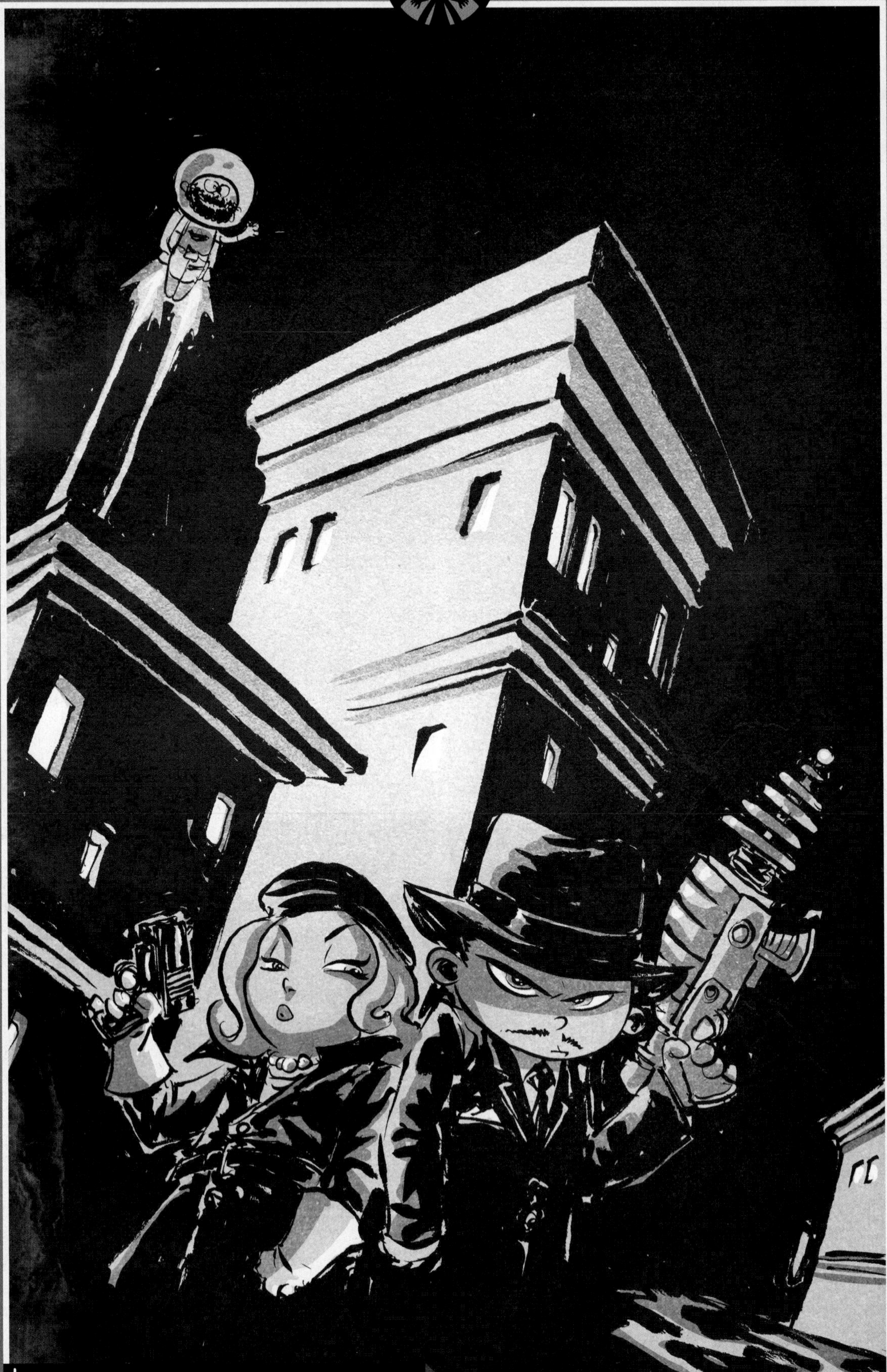

Operation: S.I.N. #1 Variant Cover by Scottie Young

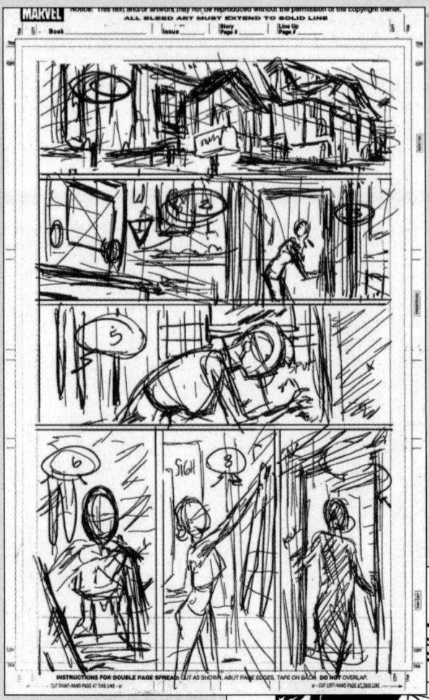
MARVEL
ALL BLEED ART MUST EXTEND TO SOLID LINE
SIGH

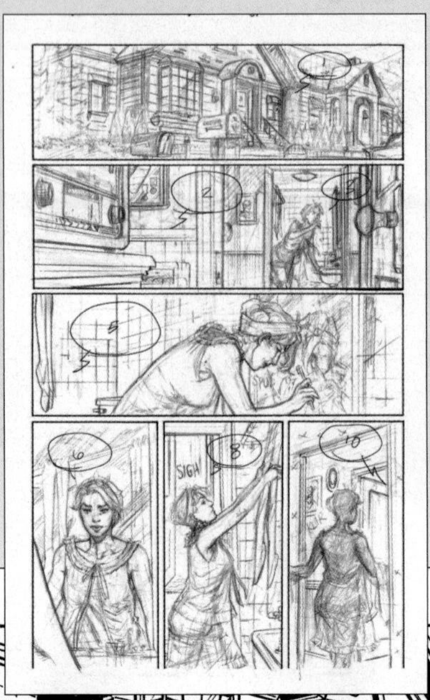
SIGH

Operation: S.I.N. #1,
Page 1: Layout,
Pencils and Inks

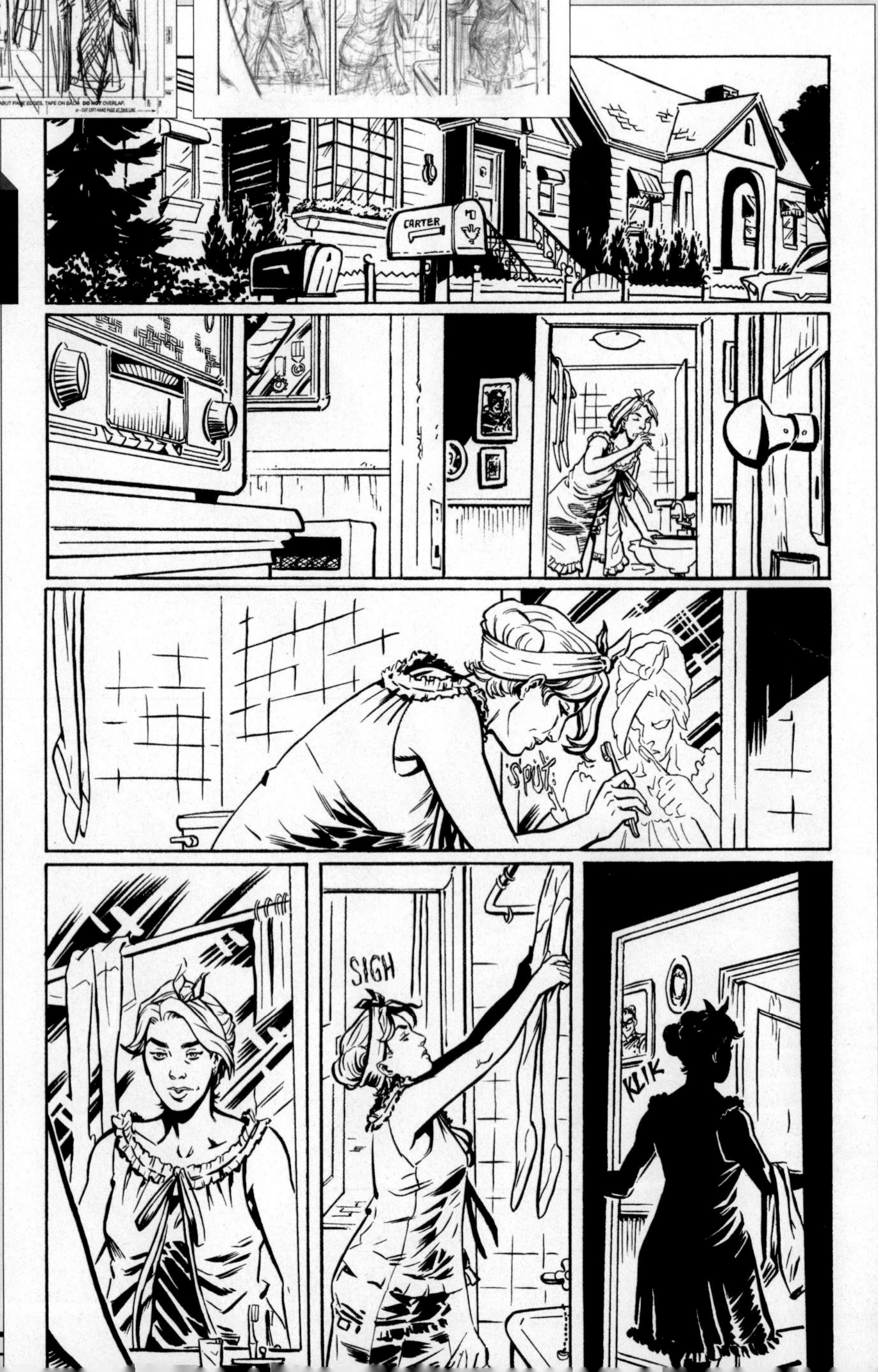
CARTER
SPIT
SIGH
KLIK

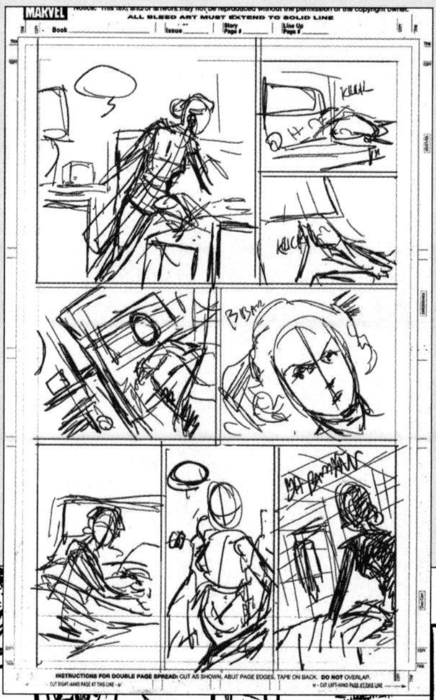

ALL BLEED ART MUST EXTEND TO SOLID LINE
INSTRUCTIONS FOR DOUBLE PAGE SPREAD: CUT AS SHOWN. ABUT PAGE EDGES. TAPE ON BACK. DO NOT OVERLAP.

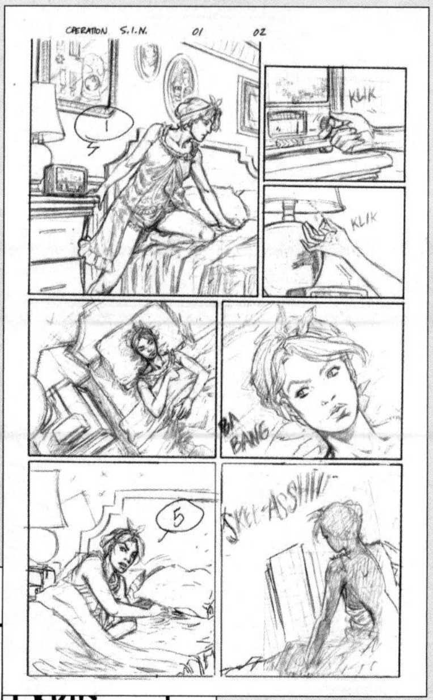

OPERATION S.I.N. 01 02
KLIK
KLIK
BA BANG
5

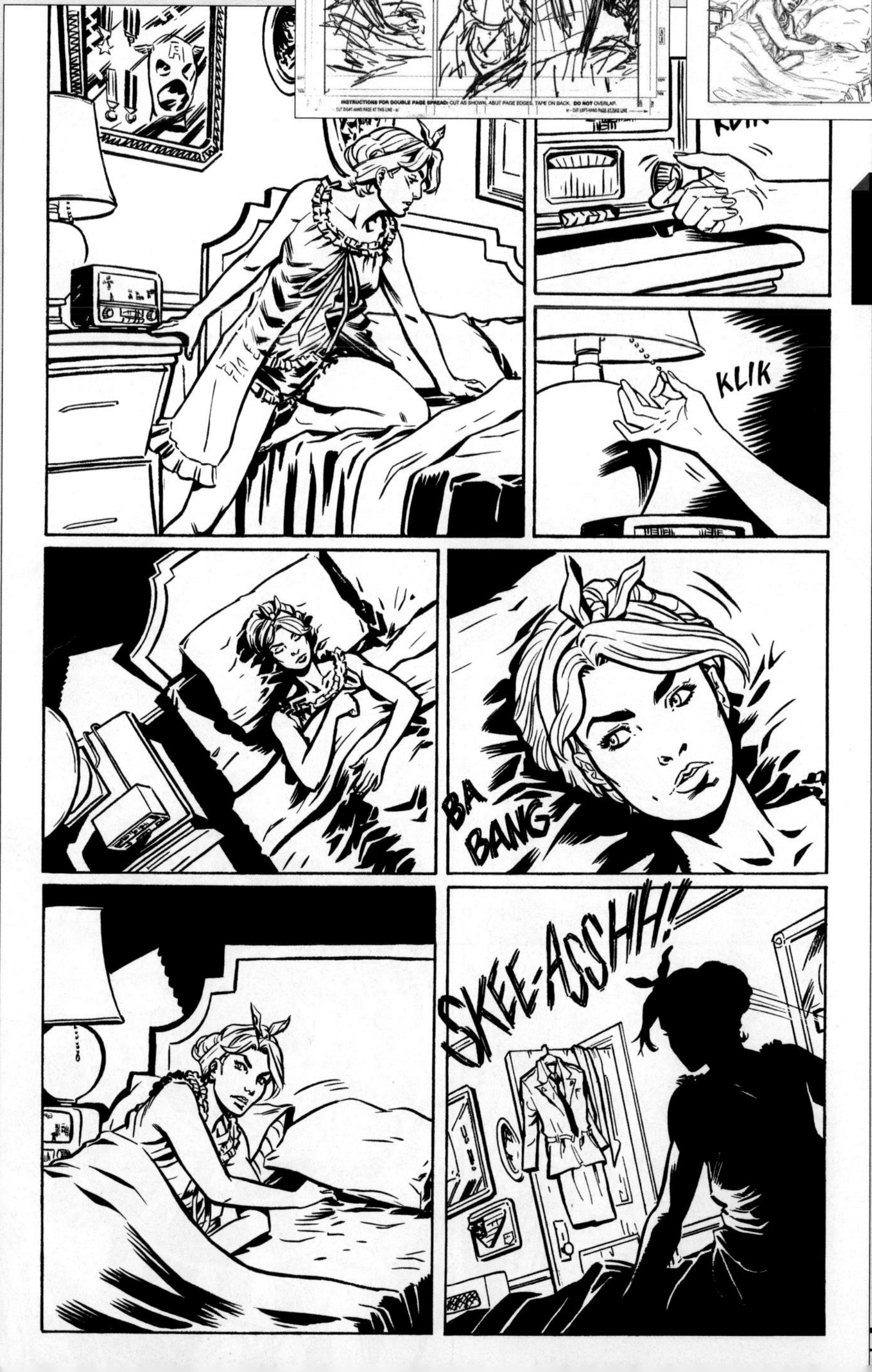

KLIK
BA BANG
SKEE-ASSHH!

Operation: S.I.N. #1, Page 2: Layout , Pencils and Inks

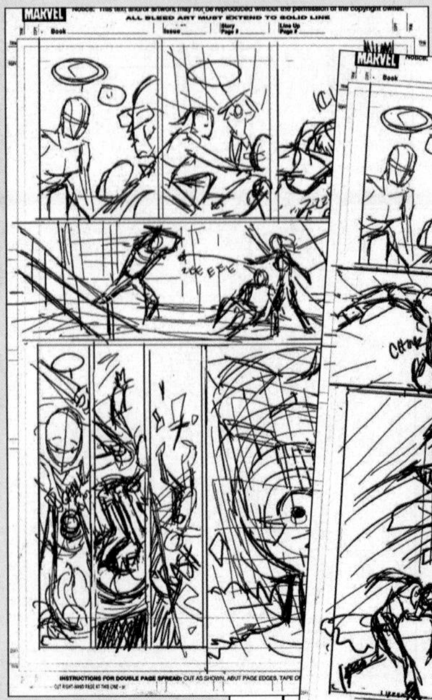

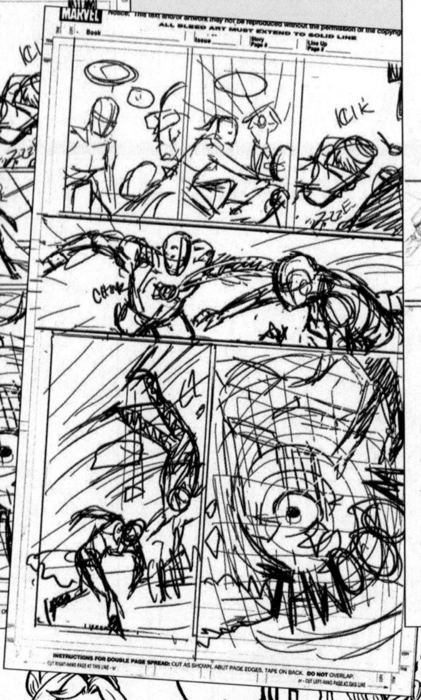
KLIK
CHINK

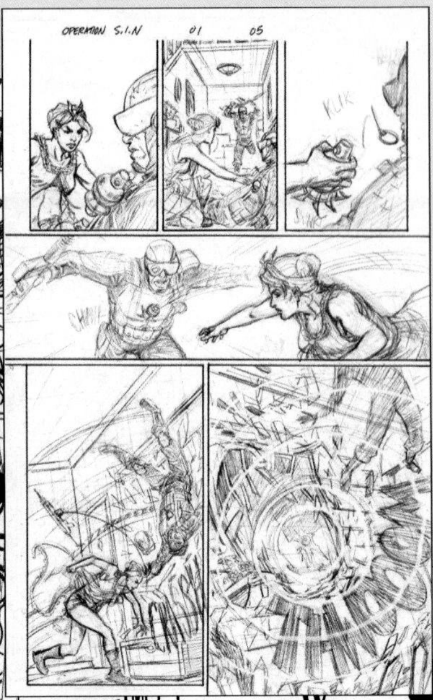
OPERATION S.I.N 01 05
KLIK

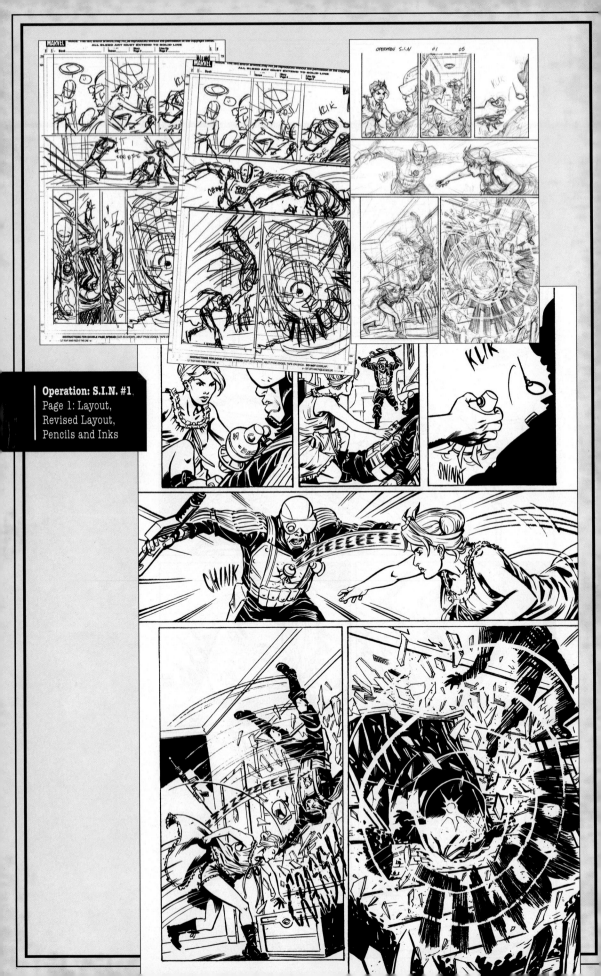

Operation: S.I.N. #1, Page 1: Layout, Revised Layout, Pencils and Inks

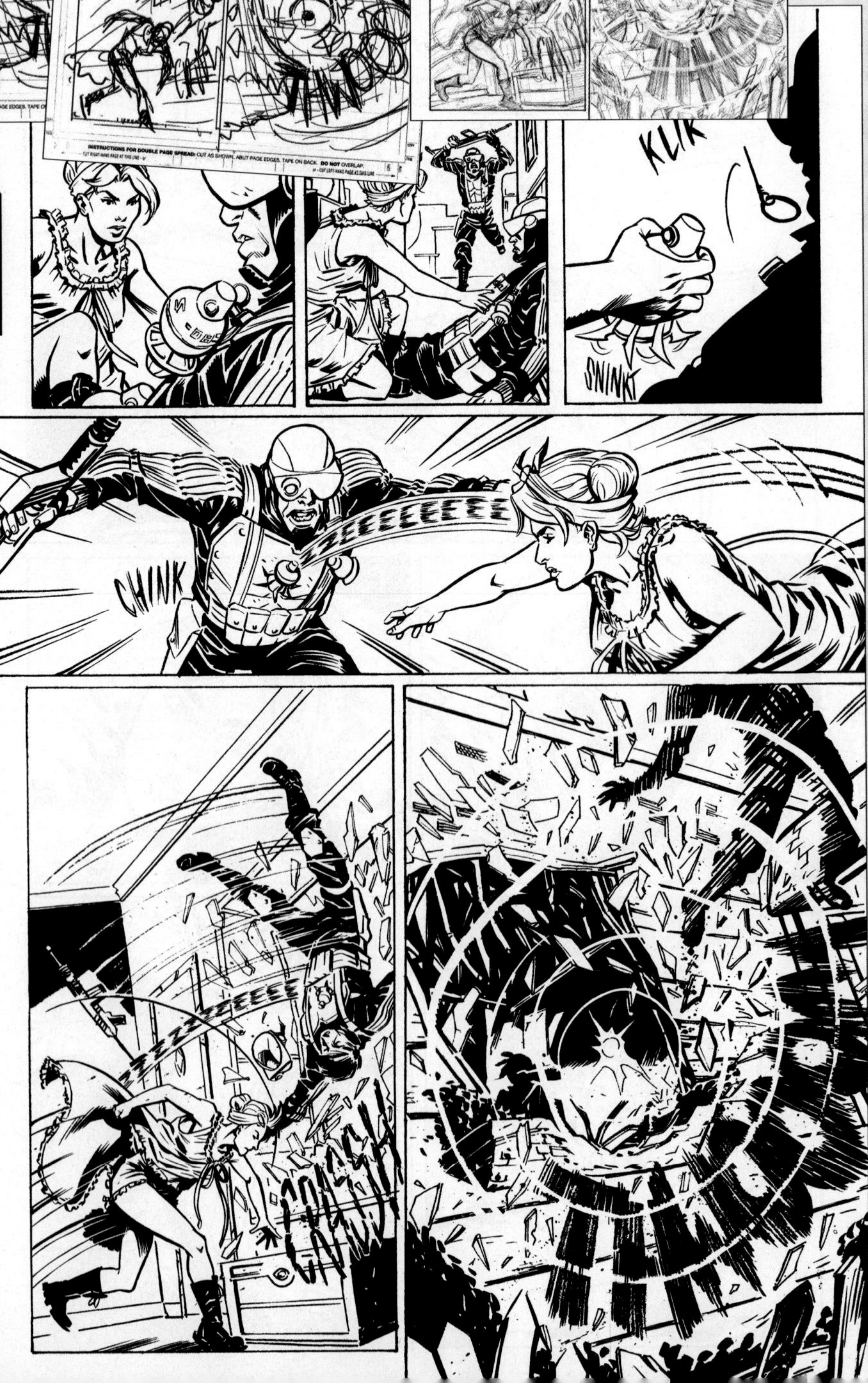
KLIK
SNINK
CHINK
CRASH